635.9/CAR

Hertfordshire
COUNTY COUNCIL
Library Service

**Please return this book
on or before the last
date shown or ask for
It to be renewed.**

Please renew/return this item by the last date shown.

So that your telephone call is charged at local rate,
please call the numbers as set out below:

32

	From Area codes 01923 or 0208:	From the rest of Herts:
Renewals:	01923 471373	01438 737373
Enquiries:	01923 471333	01438 737333
Minicom:	01923 471599	01438 737599

L32b

Hertfordshire
COUNTY COUNCIL
Community Information

1 3 APR 2004

2 7 JUL 2007
2 2 SEP 2009

L32a

CARNATIONS AND PINKS

CARNATIONS & PINKS

The Complete Guide

Sophie Hughes

The Crowood Press

First published in 1991 by
The Crowood Press Ltd
Gipsy Lane, Swindon
Wiltshire SN2 6DQ

British Library Cataloguing in Publication Data

Hughes, Sophie
Carnations and pinks.
1. Gardens. Carnations. 2. Gardens. Pinks. Cultivation
I. Title
635.933152

ISBN 1 85223 413 X

Acknowledgements
Line illustrations by Lynn Hodgson
Photographs by John Ryan

Typeset by Footnote Graphics,
Warminster, Wilts.
Printed in Great Britain by
Redwood Press Limited, Melksham, Wilts.

CONTENTS

ACKNOWLEDGEMENTS

Many people have given generous help in the preparation of this book. Remaining faults are mine but I should like particularly to thank Dr John Harvey, Ruth Duthie and Jim Gould for their reading and detailed comments on the historical sections and for permission to quote from their work. I should also like to thank Mr and Mrs Arthur Robinson, Fred Smith and Colin Short, all of the BNCS, for looking at the sections on culture and giving me the benefit of their practical experience. Mr Short has generously lent a transparency of 'PF' carnations. I am grateful to growers John and Carolyn Whetman and Donald Thomas for their invaluable help, also to Martin Rickaby of Allwoods, and David Hitchcock of Three Counties Nursery. My thanks to Hilary Spurling, David Stuart, James Sutherland, Steven Bailey, Blandford Press Ltd, Mrs Will Ingwersen, Faber & Faber and Penguin Books for permission to quote from published work. My thanks to the NCCPG, particularly Susan Farquhar, original holder of the 'National Collection' of old pinks, for sharing her knowledge and her plants. I am grateful to Peter Dennis-Jones and Win Ashmore for help with interpretations from ancient Greek and Latin sources, and to Dr Elliott at the Lindlay Library. My thanks to Bridget and Carol Like, professional florists, for their advice and arrangements on the plates, and to flower arrangers Peggy Hughes and Julia Wilde for their talks with me. I am grateful to Gloucester Women's Institute Market for fostering the early days of my interest in this subject and to the members of this and various horticultural societies met while lecturing who have made suggestions, helped with research and exchanged plants. My thanks to Audrey Hodgson, Jean Mooney and Angela Collett for companionship as we have shared the hard work of a small nursery, to Lynn Hodgson for her beautiful drawings, and to John Ryan for all the good photographs. Above all thanks to my husband Michael, children Emily and Oliver and mother Wendy Grugeon for allowing me the time this project has absorbed. Finally thanks to my present professional colleagues for their tolerance and encouragement.

FOREWORD

Given their enduring popularity with gardeners it is difficult to understand why we have had to wait so long for an up-to-date, authoritative and comprehensive book about dianthus.

Happily with this fine blend of scholarship and practicality Sophie Hughes has now filled the gap. Her observations about the history and mythology of the genus are both informed and fascinating. The detailed descriptions of the individual species and the major varieties and methods of their propagation and culture stem from a wide experience of working with them as both the proprietor of a nursery growing pinks and one of the custodians of the National Collection, nourished by those vital characteristics of the true amateur – love and dedication.

Gardeners who have previously made gardens under constricting circumstances will know that with copious dressings of lime it is possible to reduce the acidity of some of our garden soils temporarily. On the other hand, massive loads of peat or additions of acid fertilizers will only alter the pH of truly alkaline soils for a very short period.

Gardeners forced to work such soils are wisest to accept their limitations and allow them to dictate the plants which they grow. This is perhaps a useful discipline because what is created will tend to harmonize with the natural flora of the surrounding landscape and seem appropriate. Apart from, in the case of alkaline soils, abandoning any hope of rearing blowzy rhododendrons or azaleas they will not be able to plant some of the established border favourites.

But if their land is well drained they will discover that their soil provides ideal conditions for members of the dianthus family to prosper. And this is as well, because without the alpine and lowland pinks, carnations and sweet williams the palette of colours available to them would be severely reduced. Within the genus there are enormous varieties of forms and patterns of colour which makes it possible to use them to brighten borders throughout the season.

I think that it is a splendid book and I wish it well.

Graham Rose
Gardening Correspondent of *The Sunday Times*

INTRODUCTION

When offered the opportunity to write this book on the history and culture of carnations and other dianthus I was intrigued, for the subject has long fascinated me. Much scholarly research has been carried out recently into the history and development of the species by Dr John Harvey. However, surprisingly for such well-known plants, few books appear to have been written about their development since the Renaissance and their culture in the present day.

For centuries the dianthus has appealed for the same qualities that we know today. When we enjoy the fragrance of a simple wild pink or sophisticated carnation the experience unites us with many who have gone before. The challenge of presenting an authoritative account of the origin and evolution of these flowers has been irresistible to most writers on the subject, but I believe a true understanding of their early use, cultivation and symbolic meaning is still elusive. While scentless or small-flowered species grow wild in many parts of the temperate world, attempts to trace the threads of their development to the sophisticated carnations of the Renaissance often lead to an inextricable tangle of fact and myth, confusion and guesswork. There is much room for further work if we wish to unravel the absorbing history of their culture and meaning; the challenge will doubtless continue to lure us on, for the flowers remain charged with symbolism to this day.

The story of the development of the dianthus continues. It remains compelling and full of incident, since the genus is an easy subject for the hybridizer and countless new forms appear yearly, by accident as well as design. Some years ago a friend sent me seed from wild pinks gathered in the Canadian Rockies, of a type and location as yet unrecorded as far as I am aware. In my garden the small plants prospered, looking and behaving very much like one of our own native dianthus, now known as *deltoides* or the 'Maiden Pink', described by John Gerard in 1597 as a 'wilde creeping Pinke which groweth in our pastures neere about London, and in other places, but especially in the great field next to Detford, by the path side as you goe from Redriffe to Greenwich, which hath many

Dianthus deltoides *redrawn from John Gerard's* Herball, *1597 labelled by him* 'Caryophyllus Virgineus, Maidenly pink'. *Gerard describes the plant growing in London meadows and it remains widespread, though local. Easily grown from seed it will colonize and hold its own in many garden settings.*

small tender leaues shorter than any of the other wilde Pinkes.'[1] The Canadian introductions soon naturalized together with their English cousins among the beds, paths and steps of our garden. New plants sowed themselves, some apparently vigorous hybrids of these two and perhaps others, for we hold a National Collection

1 The plant known to botanists as the Deptford pink is the annual *Dianthus armeria*, described by Gerard as a 'Single read Sweet John' which we would recognize as a tall sweet william type. A printer's error some 400 years ago ascribed the wrong illustration to Gerard's caption. Now as then, trust in the printed word never should be absolute!

of older types of dianthus. I had done no work here and cross-pollination would have been by insects, wind, or the brushing hand of a passer-by. Last summer one of these new plants grew particularly large, brilliant flowers and I have saved and sown seed. In such a way over centuries, by haphazard or judicious means, dianthus species have intermingled one with another. Some of the resulting varieties and cultivars have been astonishing and this book will offer some ideas on their early history and significance as a cultivated flower, as well as a more prosaic account of how to grow the many forms available today.

Sophie Hughes

1
THE HISTORY OF
THE DIANTHUS

Some Unsolved Mysteries

Wild forms of dianthus, ancestors of our pinks, carnations, sweet williams and their many hybrids, grow in profusion in many parts of the temperate world. For the geographically minded, a wide arc may be drawn on the globe roughly between the 35th and the 55th northern latitudes, extending in the west to the British Isles and in the east to Siberia and Manchuria. Within this span some three hundred species or wild forms have been identified and named so far. They cluster most thickly around the Aegean, the Balkans, the Iberian peninsula and the European Alps, becoming more sparse as the terrain and climate become hot or wet. They are rare at the outer extremities, Britain and Russia having only two or three native forms. Very few of these many species have fragrance, and most have flowers of quite small size.

By way of a window into the history and development of the plants, we may begin by looking at the words 'dianthus', 'carnation' and 'pink'.

Origins of Dianthus

'Dianthus' was first used by Linnaeus in 1737, and the much-quoted notion that the name originates from the work of the Greek scholar Theophrastus, working in the fourth century BC, is a modern piece of whimsy, now discredited. There is no evidence of the dianthus in cultivation at the time of the ancient Greeks but we may suppose that then, as now, wild forms abounded on the mountains, hills and valleys of the Aegean mainland and archipelago. Linnaeus chose to call them 'flowers of the gods' (*dios* being 'divine' or 'of Zeus' and *anthos*, 'flower'). They still grow in abundance on the many-peaked sides of Mount Olympus, rising to 9,842 feet (3,000 metres) from the plains of Thessaly, a fitting home with its sudden moods, for the gods of the ancient Greeks. The ruins of many ancient sites, notably Delphi, Mycenae and Epidauros remain decorated by wild dianthus among the wealth of Greek spring flowers.

The desire to place these flowers in an ancient context is by means new, for a French source, *Les Jardinage des oeillets*, [1] suggested in 1647 that they appeared in Greek mythology in association with Artemis, daughter of Zeus. Artemis, virgin goddess of women, children and animals, was renowned for her beauty but would have nothing to do with mortals. However, she and her nymphs were much pursued by men, whose desire was to conquer and make love to them, Once, as she was walking on her island Ortygia, a shepherd came on her unawares. Artemis was a huntress, and had been given a silver bow and arrows made for her by the Cyclopes. In a fit of rage she raised her bow, shot out the boy's eyes, and flung them down at the side of the path. Dianthus, according to this tale, sprang from the site.

While there is no traceable classical source for this story, which would thus appear to be a picturesque seventeenth-century fabrication in its linking of the flower with antiquity, passion and death it is typical of a great many others. Dr Harvey's research has led him to conclude that 'The fact is that an extraordinary tissue of imagination has been woven about the carnation etc., mostly within the last century. It is essential to demolish this nonsense and begin with the known facts'. The view is, of course, indisputable for the historian. However, I find it intriguing that this and other tales, of apocryphal or otherwise unverified sources, are so widely known and readily remembered in connection with the flowers. Some of these legends and ideas are remarkably persistent, whether or not based on known facts, and have acquired an independent life of their own.

Another notion from the same source suggests that the flowers emanated from the tears of Mary, mother of Jesus, which turned to dianthus as she wept at the feet of her crucified son. The association with eyes in these stories suggests that the tellers had in mind the single, undeveloped forms of dianthus, with the characteristic circlet pattern resembling an iris framing a central receding throat, darkening towards the base like a pupil. A very early drawing of the flower, in the medieval Italian Herbal of Belluno, is of a small single flower of this type, named *occulus Christi* or 'eye of Christ'. Echoes of this Christian association may be present in the frequent symbolic appearances to this day of pinks and carnations as emblems of resurrection and hope. Much later, about 1493, the

1   Source given simply as 'L.B.'. *Les Jardinage des oeillets*   Paris, 1647.

French word for the entire species, *oeillet*, picks up the resemblance to eyes.

The Carnation

Turning now to 'carnation', we encounter a fascinating tangled skein of etymology, with many knots remaining to challenge the determined researcher. A similar word first appears in English in 1410, though it refers not to the flower but, again, to an account of the Christian mystery of God made flesh, or in our current usage, incarnate. 'The secund Adame chryste god and man reformed his ymage in his carnacioun.' There are further similar uses. The root here is obscure, but the word almost in its present form was originally used by Caelius Aurelianus in AD 420, though his Latin 'carnation' is translated as 'fleshiness' or 'corpulency'. By 1538 William Turner[2] is using 'Incarnacyon' to refer to flowers we would recognize as pinks or early carnations. While the series of associations cannot be demonstrated with any precision I feel that the appearance of blood- or flesh-coloured dianthus in medieval and Renaissance portrayals of the Christian mysteries may be more than coincidental, and that the flowers may well have had symbolic meaning which has eluded us so far.

There are alternative suggestions. Dr John Harvey proposes that the word 'carnation' may have derived from medieval Arabic as used in Turkey and Persia. The Turkish *karanfil* may, by a series of mispronounciations and mistakes in transcription have become our prefix 'carna'. This intriguing theory would dovetail with his conclusion that early development of the carnation was at the hands of the Persians and the Turks whose name for the plants as well as the plants themselves was assimilated into western Europe during the mid-fifteenth century.

Other sources conclude that the correct original form of the word was 'coronation' from the flowers' use, imagined or otherwise, in chaplets. While grave doubts have been cast over the supposed links with ancient classical practice here, there is at least one late medieval representation, in tapestry form, of the flowers' use in this fashion.[3] Henry Lyte,[4] writing in 1578, comments that the flowers themselves look like crowns, for each is 'dented or toothed aboue like to a littel crownet'. These, he observed, were

---

2 *The names of herbes in Greek, Latin, Englishe, Duche and Frenche with the commune names that Herbaries and Apothecaries use* William Turner, London, 1538.
3 Series of six tapestries *The Lady and Unicorn* about 1500, Loire region.
4 *A Niewe Herball or Historie of Plantes* Henry Lyte, 1578, London.

the finest of the range, which was already extensive: 'In English gardens are Gillofers, cloaue gillofers, and the greatest and brauest sorte of them are called Coronations or Cornations'. Edmund Spenser in 1597 echoes this image of the flowers' use to crown heads and initiates its still vibrant association with earthly lovers: 'Bring Coronations and Sops in Wine worn of paramours'. In the same year John Gerard produced his great Herbal, a massive and scholarly illustrated work. By now the word 'carnation' meant, as it did to Shakespeare, 'flesh coloured' and this meaning seems, for Gerard, to pre-date the flowers' name: 'The great Carnation Gilloflower flowers of an excellent sweete smell, and pleasant Carnation colour, whereof it tooke its name'.

The Pink

Turning now to 'pink', the word, the flower and its associations, another fascinating path unfolds. The word 'pinke' referring to the flower appears, as we have seen, in Gerard's work but does not extend to our current use, denoting colour, until 1681. However, the flower was undoubtedly known and valued in Britain from the last generation of the fourteenth century because it is mentioned by Friar Henry Daniel, described by Dr Harvey as the 'grandfather of botanical science in England'.[5] His work, in Dr Harvey's words 'has survived in a twilight world from which he begins to emerge as a pioneer'. Friar Daniel's observation of detail was acute and he writes with the relish of a true plantman of a perfumed single flower which can only have been a pink, acquired from the garden of Queen Philippa, wife of Edward III. It is, he says, 'a herb most like Cockel if cockle and that be asunder, but together not so. This was one of my 12 score and 12 herbs and at Stepney beside London had I it, and thither it was brought from the Queen Philippa's herber. It is a wonder sweet and spiceth every liquor that it be laid in, and principally red'. His transparent joy at the discovery of this treasure and its properties may remind us of our own first encounter with the scent and beauty of our own Cheddar pink, which this plant is judged to have been. Also familiar, across some 600 years, is the pleasure of a good plant given and received, in this case from a royal fellow gardener. In such a way over centuries have so many of our garden plants become part of the heritage in Britain. It is tradition we have a duty to continue.

Much further relevant material may be gleaned from studying

5 *Mediaval Gardens* John H Harvey, 1981, London (Batsford).

the etymology of 'gillyflower' and 'sops in wine', alas outside the present brief. There are also rich and as yet incompletely unravelled associations with the spice clove and our flowers, since their similarities of scent, appearance and perhaps use have invited comparison from earliest times. The Linnean epithet *caryophyllus* chosen by the great eighteenth-century Swedish botanist to describe these and other flowers, means 'clove leaved' but the association with the carnation had been established at least for three hundred years for it is used by William Turner, writing in 1538.

The Dianthus in Art and Literature

Leaving now the intriguing and unsolved mysteries of words, we may turn to a seam of art and artefact in search of the origin of dianthus in cultivation. There is possibly an appearance of a carnation in classical times (mentioned in a subsequent chapter) but this is an isolated event. Dianthus flowers are, however, certainly discernible in artistic work from late medieval times in Europe, and appearances multiply as the Renaissance approaches and unfolds.

The earliest representation of which we are aware is a drawing of a small, single pink in the Italian Herbal of Belluno dated about 1414. This beautifully coloured pink has small, single flowers and is clearly not a cultivated form; the drawing would have been executed for purposes of botanical identification. A further illustration of such a wild single dianthus is contained within the herbal drawn by Andrea Amadio, dated 1419. The original work is at St Mark's, Venice. There may well be other such examples yet unnoticed.

The earliest use I have found of the flower in a decorative setting is in work dated 1433 by Pisanello, of the Italian School. In his painting *A Princess of the House of Este* he shows the composed profile of a young woman, the outline of her pale face delineated sharply against a rich background of greenery. Sprinkled upon this dark leafy frame are red admiral butterflies, columbines, and the unmistakable five-petalled jagged outlines of single dianthus flowers. They are plain, reddish in colour, and rather larger than any wild form, suggesting that some selection had been at work. They appear again in greater detail in the exquisite Portinari Altar Piece of 1474–76, painted by Hugo van der Goes. This finely painted devotional work includes scarlet martagon lillies, with white and almost black irises in a decorated pot, and next to it in a fluted glass, a stem of deep purple columbine and three large, single, blood-red dianthus. Dark violets are strewn beneath. The lilies, irises and

columbines symbolize purity, nobility and the Holy Spirit respectively. The violets stand for humility. One may conjecture that the
dianthus now added to these established symbols may have been
chosen for good reason. The flowers, with their colour of raw flesh
may at this point have been chosen to represent the spirit made
man, the mystical 'incarnation' itself.

Certainly from about this time the decorators of the beautiful
devotional French and Flemish Books of Hours often chose to
include vibrant representations of the flowers in their work. The
Margaret de Foix Book from north-west France, dated about 1470,
depicts scenes of biblical drama as if through arched windows.
Heavily illuminated subtext embellishes and explains the pictures,
which are themselves surrounded by large, single, scarlet dianthus
flowers on branched stems among a profusion of periwinkles,
violas, strawberries, birds and strange animals. Single florets of
dianthus, mostly red but also pink and white, are sprinkled in the
margins and frames of many surviving works of this kind. A
Flemish example, dated about 1500, shows a solemn procession
including barefoot, cowled figures and churchmen in full regalia.
Around the portrait are closely observed studies of pinks, daisies,
campions, forget-me-nots, lilies of the valley and narcissi. There
are butterflies and also snails, and a perceptible sense of the painter's
wonder at the diversity of the natural world. Further such works
portray the familiar scenes from the Christian story. I have a print
of one in which the central panel shows Mary holding the infant
Jesus on a donkey being led from Bethlehem. The flowers here are
single blossoms of blue veronica, scarlet and white lathyrus, and
pale wild roses. The blood-red dianthus flowers dominate however, and one flower is shown in bud, its long green calyx just
showing emergent colour. Its shape, cylindrical with a splayed tip,
is reminiscent both of the spice clove and of the hand-forged nails
which would have been used for the crucifixion. Its placing, in a
narrow side border, is perhaps an omen of events to come and its
presence here may be one key to try as we attempt to unlock the
flowers' early significance and etymology.

Other Books of Hours are lighter in tone. From about 1500 also
comes a wonderfully comical portrait of a gardener's wife labori-
ously pushing a massive wheelbarrow, laden with a pot-grown
single carnation. Her husband, extending a hand as if to steady the
basket in which it rests, carries only a single stem of the flower over
his shoulder and looks towards the reader with a roguish grin.
Butterflies again adorn the flowers as they also do mine in summer.

Dianthus appear in many other contemporary devotional works, notably the beautiful Brussels tapestry depicting the mourning of Christ, dating from the beginning of the sixteenth century and now held in Vienna. Here, their red, single flowers appear among the plants at the feet of the solemn, weeping figures in their opulent and peaceful setting, with scenes of Calvary and the empty tomb in the distance.

Returning to secular Renaissance art, it is interesting to look again at *Primavera* by Botticelli, dated about 1478. Included in the figures surrounding Venus, mother of universal nature, is the Roman goddess Flora. Her simple, flowing white dress, edged with lace, is extravagantly decorated with flowers, drawn complete with their foliage as if from closely observed growing plants. Across her shoulders and breast are alternating brilliant blue cornflowers and full, apparently double rose-pink dianthus flowers. The hem of her dress is likewise bordered with cornflowers and, this time, single pale pink, deeply fringed wild dianthus. From a deep fold in her gown Flora is scattering open blossoms of pink, white and red roses on to the ground, which is deep green and studded with wild flowers, reminiscent of the *millefleurs* background of the great tapestry hangings of this century.

One of the finest of these, woven earlier in Brussels for Philip of Burgundy in 1466 has an almost black ground strewn with a wealth of detailed flowers worked with gold, silver and silks. Among other accurately delineated plants and shrubs, which include holly, irises, lilies, bluebells and aconites, are several large clumps of dianthus. They appear in white as well as a deep rose colour, both in tall forms of carnation type with many flowers on a branched stem, and more-dwarf, apparently double small pinks. From the latter part of this century there is a wealth of these fine tapestries, and in their closely worked backgrounds of flowers, birds, reptiles and insects it is rare for the dianthus to be missing. The themes are most often on a grand scale, and high rooms at the Victoria and Albert Museum in London are hung from ceiling to floor with fine examples. The effect of entering such a space is breathtaking. Mainly of Flemish and French origin, some of these are believed to have been made for Margaret, the daughter of King René of Anjou, on the occasion of her marriage to Henry VI of England. Others are thought to have been acquired by Cardinal Wolsey for Henry VIII who would have used them, as was customary, to brighten and warm the bleak interiors of the day.

The figures portrayed are imposing, larger than life, of classical or allegorical provenance. Others display scenes of contemporary life, giving an unvarnished and often humorous portrait of its pleasures, pastimes and work. A feature of many of these, notably *La Noble Pastorale* and the *Three Fates* are dianthus flowers showing clear flashes of contrasting pale colour within each dark petal. The great explosion of interest had now begun in the extraordinary colour forms these flowers were to produce. The scent, too, of the flowers is celebrated as a centrepiece of one of the beautiful six tapestries of the *Lady with the Unicorn* made in the Loire region about 1500. A crown of scarlet carnations is shown being woven by a lady in rich clothing, the light shimmering on the silks and velvet of her gown. She is watched by a maid, a unicorn and a lion, all of whom hover on a blue flower-decked meadow decorated with rabbits, monkeys and mice. All of the flowers in these portraits, including the dianthus, could be picked from our gardens today.

The Sixteenth Century

From 1500 onwards contemporary works of art show a flush of specimens of the growing plants portrayed in carefully placed containers in the European courtyards and enclosed outdoor spaces of the day. The early herbers, or gardens, attached to palaces and fine houses, had the feel of outdoor rooms, flanked by turfed and flower-planted benches and often walled high by trelliswork or pergolas supporting roses and vines. The ground was a patchwork of small beds, often raised, intersected by paths or spread with a green 'flowery meade' of chamomile or closely rolled grass sprinkled, like the *millefleurs* tapestries, with a variety of different wild flowers – strawberry, daisy, dandelion and violet. Small-flowered pinks of red, pink and white, tumble through low rails or sprout from a mass of neighbouring plant growth in thickly planted beds. Set apart now for pampered treatment are the cultivated and containerized carnations. They sit in decorated pots, each with its own framework of supporting canes, placed at eye-level near to a seat or in splendid isolation next to a peacock, as if for comparative display. The plants are tall, the flowers large and often fully double. They grow also from the ground, their stems held by carefully constructed metalwork or wooden supports, placed in individual brick surrounds in the formal parterre beds, among elaborately trained shrubs and admiring courtiers. Their scent would have been an important ingredient of the appeal, for in this age of vulnerability to plague and pestilence the hand of the apothecaries was at best uncertain, and perfumed spices and flowers were valued for their imagined prophylactic effects against the disease-ridden vapours.

They must at least have provided competition for the less pleasant smells of summer in this age of open sewers.

The importance of carnations among the other yet limited garden flora is clear also from many contemporary portraits showing interiors. Holbein's painting, dated 1528, of the family of Sir Thomas More, shows three vases of flowers containing Madonna lilies, narcissi, columbines, irises, peonies and pansies. The carnations among them are large, conspicuous and bright red. A further Holbein portrait of a merchant, dated 1532, shows a man in early middle age arrayed with the trappings of his prosperity. On a table by his elbow in pride of place is set a vase of three mop-headed double pinks, in pale rose colour. Their heads are held on a branched stem and they would appear to be cultivated forms, closely resembling those on the Botticelli *Primavera*. We may conjecture that, along with the other carefully chosen items in this picture the flowers had some significance for him; a living import, perhaps, at his hands, from Italy.

By the mid-sixteenth century contemporary drawings show pot-grown carnations sporting bicoloured florets and striped or quartered petals. The Elizabethan age with its taste for the bizarre, including aberrant forms of flowers, had arrived. It embraced these curious works of nature with relish. Although deliberate hybridizing cannot have taken place because the sexuality of plants was not yet understood, accidental crosses must have occurred when the plants were gathered into collections. Seed was saved from interesting forms of carnations here as elsewhere in Europe, and a profusion of cultivars began to emerge. There was much exchanging and trading of seed among the fraternity of enthusiasts, where any present day plantsman would have felt at home immediately. John Gerard writes that the carnations were of 'such various colours and also severall shapes, that a great and large volume would not suffice to write of every one at large in particular; considering how infinite they are, and how every yeare every clymate and country bringeth forth new sorts'. A merchant of Gerard's acquaintance, Nicholas Leate, clearly a fellow enthusiast, had acquired stock of a yellow-flowered variety from Poland and, in the true tradition of good gardening practice, 'gave me thereof for my garden'. This must have derived in part from *Dianthus knappii*, native to Hungary and Bosnia.

The Elizabethan appetite for novelty and innovation, thus whetted, was insatiable and must have taxed the resources of the hybridists. The symbolic qualities of the flowers appear to have dimmed as they became valued and collected in the manner of other

Carnations showing double and bicoloured flowers grown in a decorated pot and supported by canes. Redrawn from De Stirpium Historia *by J. Bock, 1552. Such plants feature in many European paintings from the end of the fifteenth century.*

extravagant items, natural and unnatural, in this exciting age. The extent of their artificiality at the hands of man drew the scalpel of Shakespeare's wit as, writing in *The Winters Tale* in 1611, he used the flowers to focus debate on the often rehearsed Renaissance tension between 'art' and 'nature'. Perdita proclaims her resolute distaste for the 'carnations and streaked gillyvors which some call nature's bastards', preferring instead the plainer qualities of 'hot lavender, mints, savory, marjoram'. She is not changed in her view by Polixenes' philosophical answer, to the effect that any man-made 'improvement' of nature is itself the creation of nature, since man and his powers are also natural. 'I'll not put the dibble in earth to set one slip of them' she says, 'No more than, were I painted, I would wish this youth should say 'twere well, and only therefore desire to breed by me'.

Perdita may be referring to or have initiated the naming of a distinctive type of 'painted lady' carnation described extensively at the time, being white-coloured beneath and stippled, red on white, above. I grow one of this type today, and it looks as if it is dusted with the finest powder; its scent is extraordinarily pungent. The colour is laid rather in the manner of hoar frost and just possibly it is of the type referred to by Thomas Tusser in his *Five Hundred Points of Good Husbandry*, published in 1573, thus:

> The gilloflower also the skilful doe know,
> Doth look to be covered in frost and in snow.

Without documentary evidence it is of course impossible to identify such flowers with any certainty, but it is noteworthy that carnations, with tulips, were the first plants to attract cultivar names at about this time and that fleshly, painted ladies, ripe satirical material for the wits of the day, should be in Shakespeare's mind when speaking of these flowers. They do, if one looks closely, seem to have been rouged with a camel-hair brush, rose colour on white. Their scent is heavy, exotic and refreshing. There is indeed a disturbing sensuality here in contrast to the wholesome pungency of Perdita's herbs and her homely 'marigold, that goes to bed with the sun and with him rises'. One can well understand the fascination of such foreign beauties against the more subdued colours and subtle scents of familiar British-grown primroses, violets, honeysuckle and aromatic herbs.

The Seventeenth Century

From the early seventeenth century the exploding popularity of the flowers is clear from their increasingly frequent appearance in every kind of contemporary artwork. Embroidered pieces are a rich source here. Night-caps, cushion covers, bed hangings and fine clothing become densely worked with intricate designs executed with the fine skills born of this time which, for some, was leisured and cultivated. Needlewomen sat long hours at their work and there are many surviving examples of their industry. Among them were Bess of Hardwicke and Mary Queen of Scots. Many of the flowers they chose to include in their work had well understood contemporary meaning; single pinks appear to have indicated betrothal. A portrait of a lady, Margaret Laton, dated 1610, shows her in a narrow silk jacket richly worked with roses, honeysuckle and delicate wild pinks on a single, coiling stem, as if from a magic plant inhabited by glittering wild parrots, butterflies, and perfectly worked jewel-like snails. Fuller-flowered carnations appear on the stiff bodiced, extravagant dress believed to have been worn by Gloriana herself, Elizabeth the Virgin Queen.

The clove scent of the flowers led to various attempts at their incorporation into the culinary dishes of the day, and several contemporary recipes appear later. The flowers' scent and essence was believed to cheer the heart and cure its 'passhione'. They were also used to stimulate, and feature in love potions of the day.

The ensuing Jacobean age was no less enchanted by the flowers. In 1617 William Lawson pronounced carnations 'the king of the flowers except the rose'.[6] The dress of the courtiers became yet more elaborate, with ribbons, spangled rosettes and heavy, embroidered flowers, often raised with appliqué and worked with silver and gold thread. Carnations, strikingly striped and sectored, oddly speckled and spotted, or delicately edged with a patterned rim are often to be found in this decorative feast. This was the first great era of the carnation, whose patterns, like those of the tulip (whose history of connoisseur-appeal is better known); became ever more elaborate.

The Florists

Groups of enthusiasts formed to share the pleasure of the culture and acquisition of such flowers. They organized themselves into societies, whose members styled themselves as 'Florists'. Carnations and tulips were the first two flowers to attract this specialist attention, soon to be joined by the auricula, and later the polyanthus, hyacinth, anemone and ranunculus, though the pink, relatively unimproved, had to wait until after 1750 to join this élite company. Records survive of 'Florists' Feasts', the earliest from Norwich where, on 3 May 1631, a play was presented for 'a conflux of Gentlemen of birth and quality'. The patron of this society is

6 *A New Orchard and Garden* William Lawson, 1617, London.

described as a man 'fervently addicted to a speculation of the virtues and beauties of all Florists' flowers'. Such fervent addiction would, I feel, ensure our immediate mutual recognition and rapport if we were to meet him today.

The Florists' meetings became substantial affairs, and as ever, when enthusiasts are gathered together, a lively edge of competitive spirit developed. Then, as now, acknowledged men of experience were in charge of the delicate matter of judging. On 16 April, 1729, 130 Florists met at The Dog at Richmond Hill, where 'five ancient and judicious Gardiners were judges to determine whose Flowers excell'd'. Such spring meetings would have been focused on auricula and polyanthus, but carnations took centre stage as the summer arrived. In public houses throughout the length and breadth of the country growers met to display their fine carnation blooms, win silver spoons and eat a midday meal together in the second half of the eighteenth century. Pinks only became the subject of feasts towards the end of the century. Church services accompanied some of these gatherings and good humour appears to have prevailed in most though 'seeds of discord' occurred in Norwich in 1645, and Thomas Hogg, much later in 1822, mentions that too much drinking on the part of participants was spoiling the shows. The Florists displayed their blooms individually, probably stuck into bottles. They were thus admired and judged at close quarters, somehow divorced from their natural habitat, where in truth their pampered lifestyle had encouraged the sacrifice of vigour for beauty. Their delicate constitution meant none lasted for long, but more were always waiting to take their places.

There was a brisk trade in seed from Holland and the seductive charms of newly raised seedlings are breathlessly described in contemporary prose. By 1629 John Parkinson lists fifty-four cultivar names, and some fifty years later his son-in-law John Rea lists 360.

We have the good fortune to be able to see superb images of the sorts of flowers which so captivated contemporary taste, for this flush of horticultural development coincided with the heyday of the great Flemish masters, several of whom devoted themselves almost exclusively to the art of flower painting. In their work a widening selection of cultivated flowers appear to have been chosen as much for their intrinsic beauty as for their symbolic meaning, and during the massive output of the seventeenth century scarcely any of these masters omit a carnation from their celebration of the beauties of the natural world. In a convention dating from about 1630, the

'Gilloflowers' redrawn from John Parkinson's Paradisi in Sole
Paradisus Terrestris *1629. Outstanding among the shaggy-petalled
double carnations of the day is the restrained outline, bottom right, of
'Master Tuggie, his Rose Gilloflower', a significant break.*

flowers are painted twined into swags and garlands with striped tulips, roses, columbines, lilies and peonies arranged to frame a cartouche or niche containing a subject of intense piety. Biblical scenes, portraits of the Holy Family and busts of saints and heroes framed within increasingly sumptuous floral concoctions. Spirals of holly, ivy and vine link meticulous studies of double poppies, narcissi, fritillaries, carnations and oddly coloured violas, organized into festoons and clusters, tied with ribbons, decorated with butterflies and held aloft by cherubs. The carnations, full-flowered doubles in white, red, pink and yellow, some exquisitely marked with contrasting colours, appear in every one. They are featured too in the massed cornucopias of flowers, fruit, animals, insects and fish typical of the genre in its later stages. Flowers in these painting are often bundled into wooden vats, ceramic pots and glass goblets, usually surrounded by an eclectic mix of treasures; coins, rings and jewels are strewn on a table together with a tortoise, a porcupine and a silkworm on an eaten mulberry leaf. A single iridescent drop of water may sit at the edge of a petal. These pieces, ever more extravagant, often seem to be simply a joyous pretext for assembling wonderful small objects, and they become ever more baroque. Tiring, perhaps, of such excesses, a painting by Philip de Marlier dated 1639 narrows its focus to one flower type only. Twenty or so carnations, each differently marked, are painted against a background of restful green. Their supple stems spring from a small transparent vase. The work is rare in confining itself to one flower; the carnation in its variety clearly seemed ripe enough for this attention, sufficient testimony to nature improved by the hand of man.

New Varieties

Such feats of performance on the part of the carnations and those who raise them were indeed remarkable when one considers that at this time plant sexuality was not understood, and the new varieties were achieved by meticulous selection of haphazard crosses. While much of this selection appears to have taken place in northern Europe, the English eye was also focused on the flowers and their detail, for they are strongly represented in the compilation of exquisite plant portraits of Alexander Marshal in the *Windsor Florilegium* which were painted during the interregnum. Marshal too scatters diverting curiosities of the natural world among his flowers, with fish, snakes and guinea pigs joining ladybirds, caterpillars and slugs among his arrays of striped tulips, auriculas and carnations. Marshal, like many cultivated contemporaries was himself a Florist, obliged to seek exile in France during the civil war where the great botanical illustrator Nicolas Robert, an early member of the Parisian *Academie Royale*, was at work on detailed plant studies for the brother of Louis XIII, Gaston d'Orleans. Royal patronage of such endeavour appears to have been whole-hearted, and the names of many kings, queens and aristocrats of the great European families are among those bestowed on new varieties of carnation. The passion for these flowers became highly fashionable. Caught in the swirling tides of European politics courtiers and politicians turned, when they could, for recreation to the culture of their plants and gardens. Sir Ralph Verney, for one, fellow Royalist with Alexander Marshal, returned home from exile with relief in 1653 to tend his Persian tulips, ranunculus, pinks and carnations and to continue work on the extension of his garden.

The intense interest in natural history, such a strong feature of the Caroline era, was fuelled by imports from the ever-widening world and found focus in the formation of the Royal Society in London, founded in 1660 by 'diverse worthy persons, inquisitive into natural philosophy and other parts of human learning'. The restored Charles himself was patron of this society, and in this year two red and white flaked or striped carnations are named afer him and his long-suffering, plain wife Catherine of Braganza. There are sumptuously embroidered satin bedcurtains of the same date, reputed to have hung round the notorious royal bed; they feature ebullient entwined scarlet carnations. Meanwhile in Eastern Europe and the Ottoman Empire more refined motifs of the flowers continued to be woven, embroidered and otherwise displayed upon carpets, hangings, prayer mats and saddle-cloths. There are two exquisitely-worked childrens' jackets from Persia in the Victoria and Albert Museum, made from crimson brocade and patterned with slender carnations, minutely embroidered with floss silk.

Dogged attempts continued through the seventeenth century to organize and classify the plant and animal kingdoms. The torch was passed briefly from the Flemings – Dodoens, Lobel and L'Ecluse (Clusius) – who had dominated the sixteenth century, to the British Parkinson, Culpepper and John Rea, who published in 1629, 1652 and 1676 respectively. In the case of the dianthus valiant efforts were made to separate sweet williams, carnations and pinks, then as now a thankless task.

John Rea distinguished the three main categories we recognize today. First 'Sweet William or Sweet John' of which he says there are 'several sorts, their form too well-known to be described'. He felt that only the 'double Sweete John or Velvet Sweete William' were worthy of esteem. Second, 'july flowers' (carnations) so called 'from the month they blow in'. They are, he states, 'the summer's glory as Tulips are the pride of spring. Their care, he suggested, merited particular attention, 'especially the nobler sorts which are called Dutch July flowers, or more vulgarly carnations, raised from seeds in the Netherlands and other parts adjoining the sea, and thence conveyed to us.' He clearly had little hope of British success in cultivating these beauties and records, with what sounds like personal chagrin, that 'Our inland endeavours to raise them seldom countervail our trouble, none or very few raising good ones that have not the neighbourhood of the sea'. The enchantment beckons however, for their colours are 'red purple, scarlet, tawny and white . . . such delicate variegations and pleasing scents to vie with any species whatsoever . . . the single colours little esteemed in comparison of those striped, flaked or powder'd upon white or blush, with darker or lighter red, crimson or carnation, sadder or brighter purple, deeper or paler scarlet'. He lists six distinct colour combinations for the flakes or striped flowers including King Solomon, a 'neat flower finely marked purple on snow white', and Pluto, a striped 'deep clove colour and black on each leaf' (petal), and six more plain sorts including the 'Giant Clove' of which he says there were two kinds in three colours. They were also useful, he says, in 'the best Cordials, extremely comforting to the noblest part of man, the heart.' His third category is pinks.

Rea's understanding and advice on the principles of plant culture is basically sound. His pot-grown carnations were lovingly set in 'mole earth, long untilled', fed with lime and dung (though this rich diet probably contributed to his frustrating losses), watered carefully, tied on canes and disbudded. The fuller pods were 'let down' or assisted, with careful nicks of a knife, to emerge symetrically from their calyces. Sometimes the opened petals were gently held in shape by a 'narrow film of gold beaters old mould, moistened with the tongue' and stuck together, concealed behind the puffed shape of the bloom, rather in the manner of a band of sticky tape. His instructions for layering and sowing seed of carnations would stand happily today. However he falls prey to that strain of fanciful credulity often characteristic of the gardener, for he suggests that young plants be set out at full moon, with 'the ashes of rotted and superfluous slips and stems of burnt July flowers', as if somehow the remains of a funeral pyre of their own kind would act as a talisman against the malevolent powers of slugs and rots. It is indeed conceivable that the gritty, open textured ash could have deterred the former and, by ensuring good drainage, prevented the latter. Present-day gardeners could wait for a full moon in April – try it and see!

The habits of acute observation, tenacious recording of detail and willingness to experiment shared by such practical men are a characteristic of the burgeoning scientific fever of the times. Among such scholars was Nehemiah Grew, Secretary to the Royal Society, who set himself to observe the sexual functioning of plants. His theories were to lead to the early experiments in hybridization of the next century. Interestingly, the dianthus was used as one of the earliest subjects, and in 1715 Mr Fairchild, a commercial gardener and florist at Hoxton, records his deliberate impregnation of a carnation with the pollen of a sweet william, the resulting progeny being different from either plant. While this particular stem does not appear to have survived there is a herbarium specimen of a flaked carnation labelled 'Mr Fairchild's Mule' preserved at Oxford, dated to the second decade of the eighteenth century. While the flower itself appears little different from those with which we are familiar in contemporary works of art, a scientific breakthrough had been made. Thomas Fairchild continued his experiments and corresponded with the young Linnaeus, whose foundation work on modern botanical classification was being formulated during the mid-eighteenth century. Linnaeus was credited by a contemporary with making 'what was before chaos order, and what was before difficult easy'. The increasingly sophisticated work of these men had laid, by the late eighteenth century, the knowledge base that was to inform the next great stage of development of our garden flora, that of the hybridists.

Attention of plant fanciers was diverted at this juncture towards the great number of fresh plants from all parts of the world, discovered, described, imported and in many cases established for good in our gardens, this was the great age of introductions and of the development of British gardens to embrace them.

The activities of the dedicated carnation enthusiast continued however. A strain of *remontant* carnations, tall-growing plants with extended flowering was developed in France during the 1750s and the Florists' Societies peaked in popularity in the 1770s. Further enabled in the new understanding of plant hybridization they continued to pursue the elusive ideal form of carnation flower, chief of whose attributes was now to become 'rose leaved' or smooth petalled. John Parkinson had illustrated and described a lone early prize of this kind raised and 'only possessed by' its owner Mr

'Picotee' carnation of pure white, each petal decorated with a fine scarlet edge. From an original engraving dated 1750.

Tuggie in 1629. This elusive and therefore desirable characteristic could now be encouraged by selective breeding.

The achievements of the Florists were recorded through the eighteenth century by new generations of botanical artists. Georg Dionysius Ehret, Pierre Joseph Redouté and Francis Bauer all made meticulous studies of the carnation beside their other work. Robert Furber, whose twelve portraits of *The Months of Flowers* are well known and widely reproduced, includes huge specimens of carnations as well as smaller, unusually patterned pinks in his over-flowing containers. He includes 'Painted Lady' pinks as well as carnations, 'Indian or China pinks' and several specimens of the newly fashionable 'Picotee'.

The early flowers of this form had serrated petal edges, soon to be all but bred away, but were distinguished by a rim of contrasting colour at the petal edge. They look like pale, flounced ballgowns edged with the finest contrasting trim. Some were 'pounced' or marked with flecks, narrow rays, or streaks of colour extending from the dark edge towards the centre. Others were of pure white or pale yellow ground, marked with contrasting colours of near black, purple, deep crimson and scarlet. The striped 'flaked' or bicoloured carnations of the previous century were joined by 'bizarres' of three or more tones.

All such novelties continued to receive a rapturous welcome, and were much patronized by royalty and the aristocracy in Europe as well as Britain. Empress Josephine and Queen Caroline of England were both renowned collectors and had cultivars named after them. The plants themselves however were of poor constitution and short lifespan, being often replaced with new seedlings, now from Germany, where contemporary plantsmen began to record the plethora of new cultivars by detaching a single petal from the bloom for the individual attention of the painter. An exquisite compilation of such petals was made by Dr Rossig in 1806, showing 120 different named forms of carnation. The palette of colours and range of patterns is wide. Shades range from near black, steely purple-grey and rich mauve, through the reds, pinks and white, to primrose and brilliant yellow, flame and tawny shades. Patterns are of streaks and spots, speckles and contrasting edges. Their names are reminiscent of the age – 'Grand Admiral', 'The Elector of Saxony', 'Tzar Peter der Grosse', and 'Rousseau'. The latter was a carnation lover and keen-eyed collector. On rescuing a plant of wild *Dianthus superbus* from a hungry cow in a field he sent a piece to a friend with a note: 'Do you grow *Dianthus superbus*? If not, I must send it to you. It is the most exquisite carnation, and deliciously scented. Only the Horses of the Sun should be allowed to graze upon it'.

Pinks had also come into their own by now and became included in the august company of Florists' flowers from the mid-eighteenth century. For many years Florists had valued an outlined edge to the petals of their auriculas, primulas, ranunculus and anemones. Now the pink, uniquely among dianthus, began to demonstrate this talent for itself, immediately securing a hold on contemporary taste and a plethora of named forms. From its traditional home in the open air, a humble, easy and unassuming part of English flora, the pink in its laced form, was now to become elevated to the smart circles of its cousin the carnation. No pains were spared to secure the comfort and well-being of the plants and the safe opening of the flowers. James Maddock, of whom more will be heard in Chapter 7, was a man with an eye for detail and a love of harmony. He made elaborate arrangements for the staging of his pot-grown treasures, shading them with a cloth awning 'to be let up and down by means of lines and pulley', chasing earwigs from the petals at night, and painting his flower pots white and supporting plant sticks green.

Contemporary illustrations show near-perfect confections at the hands of such men. Idealized and lovely, their names reflect the transparent enthusiasm of their raisers: 'Barratt's Conqueror', 'Styles's Hero', 'Smith's Champion'. Carnations, meanwhile, in yet another renewed flush of Victorian and Regency popularity, continued to attract the nomenclature of the noble and great; among the five hundred or so show carnations recorded between 1819 and 1858 are 'Prince Albert', 'The Marquis of Bath' and 'Lord Castlereagh'. A 'constant blooming' or repeat flowering carnation, ancestor of our modern 'perpetual-flowering' types, was raised in 1842 in France and the 'Malmaison' strain was developed in 1857 by M. Lasie under the patronage of Empress Eugénie. With their opulent scent and rich, pink, fringed petals bursting from a jade green calyx these 'Malmaisons' graced the bosoms of Edwardian beauties and the tables of fine houses. Few large establishments were without a house devoted entirely to carnations in this age of flushed prosperity and extravagance. Only a handful of cultivars how remain and have their own national collection.

Many French hybrids were exported to America and were to form the basis of further races including 'American tree carnations' developed from the tall European types which are reported to have extended to the roofs of glasshouses. From this point onwards precise progenitors and pedigrees become obscure, for, as an American breeder, Lambourn, wrote in 1892, 'By hybridizing and cross-fertilizing their distinction is gradually disappearing, the races are being mixed.' Lambourn, like others before him, combined a passion for carnations with a passion for politics. He ran for Congress in 1876 using carnation flowers prominently in his campaign. The flower remains emblazoned on the crest of Ohio, his home State.

While the amateur florists continued to raise and name favourites for the showbench and conservatory – and many prints of their blooms survive – commercial growers now entered the field in force. The carnation as a flower to cut and sell was becoming big business, and the breeders now aimed to attain a combination of large flowers, ease of culture, but above all length of flowering. 'Perpetual-flowering' strains of carnation appeared in 1842 in Southern France. These plants were tender and needed to be grown under glass. Scent – that most essential part of the charm of these flowers for many of us – was, alas, often sacrificed for brilliance of colour, abundance of crop, and robustness of temperament in a competitive market place.

Continuing work along these lines has resulted in the main forms

Laced pinks redrawn from The Florist, 1848. *'Mr Edwards' (left) and 'Young's Double X' (right). Such illustrations abound, to our mingled delight and despair, for all such old cultivars are lost to cultivation.*

of dianthus that we know today and which the following chapters will look at in more detail.

NOMENCLATURE

The use of Latin in the naming of plants may seem confusing to a beginner, but the principles are simple and important to understand since they form the basis of an internationally-agreed systematic code with which to identify any plant, whether wild or cultivated, from anywhere in the world.

The Latin name of a plant usually consists of two words. The first, spelt with an initial capital letter, is the generic name, indicating the group into which it falls – in this case, *Dianthus*. The second word is the specific name, usually spelt without an initial capital, for instance *alpinus, fragrans* etc. A third name may denote a subspecies or variety within a species, for instance *Dianthus superbus speciosus*, or more commonly commemorate an individual's selection of a good form, for instance *Dianthus deltoides* 'E. A. Bowles'. Finally, hybrids, or intentionally crossed and selected cultivars, are properly indicated by a mark x, (though for convenience this is generally left out in ordinary text), thus *Dianthus* x 'Mrs Sinkins' or *Dianthus* x *allwoodii* 'Doris'.

Taking a step back for a wider view, we need to understand that all dianthus belong to the botanical order Caryophyllaceae. This is a large and quite important family including such genera as *Arenaria* (sandwort), *Silene* (campion), *Saponaria* (soapwort), *Lychnis*, *Gypsophila* (baby's breath) and *Cerastium* (snow in summer) to mention only a few.

Within the genus *Dianthus* are some three hundred species forms, extending in their natural habitat throughout Europe and into Asia, skirting the north of Africa and making occasional appearances in the south of that continent as well as North America. Others no doubt await discovery and description elsewhere, and travellers believe there may be yet unrecorded wild forms in China and Japan. Nearer to home a hitherto unknown form of dianthus was discovered growing wild on the Gower coast in 1984.

For convenience, they are divided here into two main groups: those whose natural habitat is the rocky or scree terrain typical of high altitudes, and those whose chosen home in the wild is of a gentler more lowland type.

CHARACTERISTICS

Annual, biennial or perennial in habit, dianthus bear slender, smooth, opposite leaves, parallel-veined and often greeny-grey in colour. Species forms are both tap- and fibrous-rooted. Stems are smooth, rounded and upright, bearing five-petalled, flattened flowers in solitary, loosely-branched or densely-clustered heads. In species forms the flowers' calyces are narrow, cylindrical and five toothed, with opposing pairs of scales at the base. Petals are red, shades of magenta and pink, white and, more rarely, yellow, toothed or deeply fringed, often fragrant. Species forms have, typically, ten stamens and two styles. Pollination is by insects, mainly bees but also butterflies.

Several of the wild forms will readily cross with one another, resulting in similar varieties within the species, many hybrid forms having occurred as a result of natural cross-pollination in the wild. Some of these hybrids in turn will produce pollen and are themselves fertile. Will Ingwersen, whose monograph on the species forms, written in 1949 is a foundation work and describes encountering rocky slopes of many acres in a high valley in the Franco-Italian *Alpes Maritimes* where the ground was 'stained crimson' with *Dianthus neglectus* and it was 'impossible to tread without destroying the flowers'. He describes how there was 'every conceivable variation of shape and colour to be found among the myriads of plants' which were in a wide range of colours, from brilliant crimson to washy pink, on stems of differing lengths and with petals of different sizes. Many wild pinks, then, may naturally have undergone countless cyclical changes over centuries while growing in their own habitat, and plants or seeds reaching nurserymens' stands or even specialists' seed lists, are thus unlikely to be perfectly consistent in form, colour and nomenclature.

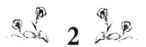

2

THE ALPINE DIANTHUS

The smallest of the species forms of dianthus are to be found in the high Alps and other mountain ranges in the northern hemisphere. Their natural habitat is scree, rock face and crevice, on limestone or chalk formations. Reproduction of their exquisitely miniaturized growth habit has connoisseur appeal and draws the true enthusiast to devise elaborate, simulated versions of their natural habitat. Such efforts will be rewarded with superbly tight hummocks of leaves and dense mats of foliage, ornamented in due season with the typical five-petalled flowers on short stems. Many of these forms are sweetly scented and are excellent subjects for the alpine house and cold greenhouse. Fine examples of well-grown alpine dianthus may be seen at Kew in London and at many other major botanical gardens. They are worth seeking out in April and May when the plants are at their best.

ALPINE-HOUSE CULTURE

Dianthus of this type are often grown in pans, or wide-rimmed pots of relatively shallow draught, which are set out in the open during the summer in a plunge bed, and removed in autumn to the cold, light, but well-ventilated conditions of a frame or alpine house. Guidance on the construction of such beds, houses and frames and the detailed care of their inhabitants is widely available in many specialist books, and those particularly interested in these and other alpine plants may find it well worth while to join the Alpine Garden Society, a flourishing organization with international links and a network of local groups. This society's publications are of high quality and they produce an annual seed list, often offering the opportunity to acquire rare treasures. There are also lively and well-attended local meetings where knowledge and new acquaintances may be rapidly acquired by an interested newcomer.

Alpine-type dianthus will tolerate any amount of cold, but tend to flounder in the face of direct exposure to the British winter, whose cold, sodden soil and muggy atmosphere could hardly be more different from the dry snow cover and quick, airy spring of their natural mountain habitat. It may be helpful to consider for a moment the annual cycle of a plant such as the alpine dianthus in its natural setting, because an understanding of a plant's character and behaviour in the wild will often prove an essential foundation for sensitive culture of its hybrids as well as its 'improved' forms in our gardens.

For many months the plants are snow-covered, and thus provided with important winter protection against both cold and excessive humidity. The soil temperatures under snow do not fall much below freezing point, but these temperatures are low enough to ensure that there is little unfrozen moisture around the leaves and crown of the plant, which is thus kept dormant and relatively dry until the melting of the snow. At this point the plants are flooded with sudden abundant ultraviolet light, encouraging an immediate resumption of growth, and the formation and unfolding of the flower buds. One of the main problems for dianthus of such provenance and for their progeny in temperate gardens is that they tend to make new growth in warm and moist spells during our odd and unpredictably changeable winters. This growth is highly vulnerable to hard frosts or cold drying winds that damage plant tissue which is then prey to fungal infection. Protection from these extremes of damp and humidity will permit these plants to perform at their best in cultivation.

Soil

The soil of their natural habitat tends to be austere, often in the form of a thin-skinned layer over a base of broken stone, shingle or rock. We may imitate this with a soil consisting of a high percentage of sharp sand or fine grit mixed with a standard John Innes or soil-free compost. Such a diet will support healthy, vigorous and tight-growing plants which will do themselves justice and be a joy to own.

In the wild these plants are often showered with rock falls or have their cushioned topgrowth pulled yards from their original roothold by moving screes. Taking a cue from this, top dressings of limestone chippings may be successfully applied to pot grown plants in our own culture, serving the double purpose of maintaining a clean, dry joint between root-stock and top-growth, and also keeping the plant tidy looking by disguising any scrawny-looking growth at their skirts. Handfuls of limestone chippings can be carefully spinkled over and worked down between the leaves from above, and packed beneath the cushion and around the collar of the main stem. I have often removed an unattractive-looking, lax-growing specimen from pot or garden, removed its soil, bunched the top-growth together and replanted it in a gritty mix to conceal the ungainly stems, only to find the plant takes on a new lease of life and springs again sturdily from its new foothold. These are tough creatures and one must not be afraid of drastic action if they are not performing with the health and vigour we might expect.

OUTDOOR CULTURE

While the owner of an alpine house may choose to cherish a collection of species and hybrid alpine-type dianthus exclusively within its shelter, many growers find that plants of the less temperamental varieties will do well enough in the open garden on a rockery or scree bed. However, before offering any plants of treasured or unknown character to the elements it is prudent to ensure a back-up stock in case of failure, and suggestions on propagation are offered in the following section. No guarantees can be given on the performance of choice alpine dianthus in the open garden, and plants which succeed in one season or position may fail unaccountably in another. Dianthus, not unlike every other type of plant, have individual temperaments; experience teaches one to regard them with increasing respect.

Raised Beds

The construction of raised beds, rockery or scree areas in the garden is a lure which tempts almost all gardeners at some stage in their careers, and is well worth while if you wish to offer a con-genial home to the true alpine dianthus as well as their more vigorous hybrid children and grandchildren. The beginner and experienced gardener alike may learn much from the many special-ist works on the building of such areas, and the use of stone in their making to create seemingly natural areas for the plants. A west- or east-facing natural slope is an advantage, preferably clear from the canopy, leaf fall and root run of trees and from the shade and drip of buildings. The position needs to be convenient and accessible for the gardener and should be sited to blend into the general design of the garden as far as possible and invite the close attention it deserves. A successfully-constructed plant area involving stone-work should give the onlooker the impression that the whole garden is sited on a bed of rock and not vice versa.

In such projects observation, research and experience are crucial but personal preference and practical limitations will inevitably have the upper hand in your result. If there is a choice of rock and you wish to grow dianthus, limestone is ideal and your soil base needs to be as free-draining, gritty and alkaline as can be managed. Your dianthus may be planted to nestle, drape or form hummocks as habit or your preference dictate, and should become a mainstay of the rock garden, remaining clean and fresh-looking at all seasons. A pane of glass for the protection of more delicate subjects during spells of cold and damp may be desirable.

Dianthus of alpine type may equally well be grown in raised beds, where they have the advantage of being physically elevated for the close scrutiny and increased enjoyment of the gardener, as well as being assured of the good drainage and favourable conditions implied by a specially constructed bed. Small boulders or lumps of stone may be placed judiciously among the plants and will look well among small dianthus. Assuming the gardener has access to plants and has the courage to halt the builder of walls for raised beds or indeed other walls in the garden, vigorous small individual plants may be placed horizontally between gaps in the stonework, and often do well in such a position, hugging the exposed vertical face as they spill out neat top-growth from this protected root-hold.

Troughs, Sinks and Containers

The smaller alpine dianthus and their hybrids do very well in containers, often serving to drape an edge or form a neat carpet for spring bulbs. Natural stone troughs are expensive and hard to come by but excellent replicas are available as alternatives. Deep, old porcelain sinks still may be obtained for next to nothing and can make very effective containers if covered with a sticky mix of cement, peat and sand, first wiping over the surface with PVA glue. Painted with milk or manure water when dry, this surface will soon acquire a patina of apparent age. Attractively moulded containers of pottery and reconstituted stone are available from garden centres, and assuming a depth of 6in (15cm) and the presence of drainage holes almost any of these is suitable. A container garden, well sited and well planted, can be a joy in a small space and if those containers including dianthus can be raised the close access to their scent and delicate patterns will be an added bonus. Window-boxes may also be planted to advantage with small, sweet-smelling dianthus, which have thrived in such containers on London balconies since the eighteenth century.

Perfect drainage is crucial for success with container gardening, as is keeping a close eye on the plants during spells of drought and dry wind in summer; in this artificial habitat their dependence on the cultivator is total. A thick layer of coarse gravel, broken crocks or coarse slates should be laid over the base of the container, which should be raised if possible to prevent worms and predators from assuming residence, blocking drainage holes and damaging roots. A good fresh John Innes-type[1] mix, perhaps opened up by extra grit or peat, is worth investment for it may not be replaced for many years.

Ideas for attractive companion planting with alpine dianthus and their hybrids may be picked up and adapted from many sources. My own preference is to place the plants in close association with neighbours of complementary foliage and habit with the aim of creating a densely woven mix to cover the visible soil surface and spill over stones or container edges. Sedums in variety make trouble-free neighbours, those with deep-red foliage colour being particularly effective foils in all seasons. For spring, the more compact, mossy saxifrages and any of the encrusted and *aizoon* forms are excellent companions because they flower at roughly similar times, and for May the heavily-scented *Erinus alpinus* is a good choice as it will naturalize unobtrusively in and among your dianthus and other residents, being always welcome with its neat habit and miniature spires of pink and white flowers. In mid-summer as the hybrid forms peak in flower the alpine aquilegias, campanulas, violas and scabious are all good foils, with their soft blues and lavender mauves making pleasant harmony with the stong colours of the 'improved' forms of the alpine dianthus.

PROPAGATION

Propagation of the species forms is easiest and most readily achieved from seed. The mainstream seed companies offer mixed packets of 'alpine' forms but more satisfying results are likely to be obtained from a more discerning approach. Specialist alpine nurserymen often publish their own lists of seed or produce their own packeted selections at the shows, and such sources are well worth investigation. Alternatively the Alpine Garden Society, The Royal Horticultural Society, and The Hardy Plant Society all produce lists of seeds for distribution to their members. Such

---

1 'John Innes' is a loam-based compost formula.

sources often include notes indicating the exact provenance of the offered seed, some of it being the fruits of plant hunters' expeditions far afield. These seeds should be fresh, and it is generally wise to settle to the task of sowing them straight away, for they are sent out in March or April and should get away quickly if you do not delay.

If gathering one's own or acquiring seeds from others' plants, the seeds should be collected carefully when the pods are beginning to show signs of ripening. There is usually a change in colour, the seed pods turning straw-like in texture, curling their tips upwards and outwards to reveal black seeds which rattle within the dry husks. The stalks should be cut with scissors or knife on a dry day, and the contents shaken directly into paper envelopes which should be marked with the date and identity of the mother plant. If not quite ripe the stems may be bunched loosely together and held, face down into paper bags with a rubber band or other tie round the neck. They can be left in a dry, well-ventilated position and will fill, in their own time, with the brittle seeds which are like small, flat, twisted lemons in shape. Recording, so often a casualty of the busy summer season, should be done at once, and I find it easiest simply to write a label and enclose it with the package. If the seeds are not to be sown at once they should be stored in a cool, dry and dark place.

The first essential for successful seed raising is cleanliness, as the main hazard facing any seedling in a warm, relatively still atmosphere, is attack by spores of fungal disease. Main offenders are those causing a condition known as 'damping off', symptoms of which are the rotting of apparently healthy seedlings at ground level, with their subsequent collapse. While dianthus seedlings are relatively tough, the risk is lessened by using sterile containers and compost, plastic being preferable to the former as it is easier to scrub and sterilize. John Innes seed compost or peat-based composts laced with an addition of sharp sand are suitable media, although the enterprising may care to make their own compost by sterilizing garden loam. This messy and memorable performance involves filling a large saucepan with garden soil, adding water to cover, then boiling the contents for fifteen minutes. Alternatively a suitable baking tray may be thus filled and placed in the oven. In each case the smell is appalling. Once the product of this labour is cooled and dried out the gardener then assembles a cocktail by adding one part of moss peat and one of sharp sand to two parts by bulk of the soil. Children of all ages find this enchanting.

Pots or trays intended for seed raising should be prepared by cleaning, crocking if necessary, and filling with the chosen compost to within an inch of the top. Before sowing, the compost should be made evenly moist, and I find it reassuring to perform an initial drench of the filled containers with a can full of proprietary soil fungicide such as Benlate the day before sowing. Before making a start it is best to prepare sensibly by making sure all materials are at hand and labels are written. If, like me, you are often helped by small children at this exciting time of the year, some prior planning and sense of order are important if one is not to be left puzzling over the identity of trays full of young plants until they flower some twelve months later.

The compost's surface should be firmed gently with even pressure from a suitable implement and the seed should be sown as evenly as possible on to this surface, ideally by placing each one with the fingers about an inch apart. The black seeds may be mixed with pale silver sand if this helps to see what is going on, and should then be covered by a light sprinkling of sharp sand and watered over with a light rose.

The containers thus prepared may be placed under the greenhouse bench or in a shady place where they should be inspected from time to time. They must at no time be allowed to dry out, though it is equally dangerous to overwater and allow the compost to become sodden and stagnant. Some growers recommend covering seed trays with newspaper or black polythene sheets, but these must be checked with increased vigilance for they must be removed as soon as the seeds germinate to avoid unhealthy growth caused by lack of chlorophyll.

Freshly gathered seed should germinate within three weeks. As a general rule seedlings are pricked out as soon as they are big enough to handle – at the 'four leaf' stage when the cotyledons are fully developed and two 'true leaves' have emerged. The moment will be quite clear in practice. The young seedlings should be handled gently and pricked out into larger pots or trays depending on their strength and size. Avoid disturbing the roots too much; tease them out of the compost gently. I use a table fork for all such operations, but all gardeners devise their own small tools from bits of stick, split cane, notched labels and so on. Plant them gently, never burying the crown; allow them to remain fairly dry after an initial watering, and continue to watch and wait. If the seedlings begin to thrust out long spindly shoots which threaten to run up to flower these should be pinched back in order to encourage bushy foliage growth. If all continues to go smoothly you should have vigorous plants ready for potting by the following spring when there will be a maiden, or first, flush of flower. If the blooms are particularly good you may consider propagating this particular plant vegetatively in future, for, as already suggested, the species forms are unlikely to come true from seed and an individual you have raised from seed which pleases you is uniquely your own. An outstandingly good form may even be worth registering under your chosen name, and there are suggestions and comments on this process in Chapter 8.

Older seed, or those from uncertain sources, may take twelve months to germinate and some high alpine forms may have obstinate seed needing exposure to frost, or simulation of conditions it would encounter in the wild. Alpine specialists routinely reproduce such circumstances for the benefit of many seeds from high altitude or arctic regions in a process known as 'stratification'. For the gardener wishing to try this process, seeds should be placed, in dry packages, in the freezer or ice compartment of a domestic fridge for several days at a time, the aim being to reproduce an experience of freezing followed by thawing on two or three occasions. Chemical changes may now have been precipitated in the seeds which, once sown, should germinate readily. Alternatively the process may be brought about naturally by leaving sown containers (which should be perfectly crocked) outside to over-winter in a northerly aspect, if possible, away from the drip of trees or buildings, never letting the compost dry out. Watch that worms do not block up the drainage holes because stagnant compost will destroy any chance of a successful outcome. Watch, too, for the slugs and earwigs that can congregate in large numbers under cover of such containers in cold weather. The top dressing of sharp sand is particularly important here for discouraging the growth of mosses or liverworts. Seedlings may sprout spontaneously from containers so treated but added stimulus may be given by moving them to the greenhouse in spring after some period outdoors. Hopes of germination should not be abandoned for two or even three seasons.

Division

Many alpine types of the dianthus are not suitable for division since the typical growth habit of several species is for foliage to expand into a symmetrical hummock from a single neck, and one slices into this main artery at peril. Other types, however, on gentle investigation in early spring, may show themselves more amenable to such methods, and new growth towards the outer edge of the mother plant may already be sprouting independent rootlets. In this case, future small plants may be carefully teased away from the mother stock and potted on separately.

Cuttings

Cuttings are usually the quickest and most reliable method of increasing dianthus hybrids. However, I find many alpine forms intractable in this respect, offering as they do such scant conventional cutting material. I find spring and autumn the best times to try, when tufty, non-flowering shoots should be removed with a very sharp, sterile knife or scissors. Cut just below a node, remove lower leaves if possible, dip into hormone rooting powder or gel if desired, insert into very gritty compost and leave in a closed cold frame or draught-free spot, allowing free ventilation once roots begin to form some three or four weeks later. Mist units and under-soil heating which brings basal temperatures to approximately 65°F (18°C) increases success rates at this point; the different forms vary in their willingness to root. Damping off and other mould attacks are, as ever, a constant threat but the true gardener's desire to increase stock of his own good plants and acquire new treasures from the generosity of others are powerful impulses, and the proportion of successes is high enough for the average amateur.

HYBRIDIZING

As already indicated, dianthus species forms hybridize with the greatest ease and many varieties are to be found in the wild, several of which have been selected and bear the names of their finders or growers. The interested amateur may care to exploit this natural tendency, to select his own parents and to raise his own progeny. It should be stressed, however, as it will be throughout succeeding chapters, that the dedicated hybridist may cast out many hundreds of inferior offspring for one individual he may judge to be worth while. Even this will be subjected to the opinion of other experts in the field and may only be deemed worthy of propagation if it exhibits qualities generally acknowledged to be a significant advance on other cultivars. One of the consequences of being designated a 'National Collection' holder for the National Council for the Conservation and Preservation of Plants in Gardens (a mouthful commonly recognized as the NCCPG) is the receiving of many unsolicited presents from fellow gardeners and keen amateur hybridists. I have many pots and bits of the garden planted with 'Mr A's dwarf double' or 'seedling from unknown lady in Sussex'. As well as some real gems among the older cultivars acquired in this way there are numbers of home produced alpine type seedlings, of greatest value to their raisers and to me because of that, but often similar but inferior in habit, flowering and temperament, to already named crosses.

Having said that, it should be acknowledged that most raisers begin as amateurs, and it is to their dedicated work over the generations that we owe the great wealth of dianthus cultivars available today. Many of these are of alpine origin, and these small, simple flowers are perhaps the easiest place to start experimenting with this oddly seductive process. Lindlay, founder of the Royal Horticultural Society, described it thus some two hundred years ago. 'Hybridizing is a game of chance played between man and plants. It is in some respects a matter of hazard and we all know how much more excitement is produced by uncertain rather than by certain results. What increases the charm of the game is, that although the end of it may be doubtful, . . . a good player can judge of the issues with tolerable confidence and skill and judgement have in this case all their customary value.'

The selection of parents is clearly the first step, each being chosen for some virtue of habit, scent, colour or quality of flower you would hope to accentuate and perpetuate. Disappointments will be many, and some features, notably the clear yellow colour possessed of the Eastern European *Dianthus knappii*, prove genetically recessive and unwilling to perform as one might fondly imagine, in place of the dominant pinks and white.

Texts may be consulted on the Mendelian principles of plant genetics in general, and there are classic accounts of the detailed process by the great dianthus specialists of the last generation, Ingwerson, Allwood and McQuown. However, a sense of the relative limits of scientific understanding prevails in them all. As Montagu Allwood, instigator of the race of hybrid pinks which bears his name, wrote towards the end of his life 'There cannot be any rule or guide how to obtain hybrids; it is simply evolution and we are the instrument. Experience must help, and I consider myself exceedingly fortunate to work in such a wonderful field of horticulture; but it behoves us to realise the marvellous privilege extended to us, so to be very humble, very persevering, and very prayerful'.[2]

In order to ensure that the insects or elements have not pre-empted

2 *Carnations and all Dianthus* Montagu Allwood, 1936.

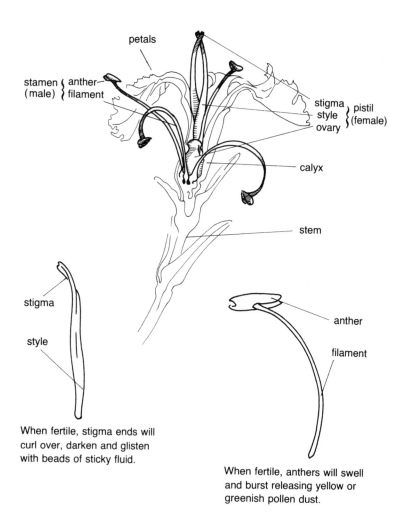

petals

stamen (anther—
(male) ⟨ filament

stigma ⟩ pistil
style ⟨ (female)
ovary

calyx

stem

stigma

style

anther

filament

When fertile, stigma ends will
curl over, darken and glisten
with beads of sticky fluid.

When fertile, anthers will swell
and burst releasing yellow or
greenish pollen dust.

Cross-section of a single flowered dianthus showing internal structure. In some cultivars stamens may be infertile, reduced or absent and stigmas may be bifurcated or distorted. Rudimentary seeds (ovules) are usually present within the ovary but may prove sterile. Sexual organs are typically absent in the 'mule' pinks.

our efforts, effective isolation of the flowers of potential seed-bearing plants is essential for several days before and after the transfer of pollen to stigma. If the plants are container grown in the cold frame or alpine house the entire growth may be enclosed in a light textured, finely woven bag of muslin or silk. If working on outdoor growing plants a greaseproof paper bag may be bunched and secured around the skirts of a small plant, or held aloft over the heads and around the stems of a larger one, fastened as securely as can be managed. Needless to say, the spring rock garden, at its magnificent peak at this time, is little enhanced by these devices.

A watch should be kept for the ripened pollen which will be borne on the anthers some days after the flower has opened. This is a fine yellow or greenish dust and is the active male element without which matters cannot proceed. In dull or otherwise inclement weather it may be hard to find good supplies of pollen, and in hybrid forms this is often a real problem. However, alpine dianthus usually produce it with a will, and around midday the anthers gently burst to release the fine dust, sometimes in great quantity. Some hybridizers use only pollen which is absolutely fresh, and must therefore now seek out a receptive female partner to the process. Chances are, however, that at least some of your intended recipients will not be at the correct stage of fertility, and the pollen will then need to be stored. In order to do this the entire stamen may be gently removed from the flower, using tweezers or steady fingernails to pluck and hold the thread-like filaments. Take care not to disperse and waste the pollen (the whole process is best done with a picked flower under cover if it is windy outside) and shake it into a glass tube which should be labelled and corked when perfectly dry. Viability should be retained for several days, and some growers have successfully impregnated partners to the process with pollen that has been kept frozen for extended periods. Others, however, maintain that only poor results will be obtained from less-than-perfectly fresh pollen, which in any event can remain in good condition on the growing flower for several days.

A search can now begin for a receptive female flower. A watch should be kept on the two pistils, extending then curling from the throat of the blooms, for a certain stickiness, indicating readiness to receive the male pollen. This normally occurs some days before the anthers on the same flower ripen, but as this is not always the case the purist may wish to emasculate the potential seed-bearing flowers and thus avoid risk of self-fertilization. If this is felt to be desirable tweezers or fingers may be used to pluck out the filmy, undeveloped stamens or at any rate tweak off their small unripe heads. Flowers differ in their shape and the disposal of their parts and if the calyx is particularly long and narrow this operation will need steady hands and perhaps a magnifying glass. If the subject is very small or otherwise awkwardly arranged some petals may need to be removed to expose the inner structure. If this is done delicately it will do no harm.

Judgement of the readiness of pistils comes with experience, and a close look at a plant in full bloom will soon give you an idea of the different stages of the flowers' sexual development. If we were to look at the pistil of a dianthus through a strong magnifying glass or small microscope we would see tiny hair-like growths standing out along the entire length of the upper edge of the stigma. When the fertile stage is reached, these become covered with droplets of viscid fluid, which serve as an enabling medium for the pollen grain which can then penetrate the softened cells of the stigma. In the wild this introduction is effected by the brushing action of insects as they search out and collect nectar and pollen from deeper inside the flower structure. It is the aim of the hybridist to reproduce this process artificially.

Practised hybridists all have their own pet methods and devices for the task. Some simply pick a flower bearing ripe pollen, strip off the petals and calyx if necessary, and brush the pollen-bearing stamens directly on to the the ends of the sticky stigma. The alpine species forms with which we are presently concerned tend to set a succession of flowers, so there is a good chance of finding an ongoing supply of fresh pollen for this method. Midday is the ideal time to engage in the work, for pollen will have been freshly released and there is plenty of time for events to take their course in a warm and dry state before the atmosphere changes at dewfall.

If stored pollen is to be used, or the hybridist is a tool user by temperament, some device will need to be found to assist in the process. Many hybridists use finely cut strips of blotting paper for the purpose, a fresh piece for each transaction. Alternatives are a fine, soft paintbrush or the frayed end of a stick or piece of cane, though all of these are hard to cleanse reliably between each process and the minute pollen dust may be trapped and inadvertently included where it is not intended, thus ruining the desired precision of subsequent operations.

Once the process is completed the flowers should be re-enclosed, with individual bags over each head if different male parents have been introduced. If fertilization has occurred they will collapse within two days, showing that the ovary has been entered by the elongating pollen tube, which will reach into the embryo sac and the nucleus of the ovules. The seed pod now begins to swell, and the calyx should be torn down to avoid rot if weather conditions are muggy and there seems any danger of this. Seeds will be forming within the pod, at first white and sappy, but progressively separate and dry. At every stage until the final harvest of seed the careful hybridizer will be labelling and recording, with details of each cross and its progress noted down.

PESTS, DISEASES AND DISORDERS

Moulds and fungi are the main dangers to the natural health and vigour of the alpine dianthus. The alpine house or cold frame can never exactly reproduce the cycle of conditions to which the plants have become adapted in the wild but there are key factors over which we may exert control in order to afford them the best possible environment.

First, we can limit or, in winter, entirely eliminate overhead moisture, thus reducing the chance of water gathering and sitting on the leaves and crown of the plant. Second, we can ensure good ventilation, aiming to prevent the accumulation of stagnant air as far as possible. These two measures, together with keeping the plants well groomed and rather dry during cold spells, should reduce the opportunities for mould spores, always present in the atmosphere, to take hold. The sophisticated alpine grower may have an assortment of fans, heating equipment and plunge beds to protect choice treasures from the effects of periods of muggy or very cold weather, but for the amateur grower of alpine dianthus these are unnecessary. Ordinary hygiene precautions when handling and potting the plants, the use of fresh compost, clean pots and so on, should pay off in vigorous, clean, growing specimens.

Having said this, few growers will avoid casualties from time to time however experienced they are. Mature plants may fall subject to bacterial attack which can enter wounds on woody stems, and rot and leaf senescence may follow. Any obviously affected parts of the top-growth should be cut hard back and the surrounding tissues treated with a fungicide powder or drench. Unsightly discolouration of older leaves will occur in all dianthus throughout their lifespan. Lower leaves will turn yellow, then mottled-brown before becoming dry as crisps. They should be gently pulled away when they are ready to part easily from the plant and should not cause concern.

Rusts may also appear in the form of yellow spots or blotches on the upper surface of the leaves. More detailed comments on the identity and treatment of such conditions are offered in Chapter 8, but for the grower of alpine types it is sufficient simply to remove and destroy any affected leaves and water the whole plant with a fungicide such as Benlate. Such disorders should be rare or rapidly left behind if the plant's growing conditions are open and healthy. Soil-borne pests should not be a problem as long as common sense prevails.

Worms, Woodlice or Earwigs
These may enter the pots from below while they are plunged or otherwise sited in the open and the soil ball needs to be turned out for inspection from time to time to check that neither these nor other untoward passengers are present. The creatures should obviously be removed by hand or they will clog drainage holes and disturb roots.

Larvae
Larvae of the Carnation Fly and other insects may occasionally be found and, as in any other pot grown plant, may be treated with a drench of insecticide.

Slugs, Snails and Caterpillars
These can be a problem and should be watched for and treated according to the individual gardener's own code of practice.

Aphids
Sap sucking aphids both green- and rust-coloured, may be visitors to your dianthus during warm spells and can badly disfigure growth. If plants are seriously afflicted I spray with a proprietary insecticide, but others may prefer to use finger and thumb. More detailed comments on control of other pests are offered in subsequent sections, but in general if the hygiene and sensitivity to detail within the alpine house are of a high standard then serious attack by predators has little chance to take hold.

EXHIBITING

Alpine dianthus and their hybrids are rewarding plants to grow for exhibition, competitive or otherwise. Finely grown flowering specimens often feature in the staged rockwork gardens at Chelsea and other large horticultural shows, their containers artfully concealed beneath the elaborate underpinning structure. Pot-grown exhibits appear almost universally on the display stands of nurserymen specializing in alpine and other choice plants. They make fine subjects, looking happy plants as they sit in wide-rimmed terracotta-coloured pans of Victorian pattern, with their cushioned growth extending neatly over a top dressing of clean, gravelly stone and their classically-shaped five-petalled or fuller double flowers opened for display. Often they are scented, and contribute to the unique atmosphere of the muggily fragrant, grass-carpeted, tented displays which spring to life at greater and lesser county and village shows throughout Britain during the summer season.

Growers wishing to prepare similar specimens for their own enjoyment may also become interested in submitting such plants for competition. The local Alpine Garden Society may hold its own regular displays, for competition or otherwise, and may often stage exhibitions of plants at local events for the enjoyment of the public. Fellow growers, once acquaintance is made, are usually generous with their know-how and much may be learnt from observation of the techniques of practised hands. Plants intended for such exhibition are generally pot grown in alpine houses or with similar protection, for while it is theoretically possible to lift a plant from the open ground and pot it for exhibition in practice this is seldom done.

Attention should be paid to every detail when considering the preparation of plants for exhibition, with considered thought being given well in advance to choice of pot and top dressing. Over- or under-potting will enhance neither the health nor the appearance of the finished article, and generally a 'half-pot' of traditional clay with a top diameter in pleasing proportion to the cushion of the plant will look well. Plants must be kept groomed for pin-neat appearance, with any failing leaves tweaked away and dead or dying flowers or stems removed with blade or small scissors. The plant should be pruned as necessary to keep a shapely appearance, and the soil surface dressed with clean grit or chippings whose colour and form may be chosen with care to complement the subject. Pieces of stone may be introduced to the small landscape of the pot, for dianthus can look well clambering as if through and over small rocks, which if skillfully inserted may also serve to disguise any deficiencies in growth or habit. Tufa, which retains moisture and can thus attract mossy groth is best avoided in this context.

HYBRID ALPINE DIANTHUS

Hybrid forms of the species alpine dianthus are widely sold today. They make easy, good-tempered subjects for the grower who has little interest in providing the specialized conditions of the alpine house or scree bed which are often needed in order to encourage the more delicate wild forms from the high mountains to perform at their best. Many fastidious plantsmen deplore the general label 'alpine' which has become commonly attached to these hybrids, for, as one expert grower has recently commented to me 'None of them have ever been near an alp in their lives.' However, it is as 'alpines' that they are marketed and known by the general public, and so be it. Many have pedigrees now impossible to untangle, including 'blood' from the *allwoodiis*, covered in a later chapter. The modern named hybrids are often vigorous in growth, producing abundant bright flowers over a long period. They will survive well enough in less-than-perfect situations, and may be relied upon to hold their own in any moderately well-constructed rock garden, raised bed or container. They are typically dwarf in habit, sometimes with double flowers born on stalks little more than 4in (10cm) in height. They have similarities but also important differences when compared with their wild relations, and thus further information will be found useful with regard to their propagation and general care.

Propagation

The hybrid alpine dianthus will grow happily outdoors. They are typically vigorous in leaf growth and are therefore easily propagated by cuttings, always the preferred method of increasing good, named forms of dianthus. Cutting material should be collected immediately after flowering, selecting non-flowering vigorous shoots which should be severed just below a leaf joint with a clean blade or sharp small scissors. Experience will tell how far down the stem this should be and different cultivars require individual judgement. As a general guide there should be at least three or four leaf joints remaining on the stem after a lower section of some ½–¾in (1–2cm) has been stripped of growth. This section can be dipped in hormone rooting powder or gel and inserted, with the aid of a label, knife blade, or whatever suits the individual, into a gritty mix. Thermostatically controlled mist units, with an electronic 'leaf' determining humidity are used by professional growers and can be a bonus to the keen amateur, though I have only polythene covered cold frames and find these quite adequate for most types. Further comments and suggestions on the details of handling and after-care of cuttings are to be found in the sections on older and modern pinks (see pp 83–159) and are not materially different for these dwarf forms. The principles for hybridizing, seed gathering and seed sowing have already been outlined above and apply without change to these types, though it may be discovered that some cultivars bearing dense double flowers are shy of producing pollen and are less easy subjects for the beginning hybridizer.

PESTS, DISEASES AND DISORDERS

As with dianthus grown in the alpine house or frame, healthily cultivated plants should resist, or rapidly grow through, troubles generated by pest attack or disease. Assuming drainage is good and the aspect open the plants should remain healthy and in good heart for many years. However, the rock garden can become host to particular menaces and it is worth looking out for these should untoward symptoms appear in your plants.

Slugs and Snails
Likely to seek shelter in the shady damp spots of the rock garden and often may be found under the spreading fans of mature dwarf dianthus foliage. While they do little damage to the leaves of established plants they can graze away fragile opening buds and are thus an enemy to be challenged steadfastly. Regular scattering of small pellets non-toxic to domestic animals should control numbers adequately and during wet spells large individuals, who seem impervious to the poison or at least capable of recovery therefrom, may be picked off and dealt with as desired.

Woodlice
May likewise lurk among leaf litter in dark places on the rockery, though their interest is primarily in dead vegetative material and depradations on living plant tissue are probably insignificant.

Larvae
Soil-dwelling larvae can occasionally infest this as any other area of the garden, and fat, dull-coloured leather jackets, the larvae of the crane fly, may occasionally be discovered as the culprit destroyer of roots and even whole stems of suddenly ailing plants.

Cutworms
The often unidentifiable larvae of various moths and other insects, likewise can saw through foliage and growth points at ground level. Surrounding soil should at once be drenched with

dilute insecticide or Bromophos powder, for these attacks can be fatal.

Aphids

Aphids and frog hoppers, the sucking insects responsible for 'cuckoo spit', are often attracted to the sappy new growth of dianthus in early summer, and a watch should be kept here and on other neighbouring plants. Without control, leaves may become distorted, flower buds damaged, and viruses may be passed on between plants from other areas in the garden.

Millipedes

Though predators of roots and shoots, millipedes probably do little damage and may be picked off when seen.

Ants

Finally, and perhaps most tiresome to those of us gardening on sandy soil, are colonies of ants, attracted to just the same well-drained, sunny walls and pockets we have carefully designed for the comfort of many sun-loving plants, including dianthus. The watchful gardener may notice finely powdered soil mounting progressively around the crowns of plants, with a scattering of small tunnel entrances and the scuttling black or brownish insects themselves. A drench of insecticide is probably more humane and effective than the old-style kettles full of boiling water, and treatment is best carried out without delay. Left to themselves ants will establish large earthworks with extensive runs, causing starvation and withering of the root systems of quite well-established plants which may suddenly collapse, dry out and fail just as they are in full flower.

Occasionally a plant may show symptoms of ill health not readily recognizable as being any of the above. If a knowledgeable local friend or neighbour cannot help with a diagnosis, members of the Royal Horticultural Society may send a sealed piece of plant for expert examination at Wisley, where suggestions and solutions will be offered. Alternatively, members of the British National Carnation Society may seek advice from this quarter. Any member of this society will be quick to help you to diagnose attack from the Carnation Fly, a pest uncommon in my experience in the open garden but familiar enough to all those who grow the dianthus extensively under glass. This insect, similar in appearance to a miniature house fly, lays eggs which hatch into yellowy-white grubs whose presence may be suspected once their silvery tunnels are visible in the leaves. Infected leaves and sometimes whole plants are often burnt since this pest, once established, can be a real menace to members of the dianthus family.

PLANT LIST

Published lists of recommended plants often cause frustration to gardener and grower alike, for availability can seldom be guaranteed in successive seasons and often varieties and cultivars are dropped from nurserymens' lists as new ones appear or older ones lose their vigour or appeal. The following is a list of smaller growing alpine-type dianthus, all of which may be cultivated successfully outdoors but may equally well be accommodated in the alpine house or frame where they can be container grown to superb effect. Heights are given denoting typical length of stem, with the proviso that different diets, growing conditions and seasons can cause atypical behaviour and appearance. Plant habit and diameter of flower is also noted, with comments on particular cultivation needs as appropriate.

Dianthus alpinus
From the Austrian Alps, and in cultivation since 1759, its best forms are considered by respected plantsman Will Ingwersen to be 'the glory of the race'. Colours vary from pale flesh-pink through to deep magenta and red, and there are albino forms discernible at the seedling stage by their paler foliage. Single, scentless flowers of some 1–1½in (3–4cm) diameter are born from May to July on 4in (10cm) stems, often completely obscuring neat carpets of shiny dark-green foliage. Petals are overlapping, toothed, and the central eye is emphasized by contrasting shades. Happy in a well-drained bed or rockery it will do well in a container and may be relied upon to dispose itself elegantly for three or four years. A good subject for the beginning hybridist, it is a prolific seed bearer. Naturally-set progeny are frequent and may be of interest, and worthwhile varieties may be easily propagated from cuttings.

Dianthus arenarius
An easily grown mat-forming species with slender grass-green tufted foliage. A plant of this species growing in my own garden has become, over some ten years, inadvertently shaded by a deciduous tree but continues to perform remarkably well, now hanging gracefully down a north-facing wall. It has grown about a

metre in diameter and spring bulbs push their way through to excellent effect. The white, green-throated, deeply serrated flowers are exquisite as individual specimens and are borne over a long period during the summer. The scent is sweet and penetrating. Stems are some 22cm long, turning in a supple curve to seek out the sun.

Dianthus arvenensis
Found wild only in the Auvergne mountains of France, this is a splendidly easy species form bearing ¾in (2cm) sweetly scented, toothed flowers of pale pink above robust green-grey foliage.

Dianthus deltoides
Similar forms of the well-known species are native to many parts of Europe and still may be found growing wild in Britain, on chalky hill pasture or dry banks near limestone formations. It is commonly known as the 'maiden pink' possibly because of its habit of modestly closing its bright petals in dull weather or at dusk. There are many named and widely available cultivars, notably the brilliant crimson 'Flashing Lights', the rose-pink 'Brilliant' and the carmine 'Wisley Red'. There is also a fine old surviving cultivar named after the great plantsman 'E A Bowles'. These fine small dianthus are perhaps the easiest of the species forms to grow and will give a good account of themselves in almost any reasonably open, well-drained garden location. Seedlings will set themselves into paths, cracks of walls, and gaps in steps or paving, surviving wherever they find a congenial home. They will often fill awkward places more effectively than the best-intentioned gardener, whose carefully wedged treasures are more often than not desiccated or washed away by the elements or picked off by nest-building birds. I find the vigorous, dark-green foliage of *Dianthus deltoides* a pleasing foil for other plants at all seasons and the plants will spill over edges and trail between neighbours to excellent effect. A particularly successful combination we have developed in a flat bed of parterre type has been a long-established colony of this dianthus now interwoven by *Campanula cochlearifolia*. The bright flowers of the former, including many naturally set varieties, among the pale blue bells of the latter are a delight. The single blooms of *D. deltoides* are small, less than ½in (1cm) in diameter, but very freely borne on branched stems some 4in (10cm) high. Each floret has the typical well-delineated eye, etched in red. Flowering extends for many weeks and though individual plants may not survive more than three or four years their progeny will ensure a succession of brilliant flowers if you delay a total haircut until early August.

Dianthus gratianopolitanus, *previously known as* Dianthus
caesius *and familiarly in Britain as 'The Cheddar Pink'. It still
clings to a foothold in the Cheddar Gorge and is now a rare and
protected species.*

Dianthus gratianopolitanus

Previously known as *D. caesius* and familiarly known as the
'Cheddar pink'. Our native species form still clings precariously to
a natural foothold in the poor limey soil and steep cliff tops of the
Cheddar Gorge in the west of England. First brought to public
attention in the eighteenth century by Sam Brewer, a Wiltshire
man, it has since been much admired by visitors to Cheddar many
of whom, alas, have indulged the gardeners' rapacious desire to
return home with a plant for themselves. As a result it now retains
only a tenuous presence, in ever-decreasing colonies which lie out
of reach of the marauders. Such collectors are in any event likely to
be disappointed in their trophies as, in common with many species

forms, the roots of the Cheddar pink stretch long and far back into the rocky terrain and most will be left behind to all but the most assiduous excavator. These wild plants must be steadfastly protected if they are to survive for future generations, and we may help in their conservation by raising our own plants from seed which is widely available from specialist nurseries. Very similar forms also occur in many places on rocky formations over western and central Europe, each hybridizing readily with near and distant relatives, with the result that variations in commercially available forms of *D. gratianopolitanus* are particularly noticeable. The most desirable varieties form a densely woven cushion of small grey-green leaves, extending and self-rooting in a neat manner to an eventual diameter of some 2ft (60cm). In the garden, plants look well near rock work and stone where they will behave as if quite at home, nestling, climbing and generally insinuating themselves to good effect. They are particularly amenable to cold greenhouse culture, and I have grown lovely looking specimens without any fuss under the simplest polythene structure. Their scent is a particular bonus, being fragrant and clove-like. Blooms are up to 1¼in (3cm) across, typically of deep rose-pink, simple and restful in appearance. The petals are toothed and this dianthus seems always the first to open in our garden, from late April onwards, being well into bloom by mid-May. I find the plant short-lived but easy to grow, and though individual specimens may begin to fail after some five or six years they will have thrown occasional well-placed seedlings before they go. Should growth of these plants become lanky or untidy looking a top dressing of gritty soil worked through and over offending parts in early spring will at once disguise matters and may promote newly invigorated cushions of growth which, on inspection, may be found to have rooted separately and reworked themselves to the crown of the mother plant. Such newly self-layered individuals can be severed with a good rootball in early spring to start new colonies elsewhere in the garden. Hybrids are many, and the species forms have probably been parents of cultivars for many hundreds of years. Worth looking out for are the forms 'La Bourboulle' with particularly neat growth and clear pink or white flowers, 'Baker's variety', of a deeper colour than the type, and 'flore pleno' a naturally-occurring double which can be excellent in form and character.

Dianthus glacialis
With flowers of similar appearance to the above, though leaves are glossy and deep green, this species form from the Eastern Alps bears fragrant bright pink flowers some ¾in (2cm) wide, on neat, short

stems no higher than 1½in (4cm). It is distinguished by a greenish reverse to the petals and, often, by a green eye. A tap-rooted species, it should be watched and protected from the alternating damp and cold typical of the British winter which can set up mould attack and fatal neck rot on outdoor growing plants. A rewarding subject for alpine house culture, this natural native of dense turf will respond well to a slightly more acid soil mix than most of the species forms, in a deep pot which should be kept very dry until spring.

Dianthus haematocalyx
A variable, sometimes tall-growing form from Yugoslavia, Albania and Greece, the dwarf growing variety, *'alpinus'* (synonym *'pindicola'*) is worth searching out for its well-shaped compact grey foliage and the particular beauty of its almost stemless salmon-pink flowers, with dark-yellow backs. The notched petals are splayed wide into the perfect five-pointed star formation with which we are so familiar as a decorative device. This classic emblem has its natural home on the summit of Mount Olympus. Bearing this habitat in mind, outdoor-grown plants are most reliably grown to their best in arid conditions, and should be placed in particularly well-drained parts of the alpine bed. They will perform superbly in the most austere scree, and are a natural choice for showy, container-grown exhibition.

Dianthus neglectus
Synonym *'pavonius'* From south-west Europe, the Tyrol and the French Alps, this is the species which Ingwersen described as forming a crimson stain in a certain valley I feel sure many plant lovers must have tried to find, so vividly is his written account. In the wild, the flowers knit themselves into a seamless mat, running together through shallow, stony turf. For those gardening on acid soil it is a good subject, being, unusually for the dianthus, happiest in lime-free soil, though garden forms will tolerate a variety of conditions pretty well. Forms are variable, and seed-raised plants which are disappointing in habit or colour should be discarded. Good forms make superb plants for the rock garden, forming greeny-grey spreading mats of needle-like leaves, covered, in early summer, by rather solid-looking flowers with rounded petals overlapping one another. The blooms are typically buff-coloured on the reverse. The best varieties have blooms up to 1.2in (3cm) across on stiff stems of some 4in (10cm). Free-flowering in many shades of pink and red they are a valuable ingredient of the garden in May and June. With their free-seeding properties and large size

they make good subjects for the begining hybridizer, and like *Dianthus deltoides, neglectus* will set its own natural offspring to find their feet in self-selected places. This summer we have had a particularly healthy plant, bearing brilliant flowers, in the riser of some stone steps. It has looked superb and its roots have obviously found what they are seeking far more effectively than had we had the time or, less likely, the idea to put it there ourselves.

Dianthus sylvestris
Synonym *frigidus*. Widespread in the European mountains and curiously named, by Linnaeus, as it inhabits dry, rocky crevices. Its small flowers of varying pink are held on stiff, erect stems. In its best forms a compact and desirable species dianthus.

HYBRID 'ALPINE' DIANTHUS

Named forms of hybrid alpine pinks, in common with named forms of all the dianthus types we shall look at, are notoriously hard to write about, for what is printed today will be dated tomorrow. At any point in the history of plant development one's perspective is inevitably defined by limitations of place, time, and personal experience. A process of change in dianthus as in all other genera has been at work for several hundreds, perhaps nearly two thousand years, and the speed of such change in plant circles, as elsewhere in the modern world, is constantly gathering pace. Good hybrid forms of alpine pinks introduced and much written about thirty years ago are no longer to be found in cultivation, their merits having proved illusory and only their names being left behind. Many of those cultivars described below doubtless will have met the same fate within a generation. In any event, below are listed some of the reliable dwarf forms I grow which should be found to be commercially available at the time of writing. All are suitable for alpine house, rock garden, or container culture, and have in common stiff flower stems no more than 6in (15cm) tall, and small flowers, usually scented, borne over a long period.

Dianthus 'Bransgore'
Single pink flowers symetrically marked with stippled deeper pink and red. Silvery, low foliage, easy to grow and equally happy in any garden setting.

Dianthus 'Bombadier'

One of a series of red double and semi-double flowered dwarfs introduced by Montagu Allwood after the last war. Others from the same stable were 'Fusilier', 'Grenadier' and 'Mars'. All still may be found, if with some difficulty, and when successfully established can be superb plants, with silvery grey foliage of strong constitution contrasting beautifully with the brightly coloured flowers. I find these cultivars can be temperamental and shy – flowering if conditions are not quite to their liking, but it is well worth persevering in their culture owing to the unique colouring. Only some thirty years ago glowing descriptions of the vigour and hardiness of these hybrids in gardens leads one to conjecture over their staying power for the future.

Dianthus 'Chastity'

An excellent white cultivar with green hummocky foliage of neat shape and semi-double smooth-edged scented plain flowers, sometimes with greenish centres. I find this cultivar easily grown in less-than-perfect conditions when it will do well enough, though when happily situated it can be magnificent. 'Chastity' propagates easily from cuttings taken in July.

Dianthus 'Hidcote'

From the renowned Gloucestershire garden, a cherry red semi-double of attractive habit and sweet scent. Its small flowers are in pleasing proportion and colour contrast to its clean growing deep-silver grey foliage.

Dianthus 'Joan's Blood'

A green-leaved dwarf growing plant with a single, rather vulnerable neck. A popular form for its large single magenta flowers with a crimson eye, said to have acquired its name after blood shed by the wife of its raiser, Jo Elliott, presumably in the cause of horticulture! This cultivar is correctly named *Dianthus alpinus* 'Joan's Blood', being a selected or intentionally bred variety from the species form.

Dianthus 'Little Jock'

An easy cultivar, bearing semi-double large rose-pink scented flowers with a dark eye on short stems over silvery neat foliage. Widely available from garden centres.

Dianthus 'Pike's Pink'

Often confused with the above, the true form has a fully double flower of pale pink dentate petals with a pale eye. Well-scented and vigorous, these last two hybrids are easily cultivated and should thrive in most gardens. I find both will form extensive matted growth which effectively smothers weeds, and will encroach gently over stonework, softening edges and looking attractive at all times of the year. Lower leaves may brown slightly in cold winter winds, and the plants, in common with all Dianthus will appreciate a top dressing of gritty soil with an admixture of a little blood, fish and bone fertilizer in the early spring.

Dianthus 'Tiny Rubies'

Tightly growing hummocks of needle sharp grey-green leaves bearing deep-pink single flowers of good shape and scent. Keeps its habit best on a sparse diet and excels in pot culture in the alpine house.

3

SUBALPINE AND LOWLAND SPECIES

Some types in this section may appear arbitrarily separated from the former, but they have in common a rather gentler, less exacting natural habitat and are characterized by a tendency to grow taller and to carry their flowers in clusters on a branched stem. Though some are graceful in habit and beautiful or fragrant in flower others are weedy in growth, odd or plain ugly in bloom and of interest only as curiosities. These latter have no place in the garden and no individual mention here. A further characteristic of these comparatively lax-growing types is that they tend to exhaust themselves in a handful of seasons and they and their progeny are sometimes grown as annuals or biennials, being replaced more often than other types of dianthus.

CULTIVATION

As always when considering how best to suit plants and their hybrid forms in our gardens it is instructive to discover as much as possible about the sorts of conditions in which they find themselves in the wild. Generally inhabiting rather lusher pastures than their high Alpine cousins, their main difference is a tendency to associate closely in a general herbiage of neighbouring plants. Their habit of holding clustered heads high on rather long stems is often an express adaptation of this habitat, and gives us helpful clues when considering how to place them to good advantage in the artificially created setting of our flower beds and gardens. It follows, then, that their culture in the garden may be in somewhat richer soil than the forms described above, and that they tend to look well when closely planted, either together with their own kind or in association with complementary neighbours.

PROPAGATION

Propagation of good species and hybrid forms of these loose-headed, free-flowering types of dianthus is to be encouraged and may indeed be essential in some kinds where established plants can easily flower themselves to death. Such individuals may produce scant cutting material, and suitable shoots may need to be claimed for this purpose in April, even March or February, before the elongation of the flower buds which can quickly overtake the plant and draw every ounce of its vigour to support the blooms. Such early cuttings will need the usual 65°F (17°C) bottom heat of a propagating unit, but will root quickly and produce good vigorous plants well worth the effort and space, both of which are precious at this time of year. The rooted cuttings will tend to produce precocious attempts at flowering shoots and these should be ruthlessly pinched back as they emerge in order to encourage tufted, leafy growth and a strong rooting system. Plants will soon outgrow convenient-sized pots and be ready to set out during early summer or autumn.

On strongly growing species or cultivars of closely tufted, 'sweet william'-type basal shoots have a propensity to throw out adventitious roots, and we may capitalize upon this tendency by encouraging the plant to 'layer'. In autumn, when the habit is naturally at its most obvious, a light covering of soil or leaf mould should be gently worked down into the plant to cover lower stems towards the outside edge of the crown. This soil should be kept watered if the autumn turns windy and dry, and within some three or four weeks freshly sprouted roots should have established a stronghold in this compost, while remaining simultaneously attached to the mother plant. Sections may by gently separated and lifted for fresh planting elsewhere. Plants behaving in this manner tend to be of even temper and good heart, and will tolerate many assaults including being transplanted when in full flower. As long as good sense and adequate watering and firming are observed, they are helpful subjects and will allow themselves to be used as 'fillers' for unexpected bare patches in the border at almost any time of year.

Species forms of this type generally come true enough from seed and the best of them can then be propagated vegetatively. Between April and mid-July (the earlier the better) sow seeds thinly in trays or pots in a greenhouse or frame. When the first true leaves appear prick out the seedlings in boxes of your chosen compost and grow on. When the young plants are well developed they may be set out either in the 'nursery rows' so loved of garden writers who assume we have all the space and time in the world, or, more realistically, planted directly in the site in which they are to flower.

HYBRIDIZATION

Most types in this section produce seed freely and have been extensively used as parents of many cultivars, old and new, now available to the gardener. The keen amateur may try his or her hand in further pursuit of developments, applying the principles already outlined. The honourable exception to this ease of fertility is the species form *Dianthus knappii*. This dianthus, having single flowers of clear yellow, has long been pressed into the role of desired parent. It is, however, disinclined to perform. Although the gardeners of old somehow must have procured its services, producing as they did so many fine carnations of clear and patterned yellow, it has proved a reluctant suitor in the hands of the modern specialists who have tried in vain to introduce a yellow pink. 'Never', wrote Will Ingwersen, with more than a touch of asperity 'has a dianthus been less inclined to hybridize'. While Montagu Allwood did produce a strain of yellow-flowered pinks during the 1930s they have quietly slipped away and the field is now open.

PLANT LIST

Dianthus arboreus
From the Mediterranean and Greece though in British cultivation from 1826, this is a woody-stemmed plant forming a straggling bush with tortuous branches to a height of 20in (50cm). Flowers are large, fragrant and bright pink. If well-suited this can be a handsome and long-lived species, needing somewhat favoured conditions, ideally against a south facing wall. Here its wiry stems will twist and elongate attractively, setting off blooms borne from midsummer to autumn against broad leaved, grey-green foliage. This species form is believed to have played an important part in the parentage of many hybrid carnations.

Dianthus armeria
A British native, this form has little garden value but still may be occasionally found growing wild on sandy soils. Stems are a lofty, erect 18in (45cm) and the leaves, coarse and green and brilliant pink, slightly-scented flowers open in succession upon a densely congested, tufted head. It grows easily from seed.

Dianthus barbatus
This is the wild progenitor of our well-known 'sweet william' and many 'mule' or sterile hybrids, subjects of a later section. A native

Dianthus armeria. *A British native, still rarely occurring today.*
Redrawn from Gerard where, victim of a printer's error, it was
incorrectly labelled 'Deptford Pink' thus initiating confusion which
remains to tax plant historians today.

of central and eastern Europe, it is known to have been in cultivation
from the early sixteenth century. Rembertus Dodoens, physician to
Emperor Charles V, described its growth in exposed, hilly places in
Bavaria in 1554. It is doubtful whether true species forms may now be
reliably obtained, but the type bears cluster-headed inflorescences of
familiar form, on stems some 1–2ft (30–60cm) high, over shiny,
green prostrate leaves. Flowers are fragrant and variable, petals being
reddish, striped and dotted with white and red at their edges, bearded
at the throat. The subspecies *annulatus* shows traces of a ring of
second colour towards the centre, this characteristic having been bred
to prominence in the auricula-eyed garden varieties.

Dianthus carthusianorum
Somewhat confused by different authorities with *D. barbatus* the
type is native to central Europe and grows tallest of all, to 3ft

(90cm). Plants are believed to have been introduced to cultivation by Carthusian monks though evidence is elusive. Easily grown from seed, an established plant forms a dense mass of sharply pointed, dark-green foliage, throwing wiry stems bearing tightly held knots of up to fifty buds, each sheathed in a brownish membraneous bract. Bright pink and, rarely, white flowers open in shy sequence. It cannot be said to be a beauty but I have grown it for its historical associations and it has an odd charm. Though said to have been grown for some four hundred years as a garden plant I find it best suited to a fairly wild habitat, where its small bursts of colour atop the lanky stems can be enjoyed amidst the exhuberant midsummer growth of similarly tall self-sown opium poppies, evening primroses and the like. The flowers have a subtle and characteristic scent which is strongest at night.

Dianthus caryophyllus

A native of southern Europe, from Spain to the Balkans, and also established in colonies in many islands of the Mediterranean. This species form is probably an original parent of all old and modern carnations. The wild plant grows up to 3ft (90cm) from a woody base, bearing 2in (5cm) wide clustered or sometimes singly-borne five-petalled flowers of variable pink. The petals are broad, with the notched or smooth edges valued and bred into the cultivated carnation, and the flowers have, of course, the clove perfume for which the species has been valued for centuries. Such plants are said to be found naturalized on old walls in this country, and though I doubted this until this summer I have now been sent material from a similar form originally found on old castle stone at Clifford in Herefordshire. This plant was propagated from a wild root of dianthus which had fallen, together with its stone foothold, from high in the ruins of a Norman castle, and was growing, by the time I heard of it, in the garden of a lady living in the village. While we cannot, of course, determine how it got there, and it could itself have been a recent garden escape, the flowers have all the qualities of those drawn by monks in the very earliest illustrations and it is, just possibly, a descendant from such flowers of hundreds of years ago. The true forms of *D. caryophyllus* flourish still in profusion in Corsica where I have seen them colonizing fertile pockets and deep crevices in mountain areas, drawing the explorer to find them with their heavy, clove scent. Plants grown from seed of such provenance will be very variable due to this species' particular proclivity for interbreeding with its neighbours, but if perfume is of paramount appeal to you this form is well worth cultivation. The plants require particularly good drainage as well as the fertile soil its natural habitat would afford.

Dianthus chinensis

Synonym *sinensis*, 'Chinese' or 'Indian' pink. Introduced to this country in about 1716, the natural habitat of this form is East Asia and the coast of Manchuria. *D. chinensis* is a parent of many widely grown annual and short-lived perennials including *Dianthus heddewigii*, much grown and used in summer bedding in its many hybrid forms. The wild plant is itself of annual or biennial habit, carrying solitary or branched heads of red or white flowers in stems of 12–18in (30–45cm). Petals are toothed and often spotted in pattern. Hybrid forms are often very free-flowering and intricately marked. The true species is rarely grown but may be easily raised from seed if it can be obtained.

Dianthus knappii

A native of Hungary and Bosnia this recalcitrant member of the group holds the elusive and therefore desirable yellow gene in its single flowers, which are the colour of bright spring primroses. Alas they have no scent, and if *D. knappii* is indeed a parent of the many yellow and yellow ground border and perpetual flowering carnations available today (no pinks, yet) it is responsible for the total lack of perfume in these beauties. The species form is easily raised from seed but is short-lived, a literally fatal trait, perhaps, accounting for so many heralded but long-gone yellow cultivars of pinks, much heralded but now laid to rest through the unsparing records of dianthus history. The flowers are born in lax clusters on 14in (35cm) high stems, looking well against the deep-green, tufted glossy leaves. An unusual form certain to cause interest and comment in your garden, it associates poorly, in my view, with its pink-tinged relations but can perform to modest advantage in a planting scheme including campanulas, violas, and other blue or white members of the early-summer garden.

Dianthus orientalis

Synonym 'Fimbriata' Jagged petalled single fragrant flowers in pinks and white adorn this native of the Caucasus. In its wild state it extends through to modern Iran, and appears in stylized form on the many ancient Persian artefacts which have celebrated the flowers' beauty and appeal to the senses for centuries. The species is woody or suffruticose at the base, with single and branched stems up to 1ft (30cm).

Dianthus plumarius

Presumed to be the main parent of the garden pink, both ancient and modern forms. The type is very free-flowering, with petals being deeply fringed and laciniated to a quarter or a third of their extent. Variants of the wild form are distributed throughout southern Europe as far east as the Caucasus. Flowers in deeper and paler shades of pink are born on 8in (20cm) stems and the plant looks fragile but is tough as leather. It is believed impossible at this stage to distinguish the true species forms from the countless introductions to and escapes from cultivation over hundreds of years. Gerard gave it the name *plumarius* on account of its feathered petals, and in his *Herball* of 1597 he lists and illustrates twelve single-flowered varieties named together as 'Wild Gillofloures'. In any form it is a desirable garden plant and, on account of its fragrance, a delightful flower for cutting. Happy to establish a foothold in any free-drained open spot, it will form a long-lived swag of blue-grey fine leaved growth to billow over a path or trail down a wall. The foliage, good on its own at any season, is overlaid, in June and July, with sweetly scented single flowers, often remarkable for their contrasting elongated, purplish calyces. Propagation of good forms is easy from cuttings though predictably, in the case of so renowned a parent, there will be many seedlings. This species form, with its exhuberant behaviour and masses of flowers, makes the best beginner's subject of all for experiments with hybridization.

Dianthus squarrosus

Introduced in 1817 from its native Russia, this is a singularly beautiful species with pure white, deeply slashed petals, forming elegant lacy flowers of sweet fragrance. Stems bear single or bunched blooms and are some 18in (45cm) tall. The matted, dark grey-green growth is dense and fine leaved, and the species is well worth while growing from seed and maintaining thus or by vegetative means. It makes a fine specimen for pot culture where its scent will dominate a conservatory or greenhouse.

Dianthus superbus

Growing wild widely in Europe, Northern Asia and Japan, this form is a parent of the distinctive modern cultivar 'Rainbow Loveliness' as well as the recently marketed, supposedly ancient, long petalled 'Japanese Florists' Dianthus' of whose history I should be intrigued to know more. Both forms are readily raised from seed and produce robust plants which are highly rewarding to grow. These cultivars merely emphasize still further the deeply slashed petals of the wild form, which is itself of frayed and cut appearance, reminiscent of our wild ragged robin, apart from its scent which is heavy and sweet. The species inhabits subalpine regions, being greenish of leaf and suffruticose of habit, bearing forked stems of some 2ft (60cm). Flowers of some ¾in (2cm) diameter and of white and pink are held singly at the tips of up to twelve loose branches per stem. This species and its hybrids are fine plants for a mixed summer border, the flowers being unrivalled for their sensuous perfume which seems particularly strong at dusk and at dawn. By the same token they are wonderful to cut for the house, and the individual flowers are of considerable beauty as a bonus. The somewhat lax habit of growth is best flattered by companion planting with tallish herbaceous perennials. I find good associations are with penstemons, tall campanulas, and the other lush herbiage of summer, through which the fragile and beautiful flowers can weave as they would in the wild. Linnaeus bestowed the *superbus* epithet with good cause here.

4
SWEET WILLIAMS

DIANTHUS BARBATUS

While the sweet william has attracted little of the fuss and glamour of its cousins the carnation and pink, it has remained a good-tempered, unassuming resident of British gardens over some four hundred years, and remains deservedly widely grown for its fragrance and ease of cultivation.

History

Sweet williams, relatively unchanged from many of those we grow today, were painted in the margins of the Books of Hours in the early years of the sixteenth century. They were used in great quantities to plant a garden for Henry VIII at Hampton Court and were well-known garden plants, sold at 3d a bushel in 1535. Henry Lyte, in his *Niewe Herball* of 1578 describes plants bearing relatively uncrowded heads, the flowers being 'three or four together at the toppe of the stalkes, sometimes nine or ten together, like to a nosegay, or small bundell of floures, of colour sometimes redde and sometimes spotted with white, and sometimes (but very seldom) all white'. Gerard writes in 1597 that 'The floures at the top of the stalkes are very like to small Pinckes, many joyned together in one tuft'. They seem to have been grown simply for the pleasure of it for, as he tells us, 'These plants are not used either in meate or medicine, but esteemed for their beautie to decke up gardens, the bosomes of the beautiful, garlands and crowns for pleasure'.

The plants, then, seem to have been commonly grown. Natural crosses appear to have been selected comparatively early on. One variety was known as 'London Tufties' or the 'Tuft Gilloflloure' and Ray comments on a double 'velvet Sweet William' and describes a spotted one.

Gerard had already separated the species into two sections, the 'Great' and 'Narrow' leaved, and his descriptions are recognizable and evocative. The Great Sweet Ioyn (probably a variety of *D. carthusianorum*) 'hath round ioynted stalkes thicke and fat, some-what reddish about the lower joynts, a cubit high with broad-ribbed leaves, like as to those of the Plantain, of a greene grassie

Dianthus barbatus. *These have been known since Gerard's time as 'sweet saint johns' or 'sweet williams'. Redrawn from Gerard, whose caption reads 'Armeria alba & rubra multiplex. Double white and red Iohns'.*

colour'. The narrow leaved form however, 'groweth up to the height of two cubits, very well resembling the former, but lesser, the leaues narrower; the floures are of a bright red colour, with many small sharpe pointed grassie leaues standing up amongst them, wherein especially consisteth the difference'. Dwarfer forms must also have been grown as Thomas Tusser in his *Good Points of Husbandry*, published some thirty years earlier in 1571, commended housewives to grow 'Sweete Johns' in pots and window boxes.

A form showing a distinct eye was described by Parkinson in 1629 but this achievement was evidently eclipsed by the performances of the carnation which, at this time and ever since, has upstaged the sweet william. However, the type has the distinction of being selected for its part in the first record experiment on any plant, for we know that in about 1715 Mr Fairchild of Hoxton used its pollen to impregnate a carnation, thus producing a 'mule'. Work on the sweet william must have continued, though in a comparatively subdued manner, for 'auricula-eyed' patterns of concentric circles similar to the laced pinks became admired and the flower was briefly elevated to the status of a Florists' flower during the mid-nineteenth century. Double forms are still obtainable from seed today; though named cultivars from vegetatively propagated stock are rare.

The Victorians loved the sweet william and in the contemporary paintings of idealized cottages and gardens a clump of the flowers is often recognizable among the hollyhocks, lilies, shrub roses, pinks and pansies forming a lush background to scenes of charmed rural life. Despite our awareness that such contrived portraits may have diverted attention from the real hardships of many true cottagers the images still have an impact and resonance which strikes deep, and the desire to emulate the apparently artless abundance of 'cottage garden' planting has never been more alive than it is today.

A love of country life lies deep in the British character, and a love of the idealized image of the cottage garden likewise. Writing in 1896 of a cottage garden in June 'A Gentleman of Great Practical Experience' included the sweet william in the ideal thus.

Along the lines of the walk parallel to the cottage, as well as the centre walk leading from the highway to the cottage door, are numbers of sweet flowers standing alone, each a clump in itself, so well grown are they. . . . the great peonies, the giants of the border, are one mass of crimson or white. The double scarlet lychnis sends up a forest of spikes. The early summer roses and single yellow Persian rose are here in numbers. . . . nestling on the ground are campanulas in blue and white, and sweet williams are opening their umbels of bloom to delight old-fashioned people who have admired sweet williams all their days. Pinks – white and pale pink – are one mass of bloom.

Purple prose perhaps, but we should not let Victorian sentimentality put us off these robust and garden-worthy plants which are now available in many forms.

ROOTS, FOLIAGE AND BLOOMS

The stiff, sturdy stems, of sweet williams should not need staking, being held firmly by a vigorous fibrous root system which will delve its way deeply into well-prepared soil. Foliage is typically rich green or bronzed in colour, the plants tending to root themselves sideways in a series of heavily leaved stems. Flowers are in crowded, flattened heads, fragrant and often beautifully marked. Colours range from crimson and deepest red through pale and salmon-pinks, to white. The auricula-eyed varieties are particularly striking, with their concentric circles inviting immediate eye-catching focus in a mixed border.

CULTIVATION

Sweet williams and their hybrids require a richer and deeper soil than most dianthus. Although they are often treated as biennials they will survive in good heart for several years in a congenial spot, behaving as a relatively short-lived perennial. Their site should be cultivated to a spit's depth and brought to a fertile, healthy condition before planting. If your soil easily grows rhododendrons and azaleas it is likely to be on the acid side and should probably have an admixture of lime to grow most dianthus successfully, though the sweet william is the least fussy of the group in this respect.

Soil structures are discussed in more detail in the following section (*see* pp. 93–5), but it is important to understand that the soil in our gardens tends naturally towards acidity, neutrality or alkalinity and before investing time, effort and money in planting out the dianthus it is as well to know which varieties will best suit you. Measurements of soil type are expressed in terms of pH value, the figure 7.2 standing approximately at the point of neutrality. Lower figures than this indicate acidity, and higher figures, alkalinity. For most dianthus we aim to find, and if not acquire, a measurement from around the neutral point upwards. Soil-testing kits are available from good garden shops and centres and if you are unsure these will give good enough results for most amateur purposes. Briefly, most of these work by mixing a little topsoil with water, leaving this to stand, and testing the cleared water with prepared litmus paper or special liquid. The resultant colour will indicate the state of the soil – pink meaning very acid, orange moderately so, green neutral and blue-green alkaline.

Sweet williams will thrive in a neutral or alkaline soil, opened up with peat or sand if needed and enriched if possible with well-rotted manure, compost or peat and bonemeal as available. Lime will correct light but not extreme acidity and is traditionally applied in autumn. The old gardeners often recommended digging in old mortar rubble and, in the unlikely event that this can be acquired it is an excellent material, serving the double purpose of distributing its lime content and contributing its rough texture to the drainage of your site.

Sweet williams seem to do best in fairly moist conditions and though they prefer a sunny position will tolerate shade better than their grey-leaved dianthus cousins. If your soil is heavy in texture and you find other members of the group do not naturally grow well for you this branch of the family may well prosper in your garden. I am told that sweet williams grow with particular vigour and abundance in the moist, fertile conditions of Irish gardens, where the old double named form 'King Willie' is said to have thrived a generation ago. I have recently had the good fortune to be given a plant of this old cultivar which, well fed and watered, has got away with great vigour. It must, of course, be increased by vegetative means and cuttings have already rooted with enthusiasm.

The sweet william is usually treated as a hardy biennial, that is, seedlings do not as a rule flower until their second season. Spring-sown young plants may be planted out in damp spells during the summer or potted on and held until autumn, to grow on and bloom the following summer. If your soil is very heavy you may prefer to sow in autumn, overwinter in a cold frame, and plant out the young individuals in spring. The established plants will last several years and remain looking good if you help them to conserve energy by removing spent stems after flowering.

Sweet williams look well in clumps or drifts in the herbaceous border or wherever else you may wish to enjoy their six weeks or so of fragrance and colour. They can be most successful in a fertile bed against a house, where their scent will waft through open windows and doors. The taller varieties should be set out about 1ft (30cm) apart and the dwarfs at a distance of about 6in (15cm). Several strains of compact varieties are available and can be excellent for window boxes and tubs.

The plants are undemanding once established but may benefit from light mulching from time to time. A top dressing of fertilizer may be given in April or May when the flower stems will be in embryo form. The aim is to encourage good strong stalks and inflorescences, together with healthy leaf growth which can be used for cuttings since individual seed grown forms may appear of sufficient merit to keep going vegetatively.

PROPAGATION

Plants are generally raised from seed sown thinly in drills in open ground in early May, or under glass in late March or early April.

Outdoors, use a rake to prepare a fine tilth over forked and firmed soil, raking in peat and sand if necessary to create an open, friable texture. Press down a rake handle or use a stick or edge of the hoe to mark out a ½in (1cm) deep drill, sow the seed evenly and water in if the soil seems very dry. When you have finished rake the bed so that the seeds are coverd with crumbly soil, being careful first to mark and label the site. After raking tread the bed carefully with your feet if the conditions are dry, or firm with an upended rake if the soil sticks to your boots. This ensures that the seeds are in close contact with the earth.

Germination should take about three weeks. The plants may need thinning out, and when they are large enough may be set out in nursery beds, some 15cm apart, if you can spare the space, where they can grow on quietly until you are ready to transplant them, in autumn if conditions are favourable or in spring if your soil seems cold and unworkable. If, like me, you are sometimes just too busy to do things at the 'proper' time, the plants will not resent being moved in quite late spring or even in early summer as they are about to flower, assuming you can arrange reasonably reliable watering and get them up with a hefty rootball. I have moved barrowloads of sweet williams already showing colour which have given excellent account of themselves elsewhere in the garden, though they have needed repeated occasional spraying from the hose on foliage which would be vulnerable to hot and dry conditions in summer.

Under glass, seed may be sown earlier, in pans or trays about 2in (5cm) deep. Assuming a temperature of approximately 55°F (13°C) germination should occur within two or three weeks. Seedlings should be pricked out when they have their third pair of leaves, about 3in (7cm) apart, in peat-based or John Innes-type compost, to be grown on at ordinary cold greenhouse temperatures, hardened off and planted out as desired.

Good forms may be propagated at any time during the summer by cuttings of leafy side shoots in the same manner as other dianthus. The plants will naturally set quantities of seed, which may be collected from the dried heads when ripe or left to sow themselves as they will. As with so many traditional biennials, once you have supported a colony of the plants for one year in your garden you will have their descendants for ever unless you are of meticulously tidy character. Seed will not come true, owing to the promiscuous tendencies of the parents, but you may discover that some of their children have interesting characters.

HYBRIDIZING

The use of the sweet william as a parent for hybridizing is, as already described, the oldest on record. Mr Fairchild appears to have crossed his flowers with those of a carnation, producing sterile 'mules'. Since the herbarium specimen labelled as an example of his work looks much like an ordinary carnation we may suppose that his work led to the 'mule' types also mentioned by his contemporaries, which carried loosely pannicled heads of bloom. These were raised and widely grown during the eighteenth and nineteenth centuries, and a few survive today. The way is open here for an enthusiastic amateur hybridizer to continue the tradition, using similar principles to those already outlined.

PESTS, DISEASES AND DISORDERS

Sweet williams' foliage and stems may suffer from attacks of rust, which produces pustules with dark powdery masses of spores. Disfigured leaves should be removed and burnt and the plants sprayed with a fungicide such as Bordeaux mixture. Leaf spot, appearing with purple margins, may also be noticed and similarly treated. While older cultivars may suffer such afflictions they are rare on modern forms, and I have seen extensive commercial plantings of sweet williams for cut flowers without a trace of disease.

EXHIBITING

The British National Carnation Society and affiliated groups generally reserve a section of their shows expressly for sweet williams, and much enjoyment may be had from visiting such events and studying the fine blooms on show. This is a relatively quiet corner of the dianthus exhibition scene and entries are welcomed. Before applying to compete the newcomer needs to study the schedule and ensure that he or she understands the requirements of the day. If unsure, ask advice which should be freely given by experienced members.

PLANT LIST

Named forms of sweet william are now rare, though a red double 'King Willie' survives. The 'mule pinks' already mentioned are representated by a handful of survivors and though they have curiosity value I find they are demanding of culture and are probably of little interest to the general gardener. They need to be propagated by cuttings which must be snatched early in the season in order to foil the plants' unfortunate tendency to exhaust and kill itself by bearing flowers on every shoot. Having thus damned them with faint praise, it should be said that, well grown, they can make a brilliant display and the following are worth looking out for:

'Emile Paré'
Salmon-pink semi-double flowers in loose pannicles. Green healthy foliage; needs frequent replacement from cuttings. Named in 1840.

'Messines Pink'
Similar in form and habit to the above, with brilliant magenta flowers. Said to have been raised from a scrap of flower found in the hand of a soldier mortally wounded at the Battle of Messines in the First World War. (Another of those romantic, unverifiable tales!)

'Napoleon III'
Bright pink, small, double flowers held in clusters. Raised by André Paré in Orleans in 1840.

A further and more lavish selection of *Dianthus barbatus* hybrids is available for those who are happy to grow plants from seed. The mainstream seed firms and specialist societies may yield many treasures, among them the following, all of which I have grown and found worth while.

'Auricula-eyed'
Strains of this type are offered under a general label roughly describing their flower pattern. A seed packet will yield plants of some 18in–2ft (45–60cm) in height bearing large cluster-headed blooms, each floret marked with an eye and contrasting rings in shades of reds, pink and white. Patterned flowers looking very like these were drawn for John Parkinson's *Paradisi in Sole Paradisus Terrestris* published in 1629 and subtitled *A Garden of all Sorts of Pleasant Flowers Which Our English Ayre will Permitt to be noursed up*. If you wish to reproduce a bit of living history for the price of a packet of seeds, here is your chance.

'Delight'
A dwarf 6in (15cm) high cross of 'Sweet Wivelsfield' (*see* below pp 77 and 78) and 'numerous parents' with extended flowering.

'Delight' has green leaves and many-headed trusses of single flowers, eyed, zoned and sweet-smelling.

'Dwarf Red Monarch'
Plants 8in (20cm) high with large scarlet heads of flower. This recently-launched strain may be grown as an annual and probably has *D. sinensis* in its breeding.

'Excelsior'
Plants grown from seed of this strain have rich colours and strong fragrance, forming compact bushy specimens some 18in (45cm) tall.

'Harlequin'
Trusses bearing differently coloured florets on one stem, growing to 18in (45cm) in height.

'Indian Carpet'
A compact bedding variety much used by municipal gardeners.

Allwoodii Hybrids

'Sweet Wivelsfield'   Until 1920 Sweet William crosses with other members of the family had always produced sterile or non–seed-bearing parents. However Montagu Allwood's work on the subject bore unexpected fruit when he crossed his *allwoodii* pinks with *Dianthus barbatus* and raised the first known fertile hybrid. His further work on this line led to double-flowered forms of this cross, known as the 'Henfield' strain. Seeds may be acquired today and are well worth trying. As Allwood wrote:

In the plant itself you can see traces of all its ancestors, the foliage and habit of growth of the Sweet William, yet rather more branching. However, the heads of blooms are larger and more loosely built, the flowers vary in size and formation. . . . the flowers are unique in markings and shadings, and every colour is represented except yellow and blue.

Carnations and all Dianthus

These hybrids do indeed have the good characteristics of both parents, having robust foliage and attractive, scented flowers which extend over a long period. The plants respond well to pot or container culture, being vigorous and forgiving in constitution and free-flowering and compact in habit. Allwood continued to use 'Sweet Wivelsfield' as a parent, crossing back with species forms and intercrossing with his new hybrids. Rapid developments were made and continuing work along similar and largely uncharted lines has led to the wide range of cluster-headed dianthus offered in the seed catalogues today. All are easily raised and a pleasure to grow.

'Rainbow Loveliness'

An outstanding Allwood cross of 'Sweet Wivelsfield' with *Dianthus superbus* and a must for those gardeners who value scent above all other qualities. The single flowers are only about 1in (3cm) across but they are the most intricately and deeply slashed of all, looking like the finest bunches of filigree lace held together with a small green central thread. Petals are white and shades of pink, with an eye of apple green. This cultivar was described by Allwood himself as 'perhaps the most fragrant of all flowers'. Plants should be raised under glass from spring- or autumn-sown seed, and are hardy though short-lived perennials. They have an extended flowering period and often carry flushes of bloom well into autumn on long, branched stems. The character of its meadow-dwelling parent is obvious from its habit, and the plants look well in a crowded, mixed planting where their faces will work themslves through supporting neighbours. Foliage is matted, slender, greenish in colour and rather sparse, affording little cutting material. Some stems may need to be sacrificed early in the season to promote enough leaf growth to ensure cutting material is available, though newly raised seedlings are invariably of good form and there may be little point in the work of vegetative reproduction. The heavy, piercing perfume is somehow reminiscent of jasmine and makes this a good subject for container culture. Pots placed on a terrace or by a window mean that the scent can be relished to the full. 'Rainbow Loveliness' is also a rewarding subject for cold greenhouse or alpine house culture, and a well-grown flowering plant would be a fine entry for any show.

5

INDIAN PINKS

DIANTHUS CHINENSIS

History

The species form of the 'Chinese pink' (inexplicably known popularly as the 'Indian pink') was introduced to European cultivation in 1716. A tall-growing plant in the wild, it bears single flowers, sometimes held on a branched stem with petals of white, bright or dull red patterned with speckles and spots. The Japanese are said to have grown and cultivated plants during the eighteenth century though the history here is unknown to me.

There are records that in about 1860 a Mr Heddewig from St Petersberg introduced plants said to have been grown from seed acquired in Japan. The presumed parents were *D. chinensis*. While details of the background have yet to be discovered, as far as I am aware, the fact is that seed strains of biennial and annual Dianthus were grown in great quantity by the Victorians and Mr Heddewig was credited with having had a hand in their parentage. The plants were of dwarf habit and had a wide range of colours, with single or double flowers of large size. They were ideal for the carpet bedding schemes of the day. Many cultivars of this type remain available through the general seed companies, being widely grown as annuals for brilliant displays in parks or gardens where this type of planting is admired. Many still bear the suffix 'Heddewigii'.

ROOTS, FOLIAGE AND BLOOMS

'Indian pinks' in their hybrid forms are completely hardy, being quick to establish on fibrous roots and forming free-flowering plants some 8in (20cm) high. Leaves are pale to mid-green and there are single and double flowered strains, plain coloured or in mixtures showing striped and ringed patterns. Shades are of red, pink and white. Flowers are born singly or in loosely branched heads, each floret ¾in (2cm) or more across. They will bloom from early summer until the first frosts. Many are scented. Hand pollinated 'F1' or first generation seed is available for particularly good forms of clear-red or variegated whites and pinks, a well-worthwhile expense if uniformity of colour and form is at a premium for a particular project. These plants are of outstanding value for extended and trouble-free flowering and generally tidy behaviour.

CULTIVATION

'Indian pinks' are particularly useful for exposed positions, for containers, bedding or edging of beds, for they are compact in habit, easily grown, and comparatively trouble-free. They thrive in any well-cultivated open position in alkaline or neutral soil. Spent flower trusses should be removed to ensure a long flowering period, though on F1 hybrids individual spent 'pips' are often hidden by newly opening buds on the same inflorescence, thus giving the impression of an ever-fresh flower head.

PROPAGATION

Early gardeners of this strain of dianthus grew their plants as biennials, sowing in early summer and removing flowering stems the first year to encourage the build up of large plants ready to support a mass of bloom the following summer. More recently however, the plants have been grown simply as annuals, being started from a January or February sowing, where germination will be successful at about 55°F (12°C). The plants are pricked out into trays 2in (5cm) apart when large enough to handle, hardened off and planted out about mid-May where they are to flower. They should be in bloom by early summer. Treated as a biennial they may be sown outdoors or under cover in early June, being planted out in their permanent positions by September for flowering the following year. If weather or soil conditions dictate otherwise however they may be overwintered in a cold frame or greenhouse and set out in April.

HYBRIDIZATION

Work continues on crossing and recrossing within this branch of the dianthus family and new named forms are launched and marketed yearly. A keen amateur may well join the professionals in this work using the principles already suggested, for the public appetite for plants suitable for bedding and container work seems insatiable. F1 seed of good hybrids is available to the public from several of the large seed companies in Britain, and though expensive will give uniform plants of predictable colour and behaviour. There have been several attempts in recent years to market dwarf cultivars suitable for indoor houseplant culture. The trade can see the obvious appeal of such an opportunity to harness the scent and sentimental appeal of the dianthus and bring them, packaged, to the window sill. So far, such efforts have not proved a runaway success and there is clearly scope for further work here.

PESTS, DISEASES AND DISORDERS

None specific to this type, which is generally rapid in growth and therefore tends to leave behind any symptoms of disorder. As with any glass-raised bedded-out subjects some care needs to be taken to avoid abrupt checks to growth which may delay the establishment of vigorous plants and the formation of their flowers.

EXHIBITING

I am aware of no schedule including specific classes for *Dianthus chinensis* and its hybrids but a well-grown pot of one of these stocky, robust-looking characters in full flower would be an unusual and delightful entry for any of the local or county shows where there is often a class for 'best pot plant' or similar. As ever, marks would be awarded for a generally spruce-looking plant with any dead leaves or flowers removed, in a well-scrubbed clay or well-polished plastic container. Flowers from the taller varieties are a valuable source of strong colour, scent and texture for flower arrangers and have the advantage of continuing availability until late autumn when the best of the herbaceous border is over. I have used them effectively at Harvest Festival to decorate the church and have also picked large bunches for funerals in November when garden flowers have seemed a particularly appropriate gesture.

PLANT LIST

'New' named forms of *D. chinensis* appear frequently in the lists of nurserymen and seedsmen, and may be tried by the interested grower in the knowledge that something different and special will result. Dozens of such names have appeared and disappeared over the years, and a search for 'old' cultivars here is of little purpose. *D. chinensis* is indeed remarkable for its part in many beautiful hybrids, a few of which are listed here. All, however, are likely to be superceded in due course by more recent arrivals, each ready to claim centre stage.

'Baby Doll'

Often written with the *'heddewigii'* prefix or suffix, this form is widely available and easy to grow, producing single flowers in a variety of colours, many with contrasting zones.

'Fire Carpet'

This vigorous F1 hybrid has pillar-box red 1in (3cm) florets covering deep-green foliage in a long-lasting sheet of colour. Seedsmen claim this cultivar may be treated as a short-lived perennial. Plants are 8in (20cm) in height.

'Snowfire'

White semi-double flowers with clearly marked vivid scarlet centres and rays. Very strong, stocky 8in (20cm) high plants. A reliable form for bedding, this cultivar will do well in mixed containers and is a useful source of summer red.

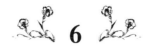

6
THE OLD PINKS

The pink is the poor man's plant *par excellence*. It is of strong constitution, and unlike the carnation, which often needs to be layered, it is easily divided. Hence it has lingered on undisturbed in cottage and farmhouse gardens so that many old varieties have come down to us today.
                    Reverend C. Oscar Moreton in *Old Carnations and Pinks*

Whenever we think of an old world garden we think of pinks.
Gillyflowers, they were called in the old days, or Sweet Johns, and they belong, more than any other flower, to the days of sun bonnets and print gowns and the little crowded gardens of the past.
                    Margery Fish in *Cottage Garden Flowers*

Nostalgia and wishful thinking are potent forces, and it is perhaps a symptom of our age that so many gardeners and writers have wanted to believe in the discovery of lost and ancient cultivars of pinks. Without wishing to discredit these writers some experts now believe that it is very doubtful that clones of Tudor and even medieval forms described growing in their gardens could possibly have survived. Others however, who have seen their own old cultivars remain in good heart for well over a generation would strongly disagree, and believe such survivals are entirely possible. While we can never know for sure we can in any event say with certainty that some forms of flower were popular at certain times and that many varieties in cultivation today bear very close resemblance to them in form, habit and constitution. They are probably descendants, replicas of those in art over the centuries, and no less desirable for that.

The search for interesting older cultivars must continue, for it occasionally yields interesting treasures which should be preserved. I would, however, agree with the cautionary remarks of David Stuart and James Sutherland that 'Stories of ancient plants found in gardens should always be regarded with some suspicion', and the sharp tone of their comments on the questionable nature of several often repeated tales of the timely rescue of various old cultivars. 'Perhaps', they write in *Plants from the Past*, 'because pinks were a flower of humble gardens (even the most sophisticated of Florists' plants) sentimental gardeners have always wanted to believe that any nice, fragrant pink must be old'.

There can be a near-compulsive quality to the quest for half-remembered or imagined things of the past. For many the scent of pinks or carnations elicits powerful recollections and images, finding focus in a search for a particular flower, perhaps remembered from childhood. Many would intuitively feel for Margery Fish's fruitless search, described in *Cottage Garden Flowers*, for the 'free flowering strain of old Clove pink' of which she was given many forms 'but none of them as generous or as strongly scented as the ones I remember in my Mother's garden'. There would seem to be more at work here than a plain search for a good plant, and by their nature such quests are perhaps bound to leave the searcher feeling never quite satisfied.

While any attempt to separate 'old' pinks neatly into their own category is bound to be impossible, suffice it to say I shall include in this section those of a kind grown before the great changes initiated by Montagu Allwood from 1910 onwards. These were basically the crossing of perpetual-flowering carnations with the older forms, to produce the 'modern pink', a plant with extended flowering and a rather heavier appearance. Pinks in this chapter then, have little or no intentionally introduced carnation blood, are bone hardy in British gardens, tend to flower once only in midsummer, have a low-growing, good-tempered habit and would be recognized as 'old-fashioned' by the general garden observer. Almost without exception they possess the fine, sweet clove scent which has proved a recessive element in many of the modern sorts.

EARLY DEVELOPMENT

While it is generally agreed that *Dianthus plumarius* was a main parent of the early pinks, a reliable account of its introduction and influence remains elusive. A fondly quoted but unverifiable tale of its arrival in Britain was offered by the Victorian Canon Ellacombe, who in 1874 observed similar single feathered pinks growing wild on the walls of a castle at Falaise in Normandy and at Dover in Kent. The stones used to build the castle at Dover had been brought from Caen by William the Conqueror and seeds of the European native had thus, he surmised, been imported to Britain. Several writers have maintained that simple wild pinks of different sorts were grown in the early monastery gardens, and late medieval illuminations of religious texts would certainly suggest that the fresh flowers were closely available for the painters. Large double pinks, with deeply lanced petals were painted by Holbein in 1532 and their relatively sophisticated development implies a fairly long period of selection, though the branched habit of these flowers suggests an early hybrid with *Dianthus caryophyllus*, the generally acknowledged main progenitor of the taller and sturdier carnation which was already the subject of close specialist attention in Europe and the Near East. The botanical and historical threads of these dianthus cousins are inevitably intertwined, and questions are frequently asked about their similarities and differences. While there is no clear delineation, their identities may be roughly separated thus: carnations are comparatively taller, thicker of leaf and stem and larger of flower, tending to bloom later and needing some special attention to perform at their best; pinks are relatively low growing, of more fragile appearance in leaf and bloom yet tougher in constitution, needing little attention and performing well in the outdoor garden. They tend to flower earlier in the season and tend to have a dark central zone looking like the pupil of an eye, though even this is not universal and has been bred out of some 'self'- or plain-coloured pinks.

By Tudor times pinks were well known, well loved and widely grown. Many seem to have been single forms recently collected from their natural habitat, and little attempt is made in the early herbals to describe them individually. Thomas Tusser, whose *A Hundred Good Points of Husbandry* was a best seller in 1557 recommends 'pinks of all sorts' as suitable for pots and window-boxes. Lyte in his *Niew Herball* of 1578 rises to the challenge of comparing and contrasting with 'cloave gillofers', apparently carnations or early hybrids:

The pynkes and small feathered Gillofers are like to the double or cloave Gillofers in leaves, stalkes, and floures, saving that they be single and a great deal smaller. The leaves be long and narrow, almost like grasse, the smal stemmes are slender and knottie, upon which growe the sweet smelling floures, like to the Gillofers aforesayde, saving each floure is single with five or six small leaves, deep and finely snipt, or frenged like to small feathers of white, redde and carnation colour.

He adds that they were 'called in Englishe by diverse names, as Pynkes, Soppes in Wine, feathered Gillofers and small Honesties'. His text is accompanied by a fine woodcut of the deeply laciniated *Dianthus superbus*. Gerard in 1597 mentions that 'sundry sorts of pinks, or wilde gellofers' grew in gardens and were 'well known to the moste if not to all,' though he baulked at the task of detailing and classifying the different forms, bundling them together in a somewhat daunted tone for there were 'many other sorts, the which were over long to write of particularly'. He does, however, pick out the first 'double purple Pinke . . . of a most fragrant smell, not inferior to the Clove Gillofloures' and observes accurately that 'Those that be wilde doe grow upon mountaines, stony rockes and desart places'. They appear to have had little medicinal value at this time, being 'not used in Physicke, but esteemed for their use in Garlands and Nosegaies'.

Scent in flowers was at a premium at this point in history, and June and July, flowering season of pinks, would have coincided with the first impact of the foul odours which must have assaulted the senses in the heat of the early summer in this age of open sewers. The selection of pinks and carnations for appearance in so many paintings of interiors would thus have had a practical as well as aesthetic dimension. The sanctuary of the garden, for conversation and pleasurable relaxation became cherished in Britain as it was already over much of Europe, and of its sensory pleasures perfume was an important ingredient. Books of advice were published and avidly read. Among them was Francis Bacon's essay *Of Gardens*, published in 1625, recommending scented plants of several types, among them pinks. 'In May and June come pinks of all sorts, especially the blush pink; Roses of all kinds . . . and because the breath of flowers is far sweeter in the air (where it comes and goes like the warbling of music) than in the hand . . .'. The sentiment is shared by William Lawson, in his *New Orchard and Garden* who published earlier, in 1618. For pinks he says 'are most pleasant to sight and smell. Their use is much in ornament and comforting the spirits by the sence of smelling'. His list of recommended 'simple flowers' for the country housewife included rosemary, daisies, cowslips, clove gilliflowers and pinks. The flowers seem, then, to have been widely known and to have had an unassuming, homely presence, growing in abundance; the poet Marston mentions lying on 'a bank of pinks' and Pepys speaks of 'wenches gathering pinks'. While their grander cousins the carnations basked in the flattery and pampering attention afforded to aristocrats of already established foreign pedigree, pinks remained relatively unnoticed, quietly biding their time; it was to be another two centuries before they, too, assumed centre stage. Even quite late in the seventeenth century John Rea affords them only passing and somewhat patronizing mention: 'Pinks are of many sorts and of little esteem, they only serve to set the sides of borders in spacious gardens and some of them for posies, mixed with the buds of Damask Roses'. They were loved by the embroiderers, painters and flower pickers of the day but clearly rather left to fend for themselves in contrast to their finely potted and cherished relations, whose delicate personalities were afforded every attention, being protected from inclement weather and removed to arbour or frame for careful nurture when not on display. Rea does, however give us a foretaste of what was to come, for some variety was already showing itself among the flowers of pinks which, he tells us '. . . have broad leaves (petals) deeply cut in and jagged at the edges, wherof there is white, light red, bright purple, and some with a deeper or paler purple spot in the middle'. There were some doubles and those with a darker eye were encouraged. This feature, together with a further tendency for colour to extend itself round the edge of the petal leaving a clear space in the centre, was to result, through a process of selection, in the magnificent laced pinks of the eighteenth and nineteenth centuries, when finally the humble pink was to come of age and receive its own accolades.

ROOTS, FOLIAGE AND BLOOMS

Garden pinks of this older type establish themselves on a fibrous root system from a centrally stemmed root-stock which is springy and elastic in youth, tending to become woody and gnarled as the plant matures. Roots are delicate-looking yet tenacious, tending to extend laterally rather than deep into the earth, often supporting a large mature plant on a comparatively small mass of finely branched pale-yellow root growth. Good drainage and an open environment are crucial for healthily growing plants, which can, if well suited, remain in good condition for a decade or more; large, mature individuals can be a splendid sight. The central crown should be kept clean of debris and organic mulching is best avoided. Poorly drained sites will put this vulnerable central stem severely to the test, for alternate waterlogging and freezing will allow ice crystals to assault and eventually penetrate the epidermis, wind rock may further buffet the plant in its foothold, cracking the woody bark and offering entry points for fungal spores. If not checked the attack may spread, eat through the stem completely, and all the top-growth may be lost. Treasured older plants succumbing in this way should not be immediately abandoned, but the site drenched with a fungicide mix; new growth can surface from points on the under-ground root-stock which may have escaped the assault. Well-estab-lished, healthy plants of some of the less sophisticated cultivars may, in ideal conditions, layer themselves independently, forming a mass of matted top growth attached to the earth as it extends on newly formed roots, eventually leaving the mother crown in redundant senescence. I have seen double 'cottage' pinks with no particular name behaving in this way beneath old shrub roses, an ideal combination.

Foliage of these older types of pinks is typically abundant and healthy, and should look spruce and attractive in winter as well as summer. Should the plants become leggy and untidy they are best given a fearless haircut in late summer or early spring, when they should resprout with clean new growth, though some flowers may be sacrificed for a season and cuttings should be taken from the prunings as a precaution lest the plant prove to have been too advanced in life to respond to this somewhat drastic face-lifting operation. Leaves of older pinks vary from slender grass-like blades to fleshier, rosette-forming bundles. Colours are from green-grey through steel-grey to pale silver. Some plants of the *plumarius* type form billowing masses of clean foliage, and may be established near the top of a wall where they will develop into an elegant and ever more luxuriant hanging swag, rather as their wild relations have done on cliffs and mountains for centuries. Slightly less exhuberant cousins may be encouraged to extend bushy foliage over hard-edged masonry, brick or gravel. Seedlings of such plants will establish in cracks or risers of steps where the restricted root run will ensure dwarfer growing cushiony foliage. More sophisticated cultivars may behave in entirely different ways, each uniquely characteristic and recognizable even when not in bloom. 'Inch-mery' has thickish leaves of pale silver-grey forming a tumbling yet decorous display; 'Rose de Mai' makes expansive, tallish bushy mounds of slender-leaved silver, seeming to fling itself into its allotted space, a reliable and substantial feature of the garden at all seasons; 'Bat's Double Red' makes steel-grey hummocks, slow growing but pin-neat and tough as leather. Some fine surviving cultivars of the Victorian age make compacted growth, 'Sam Barlow' and 'Paddington' remaining in prim and neat densely tufted mounds like curled-up hedgehogs, while 'Mrs Sinkins' spreads itself into a wide, loose cushion always chosen by one of our cats for an afternoon nap just as the plant is about to burst into untidy but lovely bloom. The wide range of foliage colour and growth habit of these plants is well worth considering for each of them can make a valuable contribution to your planting and being every-grey they are often the mainstay of an otherwise dreary-looking herbaceous border in its off season. They can also be a superb spring foil for the blues of muscari and chionodoxa and the reds of the early species of tulips.

Blooms

Singles

Single-flowered, old pinks tend to produce a mass of bloom on comparatively easy to grow, vigorous plants. They are thus very suitable for a beginner or the gardener whose soil may otherwise not seem ideal for the fussier dianthus types. In many ways I find the single-flowered varieties most satisfactory as long-term residents of the garden, being trouble-free in growth and companionable in habit, weaving their way quietly but effectively through and around their neighbours, holding their heads high to form an exquisitely detailed and brilliant piece of the summer patchwork. Patterns are often finely delineated and may be closely observed and admired on the splayed five-petalled flowers, which may be picked for small vases where their scent and individual beauty is often astonishing. The complex patterning on cultivars such as 'Queen of Sheba' and 'Coste Budde' is often almost perfectly symmetrical, looking like downy feathers of white on red or red on white, each filament painted as if with the finest camel-hair brush. 'Allspice' has regular pale pink streaks on frilled magenta petals; 'Fair Folly' pairs of flashes, white on strawberry. All are scented, and all are prolific seed-bearers, so unless you abhor naturally-set progeny a few named forms in your garden will parent many new arrivals unique to your own culture. Several forms of these dianthus do closely resemble the very earliest representations of the flowers, set in tapestry work among the feet of ladies wearing wimples and curled-toed shoes, or embroidered in silks and satins on fine fabrics. If the idea of growing living antiques appeals to you, these are a good and easy subject to begin with.

Doubles

We have seen that some doubles were noted by Gerard during the sixteenth century. They were clearly admired, picked out for comment and flattered by comparison with the more splendid gillyflowers, or early carnations. One imagines that these double flowering plants would have been separated from the rest, exchanged with other gardeners and kept going in the hope of similar seedling progeny. Present-day hybridizers find that if one parent bearing single flowers is used in their work, very few seedling doubles will result no matter how full-petalled the other partner to the proceedings. It is then a tribute to the diligence and sharp eyes of the early gardeners that an increasing number of doubles were developed, some being selected for interesting patterns as well as fullness of flower. Around the turn of the seventeenth century Charles du Bois, a gentleman, assembled in his herbarium a large collection of specimens from interesting plants gathered from around the world. One long-stemmed individual with a loosely clustered head of bloom and delicate grass-like leaves is labelled simply, in an exact and flowing hand, 'Pheasants Eye Pink. In my Garden at Mitcham'. The flowers are white, semi-double, with deeply fringed petals and a fairly large, dark, blurred patch at the centres. There are two other double pinks, both 'From the garden of Mr Stonestreet', one a double fringed white, and the other a 'double matted pink' described as 'of a fine reddish colour, spotted with silver spots'. This double, possibly of the *deltoides* type, looks very like flowers that have recently appeared in my own garden, which I believe are naturally set hybrids. Mr Stonestreet had also donated a double sweet william, as well as other sundry single pinks clearly chosen for their interesting patterns. These are the first preserved specimens of dianthus known to us.

Still growing at Oxford Botanic Gardens is 'Bat's Double Red', believed to have been raised by nurseryman Thomas Bat of Enfield in 1717, though it is impossible to authenticate the lineage and the plant is possibly nothing more than a similar seedling. The flowers are double, with bluntly toothed petals of vivid dark pink, well scented and set off by neat, dark foliage. It flowers for an extended period and appears to me to have carnation 'blood', possibly as a result of a chance carnation cross.

As well as doubles, flowers showing a smooth or rose-leaved petal edge were also noticed and selected. Among a page of 'Gilloflowers' appearing in Parkinson's *Paradisus* in 1629 is one comparatively small double flower, plain coloured with perfectly smooth edges, labelled 'Master Tuggie, His Rose Gillofloure'. Depicted by Parkinson among the ragged leaved, full-blown carnations, this restrained, smooth and circular flower stands out as the significant break it was. The desire to attain this shape was to seize and occupy carnation fanciers at once, though it was not to be attempted or achieved in pinks for another one hundred and fifty years.

The double-flowered forms of old pinks we grow today, then, have a history and tradition reaching far back. With their large heads and relatively long stalks some gardeners may wish to arrange some form of staking. I, however, find it most satisfactory to plant them closely with neighbouring campanula, iris, polemonium (Jacob's ladder) and aquilegia (columbine) and carpet them around with creeping thymes, self-sowing violas, and any other low-growing, easygoing plants to hand. Thus they are harmoniously accompanied and sufficiently supported to hold their heads high except in the fiercest of July thunderstorms.

CULTIVATION

The soil recommended for pinks ought to be rather loose, sandy and well drained; wet or moisture when over-abundant being very injurious.
Charles M'Intosh, Gardener to HM King of the Belgians in
The Flower Garden

Though the least exacting branch of the family older pinks do require a reasonably well-drained, open position in soil that is not deficient in lime. The most reliable and companionable way to establish whether they will do well for you without any particular effort on your part is to make the acquaintance of your gardening neighbours, ask their advice and observe which plants are enjoying themselves in their gardens. A British garden without pinks is an uncommon thing and if you see few or unhappy looking specimens in your neighbourhood you will need to consider, according to temperament, whether to take steps to correct matters artificially or simply to accept that nature intends other genera to grow better for you in this garden.

Soil in British gardens is either acid, neutral or alkaline and may be tested as already outlined by use of a simple kit available from hardware stores or garden centres. Extremes of acidity and alkalinity usually run between 4.5 and 8.5 pH respectively; pH 7 represents the neutral point and this reading or anything higher is fine for pinks. I am grateful to Audrey Robinson of the BNCS for her advice that 'pH 8 or more locks up trace elements'. Lower readings indicate acidity which will need correction by periodic dressings of hydrated garden lime, or if this seems too exacting by the simple avoidance technique of buying a sack or two of a loam-based compost such as John Innes and growing the plants in containers. Slightly acid soils, however, may be tolerated by several of the particularly vigorous older cultivars with no apparent symptoms of distress, and your supplier should be consulted to recommend particular plants if it is your intention to give some of these types a try in less-than-ideal conditions.

Texture of garden soil tends either to be sandy, loamy, chalky, clay-like or peaty. Sandy soils, being easy to cultivate, may seem ideal in texture for old pinks but may be acid and need correction accordingly. Their free-draining character can be a double-edged sword, for although the plants will enjoy the quick dispersal of water from beneath their skirts, they do not necessarily thrive on the starvation diet of their alpine forebears, and require a reasonably good supply of soil nutrients in order to flower freely and give of their best. A very light soil, then, may need judicious incorporation of organic material well before planting, and extra liming and feeding at planting time and beyond. The old Florists used noisome and astounding mixtures including night soil, goose dung and blood for their auriculas, and we know that rich feeding for the pinks was also recommended, producing magnificent flowers on plants which must have been lush in growth and highly vulnerable to disease and disorder. The atypical growth thus encouraged doubtless weakened their constitution and must have been a factor in their almost total demise. The contemporary gardener may emulate such recipes if he feels strongly compelled to do so but will find it more prudent to dig in whatever well-decayed compost or well-rotted stable manure that may be obtained locally, adding a handful or two of bonemeal at the time of planting for a gentle source of nutrient, and perhaps a top dressing of fertilizer in early spring, as the buds begin to elongate.

The loamy soil is the ideal blend of clay and sand, desired by all gardeners. Needing little help apart from ordinary cultivation, this is a happy environment for the widest range of garden plants. It may, however, benefit from and need an admixture of lime to enable pinks to do themselves justice, for the ground cannot be over-limed and even ideal loamy soils can become sour and depleted in nutrients over time.

Chalky soil is often shallow and/or stony, and despite its inhospitable appearance can be an excellent environment for old pinks which do exceptionally well in gardens around the Cotswolds, Chilterns and other similar areas as their need for soil depth is not great and the stony, limey conditions are similar to those of their natural habitat. Such soils may need regular mulching and forking over with a top dressing of well-rotted organic material or non-acid peat in order to maintain a reasonably fertile and moisture retentive few inches of topsoil. Care should be taken to keep any organic mulch away from the vulnerable central stem of the plants.

Clay soil which, as country people say, breaks your back as sand breaks your heart is perhaps the greatest challenge which can be turned into triumph with hard work. Unattended, this soil turns the gardener to despair, becoming slippery plasticine when wet and fissured concrete when dry; the task then is to open it up, by rough digging and liming (on a dry day) in winter, followed by manuring and further forking in spring. Friable material such as peat, mushroom compost, strawy, decayed farm manure, garden compost and sharp gravel or grit should be incorporated as available, the aim being to produce that dream of all gardeners on clay, a fine tilth. Once achieved, as it will be, given the will to do the work in two seasons if not one, dianthus plants can do extremely well, for the nutrients held in a clay soil are often rich and can support a wide range of superbly healthy garden plants. Many gardeners on clay have widened their planting opportunities still further by raising the level of their beds, a process which tends to evolve anyway with the repeated addition of bulky material, and such beds can look particularly well for they offer the opportunity for the dianthus, among other plants, to be set on a sloping face of soil, which can be colonized by prostrate campanulas, veronicas, and acaenas as a pretty and practical retaining frame for the main planting area.

Peaty soils, recognizable by local bracken, ferns and heather, are really not suitable for dianthus, though a handful of the species forms may perform well and a specialist alpine nursery should be consulted for advice. The undaunted enthusiast wishing to grow other types may grow medium-sized and small pinks in containers where they can do well, or attempt to import limestone chippings and make a raised bed or scree area. However, neither of these latter solutions is wholly satisfactory, and plants soon seem to become unhappy looking, developing long, brown prostrate stems as if trying to run away. Far better in my view to plant all the acid-loving subjects denied to so many of us, and forget the pinks which may be admired on visits to other gardens where they feel more naturally at home.

Finally, a word about the town garden, whose original character may be impossible to determine following generations of use and abuse by previous occupants, the attentions of local cats, and general city detritus. Should you acquire such a plot it may be worth while to do as we did with a London garden and simply skim off the unappetizing top few inches, dispose of it in a skip, and replace it with good loam from the country. This may be hard to acquire, but in such a garden or terraced courtyard where every inch of growing space is at a premium, it may be worthwhile labour and expense, for the scented summer beauties of old pinks in the still enclosure of a town retreat have a wholesome freshness to calm the most stressed of city dwellers.

Soil prepared, the plants should be set out in autumn or spring, depending on soil conditions, the size and availability of your stock, and the inclination of the gardener. Many expert growers insist on the advantages of autumn planting as did the old Florists; Thomas Hogg in his *Treatise on the Growth and Culture of the Carnation, Pink etc.*, published in 1822, wrote that 'Pinks moved or transplanted in the spring never do well nor shew half the beauty, which those do that were planted in September'. While I would agree with him that transplanting from one site to another (in my view at any time of the year) is likely to check and spoil the plants, common sense and practicality determine the season for all our gardening endeavours, including this one. If soil and conditions are congenial in September or October this can be an ideal moment to set out many perennial subjects, giving the young plants an opportunity to settle and establish root growth before harsh winter conditions. However, in cold, exposed gardens where prolonged winter wet, slicing winds or other local evils are known to be likely it may be preferable to overwinter the plants under cold cover, keeping them fairly dry and potting on as necessary, to wait for a congenial spring day when both soil and gardener are likely to be in good heart.

Plants should be set out about 8in (20cm) apart, according to variety, habit and desired effect and a handful of bonemeal in the planting hole will provide a gentle and reassuring source of nourishment should there be any doubt of deficiency. As a general principle, the soil should be pleasantly friable to about the depth of a garden fork, which one should be able to insert and turn over to the extent of its tines without encountering clogged or impenetrable subsoil. Plants should be firmed in gently with the fingers, and in drought conditions should be kept watered until new growth shows they are securely established. Should newly planted individuals appear to be sprouting more long flower buds than foliage, these elongating growths should be pinched out in early spring, whereupon the plant will devote a more sensible proportion of its energy to producing bushy leaf growth and may reward you with a later flush of blooms in July or August. Other newly planted subjects may establish a well-balanced ratio of flower to foliage from the beginning, and will make an effective display the first year, continuing to expand in health and vigour over many years. While many of the older cultivars will continue to present clean foliage and neat behaviour into old age, others are more prone to becoming straggly in growth and should not be allowed to dispose themselves with less than the elegance we expect from the genus.

While some degree of indiscretion on their part may be disguised for a season by flattering neighbours, for instance 'Bowles Black' violas and their progeny or other complementary annuals which can weave their way up and through the plants, individuals growing unattractively should be cut back after flowering, suitable material taken as cuttings, and the mother plant encouraged, with a sprinkling of fertilizer and a top dressing of gritty earth, to put out fresh growth. Veteran plants which may have become untidy looking over a trying winter may be rejuvenated in appearance by a similar gritty cocktail of rather lavish top dressing in March or April. This can serve the double purpose of disguising ungainly prostrate stems and leaving only fresh leaf tip growth exposed as if newly emerged from the earth, encouraging the plant's natural tendency to layer and reroot along the stems. If these cosmetic and major surgical measures fail, the plants should be ruthlessly dug up and abandoned as they are easily replaced from your own cuttings and should be protected from the indignity of a distressed old age.

PROPAGATION

While many gardening books recommend layering for the old pinks, I do not find this necessary or desirable, for almost without exception they may be propagated easily and effectively from cuttings. If you have some means of providing bottom heat and can raise soil temperatures to 65°F or 70°F (17°C or 21°C) cuttings may be taken successfully through ten months of the year, excluding November and December, though the challenge of growing on healthy plants rooted in winter may be a little exacting to the beginner. Very satisfactory results may be obtained from summer cuttings placed in a cold frame or other slightly humid environment of ones own device.

Different cultivars will vary in their provision of suitable cutting material, but generally just before and just after flowering there will be a plentiful supply of vigorous, stocky non-flowering shoots which will root easily and provide new plants by the autumn. Cuttings should be taken early in the morning on a dry day, with a sharp knife or small scissors which should be sterilized between each plant to avoid spreading any virus. If the weather has been dry the plants should ideally have been watered overnight, but the cuttings should be given a drink in any event, keeping the leaves dry, in a shaded cool place. The cuttings should be some four or five joints long, severed just below a node, stripped carefully of

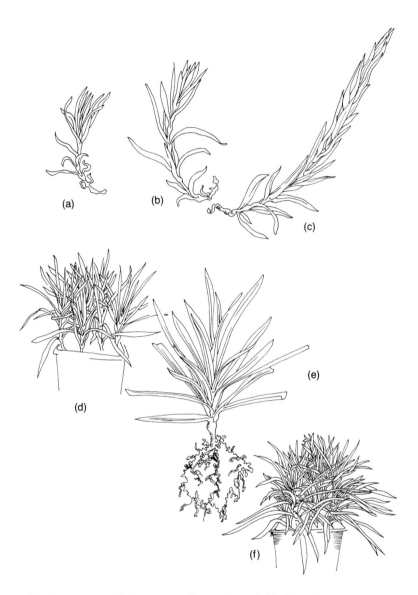

Selecting cuttings: (a) Immature small growth unsuitable for cutting. (b) Half-ripe good material should be cut below fourth joint. (c) Shooting running up to flower, unsuitable for use. (d) Cuttings stripped of lower leaves inserted into sandy compost. (e) Cutting showing bushy growth, ready for potting up. (f) Well-rooted young plant.

bottom leaves and placed as soon as possible in trays of gritty mix, or sharp sand. Hormone rooting powder or gel may be used but in good conditions I find it makes no difference, for most old dianthus are easy subjects at this stage. Cuttings will vary in character, some being stiff as matchsticks and needing no help to find their way into the rooting medium. Others, more supple or lax in habit will need careful assistance and should be individually inserted and firmed with the aid of a small knife blade, label or whatever suits the individual. As you work you will find a system which suits you, but we find that cuttings do best set about a fingertip's breadth apart in trays or pots. Close attention must be given to correct labelling at this stage, for if propagating from several plants it is fatally easy to overestimate one's powers of recall. Although foliage of the different varieties is obviously different at the time of taking the cuttings, once they have started into growth many look very similar and a whole year may have to be waited before the plants come into flower again for identification.

When finished, cuttings should be watered into the trays with a can of mixed fungicide and insecticide to firm them and guard against the main dangers of this stage; fungal attack or infestation of the sciarid fly which seems particularly prevalent at this season – a tiny insect like a house fly whose thread-like larvae can infest the rooting medium and feast upon the more susceptible, weaker rooting cultivars. If the heat of the midday sun is particularly fierce the frames, or whatever device you may be using to protect your cuttings, should be shaded with sacking or any other material to hand, for although old pinks are better tempered than many other plants they will not survive scorch and dehydration at this stage. The shading should be removed in late afternoon and the atmosphere around the cuttings kept just pleasantly cool and moist as far as possible, the covers being tipped up or otherwise judiciously adjusted in order to promote a pleasantly humid atmosphere.

Within a week or so the individual cuttings should have formed a drying skin over the cut basal edge, which will gradually thicken into a healthy callous. Foliage should remain upright and turgid, and within two to three weeks small white rootlets will begin to sprout from nodes and stem. At this point new growth will be noticed from the central leaf rosette, and air should be allowed to circulate increasingly within the frame or propagating environment. As the new leaves expand and elongate they should be pinched, cut, or gently tweaked out in order to encourage bushy growth. Neglecting this stage in the proceedings can result in tall

(a)   (b)   (c)

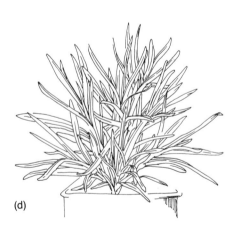

(d)

After-care of newly rooted pinks: (a) Tall-growing variety needing to be stopped. (b) Same plant with lead shoot cut or snapped out above sixth joint. (c) Plant showing new breaks from each joint. (d) Showing desirable bushy habit and strong leaf growth.

palm tree-like young plants in some cultivars, which seldom can be retrieved and will never make good stocky adults. As the young individuals firm up and show obvious signs of being established they should be removed from the frame and left to grow on in a shaded place. The trays may be fed, though this is not essential, with a weak liquid general feed, and a continuing watch should be kept for pests. Greenfly and slugs in particular are much attracted to these juicy young morsels.

Propagation with the more sophisticated tools of a mist unit is obviously a bonus if this is available, and highly scientific techniques of meristematic and micropropagation culture are now commonplace in laboratory conditions. No such methods were available to previous generations of gardeners and at the other extreme many growers have perfectly good results with their pinks by inserting and rooting their cuttings, with minimal fuss, in sandy, prepared beds in a favoured spot out of doors.

Young plants should be potted on when the rootball is substantial enough and set out in autumn if soil conditions are suitable. Should time or opportunity not present itself they will do perfectly well if overwintered under cold cover, kept on the dry side, and planted out in March or April the following year.

HYBRIDIZING

Principles already outlined in the previous sections on species pinks and those of the sweet william type will serve without significant change for dianthus in this group. However the attempt to use very full double blooms as parents may present problems to the hybridist as, in some cases, the mass of petals may have evolved by adaptation of anther to petal and on stripping down the bloom it may be discovered that anthers are either missing or sterile. For this reason cultivars like the well-known 'burster' 'Mrs Sinkins' rarely set seed; for some this may appear to be nature's statement that enough is enough, for 'Mrs Sinkins' is already unable to hold the petals she has without exploding into an untidy but glorious muddle.

PESTS, DISEASES AND DISORDERS

Pinks are grown in many gardens without any serious trouble being experienced from pests or diseases. Healthy strong plants will often shrug off troubles in the same way that fit people do.   *Jim Gould*

Though Mr Gould is writing here primarily of pinks of the more recently raised modern type, the analogy is apt and applies equally to older varieties. Provided that these cultivars are given a reasonably well-drained, open position in soil that is not sour or acid they should rarely be troubled or, at any rate, quickly grow through any setbacks caused by pest or disease. However, a sensible watch should be kept on these as on all occupants of our gardens, for particular seasons and conditions can elicit a variety of assaults to members of the plant kingdom held in unnatural proximity in the artificial habitat of our flower beds, and garden pinks, despite their famed hardiness are no exception.

Aphids

These are perhaps the most common predators, and a watch needs to be kept from early spring while dianthus and many other plants are forming their buds. Curled or distorted-looking leaves should be examined, and colonies of distinctive fleshy green or brownish bodies may be summarily squeezed between finger and thumb, or seen off with a spray of insecticide, preferably systemic, for which there is likely to be much call among other susceptible garden plants at this season. Aphids, with their puncturing and sucking habits which spoil the flowers are also responsible for spreading the virus diseases which are endemic among many of the older cultivars. While most plants make valiant and successful efforts to leave any symptoms behind, it is often only when growing meristem-cultured, scientifically 'cleaned' versions of old favourites that the extent of the disability carried by the infected old forms is evident. Some older varieties, 'Caesar's Mantle' and 'Queen of Sheba' for instance, are very badly affected and sadly, although several including 'Mrs Sinkins' have been refurbished and given a new lease of life by the scientists, they need to be returned to the laboratory on a fairly regular basis as they remain susceptible to reinfection. While careless hygiene at cuttings time may be responsible for some of this virus transfer, aphids are undoubtedly primary culprits, and certainly should be treated and kept under regular control on older pinks as well other garden plants.

Carnation Fly

These may be encountered in some gardens, recognizable by silvery tunnelled passageways on infected leaves. The maggots, if unchecked, will work their way into the stems and crown of the plant, impeding natural progress of sap and causing dieback, which may first be noticed as a sudden yellowing and straw-like senescence on part or all of the plant. The watchful gardener may scotch such fatal progress simply by removing and destroying leaves with early signs of attack, but systemic insecticide applied, say, fortnightly from the end of May should cure, or ideally prevent, assault by this predator. These, in my experience of growing old pinks in the open garden, are rare.

Earwigs

These are abundant in our gardens in June and July, when the pinks are at their best. During warm nights they may be attracted to the flowers and can eat at the petals causing jagged holes. The late eighteenth-century Florist, James Maddock used to get up in the night and catch them. If you are growing blooms for exhibition and anticipate attack you may feel moved to do the same or, like him, wrap fluffy wool around the stems to foil their ascent. However, earwigs are likely to have no opinion at all of such devices. Seasoned exhibitors recommend that buds of flowers likely to be of importance are dusted with powdered insecticide. This should be done well before they are due to open or they may be marked and damaged by the preparation itself. Other growers suggest the very old remedy of trapping the insects in an upturned pot filled with straw held aloft on a stick. Such arrangements will entertain visitors to your garden and provide a talking point even if, as in our case, they fail to interest the earwigs.

Leather Jackets

These are the fat, grey or dun-coloured soil-dwelling larvae of the crane-fly or 'daddy-long-legs' and can be numerous on newly cultivated land. If you suspect they are at work you will probably discover them easily enough for they are more or less immobile and lie an inch or two below the earth's surface. Working beneath the soil these pests can gnaw through the central stem of pinks, as other plants, and can be an occasional, but real, menace. A drench of insecticide over suspected sites of infestation should see them off.

Ants

These and ginger-coloured, scuttling millipedes are other soil-dwelling nuisances of lesser malevolence, enjoying the well-drained warm spots you have chosen for your pinks as much as the plants themselves. Their numbers may be checked by a strong mix of insecticide from a well-directed watering-can. Their presence may seem benign enough but their extensive underground activities can undermine the plants' foothold and the vigour of otherwise healthy individuals can be suddenly and unaccountably diminished as a result during July and August.

Slugs

These are a particular menace in many gardens including my own, and often may be found sheltering in large colonies beneath the evergreen and ever-grey skirts of all types of dianthus, where conditions usually remain moist and humid even in midsummer. While older plants are little affected, the slugs may graze off the tender buds or the lush growth of newly planted individuals, and a close watch should be kept for this obvious damage. They give themselves away by shimmering silver trails and often may be discovered on dewy mornings gorging themselves on your treasures. Blue slug pellets scattered randomly or strategically placed beneath sheltering stones should result in a crop of dead or dying individuals within twenty-four hours, though larger creatures may recover. The soft-hearted may prefer to provide saucers of beer in which the creatures are believed to slide into happy oblivion. The malicious may wish to venture forth at night or at dawn with a torch, catch them *in flagrante* and sprinkle them with salt whereupon they will seethe horribly, shrivel and die.

Red Spider Mites and Thrips

These are other despoilers of dianthus flowers, being tiny insect predators of petals, calyces and leaves. Serious depredations are in my experience very rare except when growing the plants under glass, unusual in the case of older pinks, and should be prevented or cured with systemic insecticides. I am told, however, that those gardeners growing extensive beds of strawberries may expect more problems with red spider mite in hot summers, for the strawberries will attract and support large colonies of this pest. Commercial strawberry growers use its natural predator for large-scale control and comments on this will be found in the following section on modern pinks grown under glass (*see* p 148).

DISEASES AND DISORDERS

Anther Smut

This is a rarely encountered fungal disease causing distorted flowers and a sooty black deposit instead of yellow pollen on the anthers. Plants showing symptoms are beyond redemption and should be destroyed rapidly, for the condition is spore-borne and drift should immediately be prevented.

Bud Rot

Some of the older, white double-flowered varieties seem particularly prone to bud rot, which is often prevalent after a long wet spring. Fat, promising-looking buds are formed but instead of producing the expected flowers in due season remain unopened and on examination seem to have been hollowed out by brown rot. Such stems should be obviously cut off and destroyed. Some particularly fine, heavily scented old clones of the white 'Fimbriata', 'White Ladies' and 'Old Fringed' are often affected in this way, whereas newly cleaned stock of 'Mrs Sinkins' is not. It may, therefore, be a virus-related affliction, to which the plant succumbs in less-than-ideal spring weather.

Fungal Attacks

These may cause purple, purplish-black or grey-brown spots and streaks to appear on leaves of many old cultivars when plants are growing in less-than-perfect conditions early in the year. Usually appearing on old leaves, the plants should grow through this complaint when climate or growing situation are more congenial. The offending leaves may be removed, for they will soon wither to a crisp and easily be crumbled away. The plant may be dusted, if desired, with Bordeaux powder or treated with a general systemic fungicide.

Stem and Basal Rots

More fungal infections, which may attack plants under stress as a result of poor drainage or other faults of cultivation. Generally incurable, the planting site should be regarded as suspect and appropriate measures taken to correct the faults.

Wilt

Another fungal predator which occurs rarely outdoors but is a specific type, namely *Fusarium dianthi*. Plants may suddenly wither as if they had been subjected to prolonged drought, and should be burnt. Diagnosis may be confirmed by scrutinizing the lower parts of the stem of affected plants which, when opened up, will show a brown, hardened centre where the xylem has been blocked causing interruption of the moisture flow from root system to stem and leaves.

EXHIBITING

Classes are reserved in several of the British National Carnation Society Shows, including the London events, especially for older varieties of pinks. In my experience fellow exhibitors in this section are comparatively few, for the main focus of competitive interest remains, at present, upon the laced and *allwoodii* pinks, and there is a stronger still following for the magnificently patterned but tender perpetual-flowering carnations and their hardy cousins the border carnations. However, the scent, charm and fragile beauty of the older pinks is acknowledged by all dianthus lovers and this small niche is accordingly reserved for them despite their shortcomings as show flowers.

Comments on selection, preparation and transport of the blooms will be detailed to more purpose in the sections on the more mainstream exhibition dianthus (*see* p 150). Suffice it to say in the case of older cultivars, as with all other subjects. it is important to study your show schedule in advance, ensuring plenty of good-quality blooms of whose identity you are certain from which to select the required number on the day.

Show officials are always ready to welcome and assist a newcomer to these sociable and fascinating events, each of which has a life and culture of its own. Much may be learnt by walking around unobtrusively on the day before the show, absorbing the atmosphere and watching the other exhibitors at work, for many of them will have been staging their flowers at similar shows for a generation or more. The concentration and painstaking attention to detail are intense, and only once an exhibit is complete should any approach be initiated to engage the grower in conversation. The whereabouts of vases, water and so on may be ascertained by observation and prudently timed enquiries, and you should find yourself some bench space to begin your work. It is crucial to take with you an ample supply of Oasis to fill the neck of containers, which may be crude or odd in shape, and a good quantity of foliage with which to mask the Oasis and give a pleasant-looking frame for your flowers. The foliage need not be from the same plant as the exhibited flower, and indeed it is preferable to avoid this as cutting material from good plants is precious at this time of year. Healthy and abundant foliage is produced in quantity on seedling or vigorous *plumarius* type cultivars, and its use is permissible and normal for this purpose.

The classes for which you wish to submit an entry will already be known to the show secretary, to whom you should have posted your proposed entry some ten days before the show. You will be given an appropriate card to fill in and place against your vases which, once completed to the best of your ability, should be presented for placement in its alloted space. Other people's exhibits should be treated with the greatest respect; should other completed vases need to be moved to accommodate yours it would be imprudent to take matters into your own hands. Always ask; such courtesies and protocol have evolved for good reasons over many years and a newcomer insensitive to their importance would not be made to feel welcome again.

The staging over, one may then relax and savour the fragrant and bustling atmosphere of a show in the making. On the following day the pleasantly dishevelled fellow exhibitors of the night before will be resplendent in best clothes, chatting over old times and new plants, modestly disclaiming their successes and grumbling good-naturedly or otherwise about the poor judging of their failures. You may even find a prize card adorning your own offerings: red for first, blue for second, green for third. It is a curiously pleasing moment.

PLANTING

Planting style and associations can only reflect the individual taste, character and whim of the gardener. For my own part I like to plant the pinks in odd-numbered, elongated lozenge-shaped groups of at least five plants of a kind, which will grow as if into one clump by their second season. The plants need no support and look well if tucked into the bed with closely associating neighbours. I find it works well to build the planting in layers, using creeping or prostrate trailing plants at the front edge, clumpier plants including pinks for the next, and taller perennials for the third. Surprises like the spired violet *Salvia haematoides* or the massive scented froth of *Crambe cordifolia* can mix with the shrubs and even small trees of the final backdrop. The prostrate thymes are excellent for use in the front layer, curving over hard edges and flowering in succession in pale pink, white and deep purple through the summer. Pinks, in drifts of contrasting colours and habits can be placed behind them, interspersed with dwarf blue scabious, *Erodium macrodenum* and the lovely older violas and their progeny which are making a comeback at present; slender irises, tall double campanulas, delphiniums and phlox all look well as a third layer, and shrub roses are a classic ingredient of a final eye-level tier. Those lucky enough to be able to garden against a wall have the opportunity of adding climbers and scramblers as a backdrop.

For early spring, I encourage violets and primroses to self-sow around the garden, for they will soon carpet and become an excellent foil for the plants and the heavy perfume will lure you out for the first weeding sessions of the season. The early flowering rosemary, purple pulsatillas, deep blue muscaris and the subtle colours of species tulips and daffodils are all set off by the pinks' silver foliage. As the season progresses auriculas, forget-me-nots, fat red peonies, self-sown columbines and tall blue jacob's ladder begin to mesh over the brown earth which will be completely hidden by the time the pinks are in bloom. By late May and early June the small blue veronicas, dusky grape-coloured old wall-flowers and rock roses in pale primrose and white are in flower, to be joined by the old dianthus. I find their soft pinks and reds easy to accommodate in early summer though I tend to avoid including hot orange in nearby planting, finding this best left to associate with the reds and yellows of its own tonal range elsewhere in the garden.

Old pinks have an obvious place in a silver border and can be contrasted effectively with the paddle-shaped glaucous leaves of *Othonnopsis cheirifolia*, the trailing lacy cushions of the *Artemisias*, and the well-known woolly ears of *Stachys lanata*. More elegant companions are the grey and white-striped swords of *Iris pallida* and the spectacular, felted-leaved *Onopordon* thistle which will grow to a giant six feet in a season. Silver borders can gleam enticingly in the dark when the perfume of many flowers, including pinks, seems particularly strong, but watch out for the thistles.

NOMENCLATURE

The task of establishing correct names for the older pinks is fraught with difficulties. There is no scientifically exact method of dating and identifying plant material and we are thus dependent upon evidence from artistic impressions, photographs and growers' memories, all of which are fallible. Several years ago I took a bunch of flowers of his own raising to F. R. McQuown, writer and celebrated breeder of the 'London' strain of laced pinks during the 1940s. While pleased to see so many of his flowers he could not help my efforts to identify them all, nor match them with the various published photographs, which we concluded had muddled captions. Our recollections of the exact details of cultivars naturally fade over the years; new named forms come and go and unless the gardener has personally superintended propagation of a particular clone its true identity cannot, over several generations, be certainly determined.

THE OLD PINKS

To compound the problem, there is much evidence to suggest that the appearance of flowers can change significantly over a generation or two. The 'true' form of 'Mrs Sinkins' has been authoritatively described as being distinguished by pure white, ivory and greenish tinged centres, and by one account had originally a strong red mark at the eye. Chances are that seedlings of similar looking plants of this among many other cultivars have got themselves labelled with a blanket name at different times and different places, and the anomalies only come to light when comparisons are made with the living flowers in hand. Alternatively, cuttings may have been taken from parts of the mother plant carrying mutant characteristics, the plants then being passed on for further propagation without this being realized. Some cultivars are notoriously 'unstable', showing numbers of atypical flowers on a single plant; 'London Glow' was one of these, and although a particular sport was selected and distributed by nurserymen in 1946 many variations are now seen bearing this name, none resembling photographs taken during its heyday.

In the years immediately following an introduction, when flowers are frequently shown for competition, any such changes soon come to light. However, many of the older pinks were never Florists' or competition flowers and are likely never to have been seen outside the immediate area where they were first developed or noticed. Such plants often bear only local names and may never have been registered. Even well-known Victorian cultivars like 'Mrs Sinkins', 'Fimbriata' and 'White Ladies' whose stock now seems irretrievably muddled are so rarely shown to the public these days that we have no proper forum to compare and contrast. Officials of the British National Carnation Society and custodians of the National Council for the Conservation of Plants and Gardens have a part to play here but their voluntary efforts can only be partial, and there is nothing to stop any grower coining a new name or appropriating an old one and attaching it to any plant of his or her choice, a practice which can only lead to hopeless confusion.

With the above provisos in mind, then, there follows a list of cultivars whose names are, hopefully, at least agreed between the two National Collection holders and the major nurserymen in the field. All are also recorded in the impressive reference work published by the Royal Horticultural Society, with the assistance of officials from the British National Carnation Society, *The International Dianthus Register* (2nd Edition, 1983) now with seven supplements.

PLANT LIST

'Alloway Star'
Large-flowered pale pink single with radial red purple markings. Free flowering, vigorous foliage.

'Allspice'
Full, frilled overlapping petals edged and mottled pale pink on magenta. 'Allspice' produces abundant, single flowers over a long period and is a vigorous and easy plant to grow, making a bushy tumbling mass of healthy silver leaves which will push over the edge of a bed, path or wall. Well-scented flowers often hide the foliage.

'Allspice Sport'
A pale pink sport of the above, with delicately feathered markings and eye of dark red. A vigorous, good-tempered plant which can hold its own without fuss in any ordinary garden setting.

'Argus'
Single, large white flowers with toothed petals and a clean, dark maroon eye. The only old example, as far as I am aware, of a type of once-popular 'black and white' pinks which had their own show class in the Florists' shows. Argus has rather small growth and is neat in its habits.

'Bat's Double Red'
Glowing red double with sturdy growth and steel-blue foliage. Believed to have been raised by Thomas Bat, Nurseryman of Enfield in the early eighteenth century. Records of a 'double ruby pink' grown at Oxford Botanic Gardens since 1717 led Oscar Moreton to suppose that this is the same cultivar. While, without the means to test plant material scientifically, we can never be sure of the age and provenance of this or any other cultivar, it is in any event an excellent plant and worth growing, with flowers lasting well into the autumn which suggests a chance carnation cross.

'Bridal Veil'
Very full, double, strongly perfumed old cultivar, which invariably splits its calyx. Petals are deeply fringed and flowers have a green and pink centre. Growth is vigorous and foliage silvery, neat and handsome. Pinks of this type were known as country girls' carnations, carried for weddings and used to deck hair.

'Bransgore'
Mottled single flowers, white on lilac. Neat growth, easy to grow and long-lived.

'Brympton Red'
Striking single, raspberry red with dark lacing and eye. Good blue-grey foliage. Found in the garden of a workhouse by a friend of Margery Fish.

'Charles Musgrave' syn 'Musgrave's Pink', 'Old Green Eye'
Believed to be an early eighteenth-century pink, though recent doubts have been cast upon the consistency and reliability of the evidence. The pure white, single frilled blooms have a cool green eye. Established plants can be a fine sight and grow well, though cuttings are hard to root.

'Cockenzie'
Early flowering, honey-scented small double flowers, deeply fringed and carmine pink. Foliage is delicate yet sturdy. Believed to date from 1720, originating from Montrose House, Scotland, and also known as the 'Montrose Pink'.

'Constance Finnis'
Named after the mother of plantswoman Valerie Finnis, this cultivar may not be old but has the appearance of the old forms, having large, single, frilled blooms of strong pink, mottled and edged white. It flowers abundantly and has good perfume, having received a Highly Commended award by The Royal Horticultural Society in 1969.

'Coste Budde'
Also named by Valerie Finnis, this single flowered pink is of considerable beauty, having regularly marked fine patterns resembling feathers, white on red-purple. It is scented and has a good healthy manner of growth, being similar in flower formation to 'Queen of Sheba' but much easier to grow successfully.

'Fair Folly'
Listed by the compilers of *The Register* (*see* p 107) as of '17th Century origin' and 'Painted Lady' type. While the pedigree cannot be established, it does resemble closely flowers embroidered and otherwise depicted from mid-Tudor times. A striking garden plant, with large single blooms cleanly splashed white on raspberry, Fair

Folly is very free-flowering and needs renewing from cuttings regularly or it may flower itself to death.

'Fimbriata'
Correctly listed in *The Register* as *fimbriatus* is in its original form a vigorous spreading, double white, larger than 'Mrs Sinkins' though stocks seem to have become muddled. Heavily perfumed flowers which split their calyx have greenish tinged centres and fringed petals.

'Fringed pink'
Common name for plants of *Dianthus superbus* or *plumarius* type. I grow an attractive form from the Queens Garden at Kew, having pale, single fringed flowers with long purple calyces carried in profusion. A good plant for trailing down walls or placing in crannies where it will, once established, form a billowing swag.

'Highland Fraser'
Free-flowering, single red blooms, regularly flashed pale pink. Raised as one of a series by Haywards during the 1930s.

'Houstan House'
Bright pink, small double flowers, sweetly scented. An old variety.

'Irish Pink'
Single crimson, patterned pale pink and white. Easy to grow but rather tall. Many interesting old cultivars are believed to have been grown in Ireland and this may be one of them.

'Inchmery'
Very pale, delicate pink described as 'amaranth rose'. Blooms are well-shaped and smooth-petalled, flowers semi-double, opening flat. Subtle, very sweet scent and vigorous silvery foliage. Believed to have been raised in the eighteenth century, 'Inchmery' gained an Award of Merit in 1946.

'Jane Austen'
Origin uncertain, but an outstanding pink for its long flowering period and neat habit. It bears a succession of small, single mulberry-coloured flowers exquisitely marked and frilled white.

'Madonna'
Fully double fringed white with clean red eye; a calyx-splitter with a sweet scent and spreading cushions of silvery, weather-resistant foliage. An old variety.

'Mrs Sinkins' honoured by appearance on the armorial bearing of Slough where it was raised and named by John Sinkins, Master of the Workhouse, in 1868.

'Mrs Sinkins'

The name almost all flower lovers know. The original cultivar was named after the wife of its raiser, John Sinkins, master of the workhouse at Slough. He named his cultivar in 1868, and the plant received a first class certificate in 1880, being exhibited by Turner and Sons of Slough. The town honoured its fame by placing a flower in the break of the swan decorating its official crest. The plants were grown very widely around the turn of the century and during the 1930s, and many people retain clear memories of rose beds and borders skirted with the silvery foliage and strongly perfumed large white flowers of this variety. Meristem-cultured 'cleaned' clones are now newly available on the market; part of the reason 'Mrs Sinkins' became scarce appears to have been widespread virus infection causing a progressive weakening of stocks. It may now be impossible to determine the exact appearance of the original flower, for during its exceptionally long commercial lifetime different descriptions have been offered by the experts. According to one account in the 1988 *Carnation Year Book*, passed on by a friend of Frank Sinkins, son of the raiser, the flowers originally had 'A lovely splash of crimson on the fringed petals, which disappeared in later years'. The compilers of the first *Pinks Register*, published between 1952 and 1955, maintain that it should be self-or plain-coloured without 'traces of ivory or greenish colouring'. However, Oscar Moreton maintains in *Old Carnations and Pinks* that the 'base of each petal is greenish'. The truth probably is that many similar seedlings or sports were propagated and passed on under what became a blanket label. Mr Galbally relates in the *Carnation Year Book* 'The late George Allwood told me how he once requested material of the genuine 'Mrs Sinkins' and that among the fifty samples received there were no two alike. In those days any white pink with a scent and split calyx was labelled 'Mrs Sinkins' and any old ragged red carnation with some pretence to scent was called 'Old Crimson Clove'.

If this amount of uncertainty can occur over a cultivar of such outstanding popularity within the relatively brief space of a century and a quarter, the margin for error and confusion on the correct naming of other 'old' sorts is evidently wide indeed. In any event, the 'Mrs Sinkins' now grown is a fully double white, with deeply laciniated petals and a smell described as of chocolate, clove or vanilla according to the palate of the sniffer. I have versions with greenish, ivory and red flecked centres and it is doubtful if anyone at this point will ever determine which, if any, most resembles the original.

'Murton'

Found in a bunch of flowers brought to the Womens' Institute Market at Mumbles, Swansea, and noticed by my mother-in-law! As is the practice for all unnamed pinks with apparent claim, like this one, to merit propagation on account of age, beauty or both, it bears the name of the village in the Gower where its owner remembered it growing for as long as she could recall. 'Murton' has large double dark-red flowers flecked and edged white, with strong blue-grey foliage. Alas it has almost no scent.

'Old Dutch'

Believed to be a seventeenth-century survival, or at least bearing strong resemblance to those depicted in contemporary paintings, the flowers are pale pink striped rose, with sharply serrated petals and a strong fragrance.

'Old Fringed'

A deeply fringed, small double white with strong perfume and good clean foliage, useful for edging or mass planting. A plant bearing this name is credited by Montagu Allwood as being a parent of the race of modern border pinks which bear his name. A pink which sounds similar was known in Tudor times as 'White

Shock' and was commonly used for edging knot gardens. 'Old Fringed' may be a direct descendant of this, a vigorous and exceptionally long-lived plant with neat habit and distinctive silvery foliage.

'Old Velvet'
While this may be a sport of 'London Glow', a laced pink raised during the 1940s by Mr McQuown, it is now listed separately. It is a semi-double of deepest maroon, opening almost black and fading to the colour of its name. The reverse and edge of the petals is silvery pink.

'Paddington'
Very double, deeply fringed pale pink, with deep purple eye, raised at Paddington by Thomas Hogg about 1830. Strong clove scent, abundant foliage.

'Pheasants Eye'
Deeply fringed, white double, with deep purple eye and traces of lacing. Very fragrant. Pinks of this type are included in herbarium specimens collected around the turn of the seventeenth century, and were one of the first types to be selected and named. Growth is small and neat but plants may be virus infected and can be hard to propagate.

'Queen of Sheba'
Uniquely feathered markings of ivory on magenta. Small, single blooms on long jointed stems. Foliage is sparse and poor but the plant is worth growing for the exceptional beauty of its flowers. Believed to be an old survival.

'Roodkapje'
From Holland, age unknown. An excellent small flowered pink double with strong perfume, vigorous growth and free flowering. Of the form and habit illustrated in the earliest representations of double pinks.

'Rose de Mai'
Probably early nineteenth-century origin. Pale mauve-pink flowers lightly streaked white. Double scented flowers held on longish but self-supporting stems above pale silvery healthy foliage. Plants will form a billowing clump and are long lasting. Always the first to flower, in May, and continues to produce blooms into the autumn.

'Sam Barlow'
Large white deeply laciniated double with deep purple, almost black eye. A Victorian calyx splitter with strong perfume. Named after contemporary horticulturalist.

'Sops in Wine'
This form is a double white with notched petals and purple centre. There are occasional traces of faint lacing and a wonderful clove scent. Early to flower, bearing large blooms on upright tufted silver foliage. The origin of the term sops in wine is expanded in the section on recipes and pot-pourri (*see* pp 202–10).

'Sweetheart Abbey'
Deep rose semi-double with white flecks and wire edge, not of particularly old raising but of the type grown in the seventeenth century. Plants of 'Sweetheart Abbey' can grow to a considerable girth and the dark flowers, freely born, can look dramatic with the evening sun behind them.

'Terry Sutcliffe'
Burgundy-red single, reflexed petals shaded pale pink. Free-flowering and easy to grow, with vigorous bushy green-grey foliage. Named after present-day nurseryman and age unknown though with the appearance of the old varieties.

'Ursula Le Grove'
Purple-red eye and striking random radial flakes on white fringed, single blooms. Very free-flowering plant named by Oscar Moreton after his daughter. Roy Genders believed it to be a very old variety, referring to it as 'Old Feathered', and conjectured that it arrived in this country with Henrietta Maria, Queen of Charles I.

7

THE LACED PINKS

A Pink called Major's Lady Stoverdale . . . [was] the first pink possessed of that singular and beautiful ornament called a Lacing, which is a continuation of the colour of the eye, round the white or broad part of the petal, which gives it a most elegant appearance.

James Maddock in *The Florists' Directory* 1792

Its principal beauty and attraction consists in the eye, which, with the lacing, forms such a beautiful contrast with the white, which assumes a sort of half moon in the interval.

'J' of Sheffield in *The Floricultural Cabinet*

The story of the development and fortunes of the laced pinks would fill a book on its own, for they were the subject of intense specialist activity and many exquisite illustrations survive from their Georgian heyday. We know from late medieval Flemish and French textile work that there was, even at this time, a tendency for splashes of pale colour to appear at the centre of the petals of the pinks. Forms showing this characteristic were chosen for portrayal in various different works of art, and, it is fair to presume, would have been gathered together and exchanged by gardeners from early Tudor times. However, it was not until the late eighteenth century that their culture attracted the attention of the Florists, or specialist growers, and started a line of development that was to gain them acceptance as a Florists' flower by 1792, and to lead them to centre stage between 1830 and 1860 when they became, as Ruth Duthie, writing in *Florists' Flowers and Societies*, has shown with her careful research, probably 'the most popular of the original competition flowers'.

James Major was gardener to the Duchess of Ancaster and is credited by his contemporaries with the raising of the first laced pink; he named it after his employer and two years later produced 'Lady Stoverdale' which sold at 10s 6d a pair. He sold £80 worth, at a time when the average wage of a working man was about £2.00 per month. The promise of finely traced markings on these pinks had an instant appeal to the Florists, ever on the lookout for something unusual and new to savour. They lost little time in raising new seedlings and applying themselves to the self-imposed task of 'improving' the form of the blooms which, it was decided, should aim to shed serrations on the outer rim of the petals and aim to become 'rose-leaved', a characteristic already encouraged over several generations with the carnation.

The taste of the Florists was to develop flowers with as near as possible a circular outline, complemented by striking regular petal patterns. Hence tulips with 'feathered' and 'flamed' markings had been bred to lose their naturally pointed petals with the aim of assuming the shape of a wide-rimmed chalice with patterning and anthers exposed at the centre of the open bowl. Smooth-petalled carnations had long been desired and to some extent achieved, those with a picotee or finely delineated contrasting edge being particularly valued. Auriculas had been develped from Elizabethan times to show off their naturally circular form with a complicated central eye, adorned with contrasting concentric circles up to four in number on subtle dark colours including green, often dusted with shimmering white 'paste' or farina encircling and accentuating the eye. Ranunculus and hyacinths were grown by the hundred for competitive display, though Florists' forms of these two genera are all but lost to us today. At about the time of the laced pink, laced polyanthus appeared and were likewise greeted with enthusiasm by the Florists. Laced polyanthus showed a gold eye and clear bands of the same colour around the edges of each deep-red petal. A century later pansies, dahlias and chrysanthemums had joined the company, each being encouraged to behave in a composed and regular fashion. Competitive exhibitors of modern roses today will recognize the quest for rounded blooms which, then as now, spurred on the competitive amateur to challenge nature to conform to man-made specifications.

James Maddock, quoted above, defined the standards for laced pinks in the authoritative (some might feel authoritarian) tone still recognizable today in the leaders of the various specialist societies:

The stem should be strong, elastic and erect, not less than 12″ high . . .
Petals should be large broad and substantial and have very fine fringed or serrated edges, free from large, coarse, deep notches or indentures; in short, they approach nearest to perfection when the fringing on the edge is so fine as to be scarcely discernible; but it would be considered a very desirable object to attain them perfectly rose-leaved without any fringe at all.

Blooms for exhibition were divided into red-laced and dark or purple-laced classes; a third section, the 'black and whites' referred to clearly marked dark-eyed whites with no lacing, a race of pinks which has all but disappeared today to the sadness of present-day lovers and breeders of these flowers. At this time the modern 'pink-ground laced' class did not exist, for tinges of pink in the background of laced blooms were considered merely run colours, a grave fault. Later, however, 'rose pinks' of this type were admitted, and these dominate the show benches today.

Maddock continues to pontificate thus:

The broadest part of the lamina, or broad end of the petals, should be perfectly white and distinct from the eye unless it be ornamented by a continuation of the colour of the eye round it,[1] bold, clean and distinct, leaving a considerable proportion of white in the centre, perfectly free from any tinge or spot. The eye should be of bright or dark rich crimson, or purple, resembling velvet, but the nearer it approaches to black the more it is esteemed. Its proportion should be about equal to that of the white, that it may appear neither too large or too small.

1 When the corolla consists of petals of this description, it is denominated a Laced Pink.

A great debate was later to emerge between northern and southern Florists as to the size of desirable blooms. While southern growers tended to aim for great size, often at the expense of an impossibly overloaded calyx which burst as the flower opened giving a lopsided appearance, northerners preferred a more moderate-sized bloom which opened evenly to display the markings. Southerners were of the opinion that the northerners' blooms had hollow, unlovely eyes, but 'J' from Sheffield replied archly that he wondered if his London friends knew what the eye was because the flowers they grew had such a mass of petals that the eye never showed. They favoured, he said, a 'full double, high crowned flower like a ranunculus'. Such differences, good-natured or otherwise, fuelled local loyalties and there are records of inter-society challenges, no doubt animated affairs. The huge blowzy 'bursters' of the south could measure up to 4in (10cm) in diameter, and had to be artificially held together by devices such as strips of glued pig's bladder, or 'let down' by the careful nicking of the calyx so as to afford a uniformly broken calyx to support the explosion of petals. Cards were allowed to support the drooping guard or outer petals of these monsters, which were then 'dressed' or rearranged with much dedicated and gentle attention. Present-day breeders occasionally produce such flowers, though they are not available to the general grower owing to the poor behaviour of the plants in other respects. Jim Gould, for one, has photographed a bloom of his own raising looking very like the old illustrated plates. He describes it as

Idealized laced pink, showing incorrect and correct single petals, left and right. Redrawn from Gardener and Practical Florist, *1843, when the Florists' interest in laced pinks was at its height.*

'A monstrous bloom, nearly four inches in diameter'. Despite its beauty its growth habits were appalling, with stems 'As stiff as wet string some four feet long'. Like all good plantsmen he was ruthless with this inferior individual despite its remarkable flowers.

James Maddock, appealing for moderation on the subject, presides thus: 'It is more desirable to have their pods large and long than too short and round, as it is hardly possible to preserve the latter from bursting, whereby the beautiful circular form which the flower ought to possess is lost'. Excesses doubtless continued, however, for carnation blood was included in the pedigree of these pinks, whose systems were clearly overloaded.

The culture of Florists flowers, particularly pinks, was the province of the gardener of modest means. While the wealthy landowners of the day had their eye on larger horizons and were courting the talents of great landscape artists like Capability Brown and Humphry Repton, these flowers belonged to the small garden or backyard plot of the artisan, where attention to detail could be lavished upon individual specimens. The art of floristry boomed and, in the words of Ann Scott-James, in her book *The Cottage Garden*:

'Became a source of much social junketing. Clubs were founded in many parts of the country and flower shows organized which became occasions for club dinners or feasts at the local inn . . . Members of a club paid a subscription to cover the costs of a show and the dinner which followed, and often a local gentleman would be patron and would provide prizes, usually silver cups, spoons or punch ladles, or copper kettles. Perhaps the gentleman's gardener would compete but most of the competitors were artisans, and wherever there were weavers, or other home-based workers, they were likely to carry off the lion's share of the prizes.'

Much detailed advice was published. Robert Sweet, writing in 1827, gave elaborate instructions for planting and recommended that growers should 'Shade the beds when they are in full bloom as sun or rain will damage the colours'. Various devices were suggested for this purpose, conical 'hats' and awnings designed to be held aloft over both individual flowers and groups of blooms.

Pink feasts were held at various inns all over the country, and records may be traced in many local newspapers. It is believed that the growers would tramp miles, flowers nursed carefully in containers held on a yoke, for this opportunity to compare and compete. Prizes offered were of immeasurably higher relative value than those available today from equivalent meetings. As far as is known competitors were exclusively men, apart from one lady grower of auriculas, and this continues to be largely the case. There would seem to be a particularly compelling lure for men in the desire to attain perfectly symmetrical patterning in flowers – a gentle and skilled pitting of wits against the caprices of nature. While Georgian and Victorian illustrations of the laced pinks are no doubt absurdly idealized, looking as if drawn with a compass, so perfect is their regularity, the achievements of present-day breeders and exhibitors are also remarkable, and a visit to their summer displays is a memorable experience.

Writing of the devotion of the early Florists to their plants, including the laced pinks, Anne Scott-James writes:

I find the skill and care given by the artisans to their flowers very moving. The weaver at his loom watched his pots in the garden as a mother watches a baby in a pram through the kitchen window. If the day was hot, he hurried out to shade his plants; if a shower threatened, he went out to cover them; he saw that they had plenty of fresh air, he fed them expertly, mixing up all sorts of horrid feeds.

The analogy is apt, for the patient attention elicited by such flowers is indeed almost parental. The anxious concentration of a present-day grower as he dresses and sets his flowers to look their best is reminiscent of a mother adorning a barely compliant child for a party. Nerves and excitement are compounded by the knowledge that at any moment a show of temperament on the part of the subject may bring the best laid plans to ruin.

A significant break came for the laced pink in about 1828, recorded by Robert Sweet in his *Florists Guide*, who gave an account of Davey's 'Juliet Pink', which was 'Of great importance on account of its rose-leaved petals, not jagged at the edges'. Mr Davey, who ran a nursery at Kings Road, Chelsea, introduced and 'let out' new laced pinks at a sharp pace from this time, and like many nurserymen today had often received these from amateur enthusiasts. Many have friendly, unpretentious names, reflecting the unassuming character of their raisers. 'Miss Cheese's Pink' was a finely laced form 'From seed of Mr Cheese, who cultivates a choice collection of Florists' flowers with great success'. Sweet is a fulsome supporter of the pinks, affirming that they are 'Of easy culture and readily increased by pipings. They are very generally cultivated but perhaps not so much as they deserve to be . . . and should therefore be preferred [to carnations] for any Lady or Amateur who wishes to make a collection'.

Maddock too had compared laced pinks favourably with their aristocratic cousins the carnations thus: 'The culture of pinks is much less difficult than that of carnations: they are hardier, more easily propagated, increase more abundantly, and are less liable to the casualties incident to the latter'.

The thirst for competitive success however seems to have led to cultivars where vigour and constitution were sacrificed for beauty. The individual blooms were exhibited in bottles to be admired from close quarters or even inserted into holes and held round their necks on a mounted display, like butterflies on a board. While one or two may have survived from the late Victorian era it seems probable that any earlier ones are now lost, and stories that old forms were rescued from Paisley, an area reputed to have particularly fine laced pinks, have recently been queried. Oscar Moreton believed he had an original 'Paisley Pink' from Mr Taylor of Longniddry, who had in turn 'rescued' several cultivars supposedly grown by John Macree, a muslin worker who died in 1804. Dr Stuart, co-author of *Plants from the Past* lives not far from Longniddry and decided to find Taylor's garden, which was empty. However, an elderly friend of Taylor contacted Dr Stuart and came to visit him. He recounts how she drew him aside. 'I'll tell ye a wee secret', she confided, and told him how there were lots of 'Paisley' pinks: 'Paisley Gem', 'Paisley Weaver', 'Paisley Delight', 'Evelyn Taylor' and more. When asked where Taylor had found them, the old lady winked. 'Och, they all came from the same pod' she said. You may believe, or chose not to believe, in the authenticity of the 'old' cultivars, according to the degree of romance in your temperament.

Having thus introduced a note of doubt, and even a suggestion of dishonour, it must be added that the debate on the authenticity of the 'Paisley Pinks' remains very much alive. The garden historian Ruth Duthie, to whom I am indebted for her careful perusal of this section, disagrees strongly with Dr Stuart's implication that G. M. Taylor, 'a fine gardener who wrote some excellent books' may knowingly have misled fellow gardeners including the Reverend Oscar Moreton as to the authenticity of the plants he grew and shared with his friends. Ruth Duthie has scrutinized the minutes of the Paisley Florists Society and has published a photograph of the fine decorated ramshorn snuff mull they offered as a prize for their blooms. She has no doubt that the Society was a substantial organization. If this is the case it would indeed seem extraordinary that none of the Paisley Florists' cultivars survived. There is doubtless more to be said on the subject.

ROOTS, FOLIAGE AND BLOOMS

We know from the early records that original pinks of the laced type had an admixture of *Dianthus caryophyllus* or carnation-type blood. Their descendants show this in their habit of growth, tending to be somewhat longer jointed than the plainer forms, making a taller and more brittle plant. Foliage is usually silvery and strong, born in tufted growths on stems which tend to early woodiness. The flowers are held on tallish branched stems of up to 18in (45cm) and open later than the plain pinks, being at their best in late June and through July. More recently raised laced pinks with *allwoodii* blood have a more compact habit and will flower earlier and for a more extended period, from late May and throughout June and July. They behave rather in the manner of hybrid tea roses in that they will continue to produce renewed flushes of bloom into autumn if spent flowers are regularly removed.

A healthily growing plant in youth and middle age will produce a satisfying crop of flowers, whose opening is exciting to watch as each is different and any one has the potential to reveal the patterned symmetry desired and admired for over two centuries. Some plants and some seasons will produce a high proportion of such flowers, perhaps one in twenty. Other seasons or growing conditions may prove more disappointing, and lacing may be faint or even, rarely, non-existent. Early morning is the best time to look at your plants, and there are moments of quiet triumph at the discovery of near-perfect flowers which have opened overnight. You may wish to cut these for closer examination and enjoyment in water, where they will last for a week or so in good condition. This is the season of the hottest sunshine and the fiercest thunderstorms, and the fleeting perfections of the laced pinks are best savoured in some small pot or jug, perhaps with moss roses, and philadelphus, blue campanulas and lavender. The flowers are much in demand for small bridal decorations, or any situation where you wish to invite the attention of the eye and nose. It is hard to avoid being captivated by the form and scent of the laced flowers, and one can well understand their addictive potential.

The nineteenth century growers advised limiting the number of stems in order to concentrate the plant's vigour and resoures on a few flowers. R. P. Brotherston echoed this advice in his *Book of the Carnation*, published in 1904: 'For exhibition purposes from one to five stems are left on each plant, and these are disbudded in due time, never more than three buds being left to expand'. However, the work of twentieth-century breeders initiated by Montagu

Allwood and George Herbert and followed through by Frederick McQuown and others has produced more robust, free-flowering cultivars, and such drastic sacrificial pruning is not generally deemed necessary today. A little judicious thinning in April or May may be sensible if the plants seem to be attempting to carry an intolerable burden of lengthening potential flowering shoots, for some modern cultivars have a distressing habit of flowering themselves to death.

CULTIVATION

As the laced pinks have the potential to yield rather special blooms, a little extra care is well worth while in preparing their growing sites. The same principles already outlined for old fashioned pinks apply; in other words, good drainage, an alkaline soil, and an open position. Beds with doubtful drainage may be raised by incorporating sharp sand or grit. Well-rotted manure or thoroughly sweetened garden compost may be dug well in to the soil, and a handful of bonemeal or blood, fish and bone may be added to the soil in the planting hole. Further granular feed or more bonemeal may be sprinkled round the plants and watered in if necessary in spring. Hydrated lime or chalk lime may be added as a top dressing, and gently raked into the soil around the plants in autumn. Organic mulching which can cause stem rot is best avoided.

New plants may be set out in autumn or spring, depending on weather and soil conditions. Plants should be well-rooted in containers before being entrusted to the always uncertain elements. Those newly arrived from a mail order source should be potted up and acclimatized in a shaded frame or cold greenhouse for a week or two as they are likely to be light sensitive and should ideally re-establish leaf and root growth in your care before being set out in the open ground. They should be placed at or a little above their soil level mark, which will be obvious from looking at the stem, and kept watered if dry or pressed back into the earth if lifted by frost, until convincing signs of re-established growth are visible. Plants which cannot be set out in autumn may be potted on and kept under cold cover till spring where they can have a head start over companions which may have been obliged to suffer the trials of a wet or capricious winter in the open. Such protected plants must be observed with care, any long shoots being kept pinched back to ensure compact habit is maintained and plenty of new 'breaks' or bushy growths form from low down on the skirts of the plant.

PLANTING

While the old Florists maintained that lacing was often imperfect or absent on spring-planted pinks, I do not find this to be a determining factor, and in my experience of the few times when this has occurred other adverse influences like drought or sudden checks to growth at the time of bud formation seem to have played the main part. Other growers, however, hold firmly to the belief that autumn-planted individuals always do best. Local conditions and soil structures are bound to have the strongest influence on your planting practice and here, as always, consultation with your gardening neighbours is likely to yield the most reliable advice.

The plants should be set out at intervals of some 8in (20cm), ideally in odd-numbered groups which will join as if into one individual by the second or third season. If well-suited they should last in good heart for five years or more, though it is prudent to take cuttings annually and ensure a regular succession of youthful individuals to give to your friends or sell on to others. It is thanks to this tradition that the British gardener has such a rich variety of plants from which to choose today. As the Reverend Oscar Moreton wrote in *Year Book of the British National Carnation Society*, 'If you have any cuttings to spare, give them away, for that is the surest way to preserve them. I have always tried to work on the principle "Cast your bread upon the waters, for thou shall find it after many days".' There is certainly no pleasanter way of ensuring that one remembers and is remembered by gardening friends and acquaintances and it is in this way that our gardens become uniquely our own. The garden of the kind friend who started my own interest in the dianthus family has greatly changed since her death but to me her personality remains as vital as ever as healthy plants raised from cuttings which she gave me and taught me to root are now growing safely in my own garden.

I find the laced pinks look happiest when afforded more elbow-room than the more tufted and tumbling 'old' pinks. Their rather tall and angular stems, sometimes growing up to 1ft (30cm) in height, can be practically and pleasantly flanked by the waved green leaves and stiff stalks of aquilegias, or the shrubby aromatic purple or tricolour sages, both of which can offer support to the plants or hide your own underpinnings if you feel this is necessary. The flowers, being detailed in pattern, can look a little dizzying in the bright light of the summer garden if not carefully placed, and I find a cool, plain background of green iris leaves or other lanceolate subjects like tradescantia works well. The familiar frothy acid-green flowers and crinkled round leaves of *Alchemilla mollis* can also be an effective foil, and the Euphorbias, *myrsinites* alongside and *wulfennii* behind, make a fine contrast.

The white, ground laced pinks with their elegant dark-red or velvety purple lacings are easy to place in almost any setting. Those with a soft pink ground are also little trouble, but the strong magenta of more modern sorts like 'Laced Monarch' needs more care, frankly clashing uncomfortably with the yellow and orange shades which tend to prevail in the July garden when the post-war hybrids are in full flower. Their vivid colours can look dramatic and effectively matched in association with the deep blues of aconitum or delphinium, and are well set off by the herbaceous veronicas, notably the spreading eucalyptus-leaved *Veronica petiolaris* with its blue nodding spikes of flower, and the silver-leaved royal blue *Veronica incana*. The bold colours of most of the herbaceous penstemons are also good partners, for instance the purplish-blue 'Sour Grapes' or the deep-red 'Blackbird'.

While laced pinks are usually and most satisfactorily grown in the open garden they can make satisfying subjects for the cold greenhouse or polythene tunnel. I often grow rare or temperamental old cultivars in this way, and for large commercial growers it is standard practice. Though the plants necessarily fail to meet their full potential in root, leaf and flower growth and behave in a rather atypical way they can do well enough and produce a good crop of flowers and an abundant supply of cutting material.

Young plants intended for this type of culture should be potted several to a container in autumn or spring. Roots should be kept fairly closely potted and the plants placed in larger containers only when the rootball fills its allotted space. Compost should contain a good proportion of sharp sand and feeding is generally unnecessary for amateur purposes, though a weak foliar feed as the buds are forming may be appreciated. There is little advantage in potting the plants on into containers of more than 2 litres, though some commercial growers aiming for lush-growing plants yielding plentiful cuttings set their plants in growbags with apparent success.

Gardeners who find themselves prevented by infirmity, disablement or simple disinclination from venturing into the great outdoors may be pleasantly occupied in the sheltered setting of the greenhouse or conservatory and enjoy to the full the laced pinks among many other plants. Ideal opportunities may present themselves for the careful and exciting work of hybridizing in such circumstances.

PROPAGATION

Cuttings of the laced pinks usually root without difficulty under the conditions already described. More recently raised cultivars will show greater vigour than their older counterparts, and several crops per year may be taken from the plants, from mid-June until the end of August. A cold frame is quite adequate for successful rooting during the summer months though basal soil temperature should be raised to 65–70°F (17–21°C) at other times of the year. Particular care needs to be taken in pinching out long central growths as the plants show signs of rooting, as it is important to encourage bushy plants from the beginning and the laced pinks are a little more inclined than any others to elongate prematurely and try to run to flower. If this is allowed they will never make good plants.

Packets of seed may be acquired from specialist suppliers and may give a proportion of laced seedlings, though it is unlikely that any particularly desirable forms will result. Far better to acquire stock of good named forms, which you may pick out from displays at shows or from catalogues of the nurseries mentioned in the Appendix (*see* pp 213–4), and take cuttings to increase your stock of plants which will have a certain claim to space in your garden.

HYBRIDIZATION

The breeding of new laced pinks remains the province of a very few growers these days, and those new forms which do reach the show bench and market place are predominantly of 'pink ground' type. During the mid-nineteenth century a Colchester man, Dr Maclean raised several outstanding cultivars with pure white ground whose beauties were celebrated and recorded in contemporary illustrations. I have spoken with plantsmen who recall these and other cultivars of similar vintage and attest to the perfection of their flowers yet, like the famed 'Paisley Pinks' there are, alas, no survivors. It is said that George Herbert, the renowned Birmingham nurseryman who ran a flourishing business and breeding programme during the 1920s and 30s had access to the old cultivars in his work. It is also said that he, Montagu Allwood and F. R. McQuown exchanged stock with each other. It is then just possible that 'blood' now running in veins of present-day laced pinks can claim an honourable pedigree dating back to eighteenth-century

Pinks are among the flowers decorating the dress of Flora, in Botticelli's Primavera.

Flower piece by Ambrosius Bosschaert (1573–1621), showing flaked and yellow carnations.

Dianthus plumarius *thrives in most situations.*

Alpine dianthus.

'Waithman's Beauty'. Small pinks with regularly marked petals are often called 'Sops in Wine'.

Dianthus superbus *originated in subalpine European meadows.*

Dianthus *'Fair Folly' against a cool background of irises.*

'Camelford' found growing in the Cornish village by Nick Schroder. A good, vigorous white ground laced pink of unknown age.

Old varieties of dianthus from
the NCCPG National Collection
including 'Pheasant's Eye',
'Paddington', and 'Old Dutch'.

Dianthus plumarius 'Queen of
Sheba' and 'Coste Budde'.

Single pinks are easy to grow and
produce abundant scented flowers:
'Ursula Le Grove', 'Allspice' and
'Fair Folly'.

'London Brocade', the favourite of
its raiser, the late F. R. McQuown.

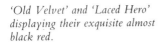

A few named varieties in your garden will give rise to many self-sown progeny like these.

'Mrs Sinkins' in pink and white forms, and laced pinks 'Gran's Favourite' and 'Laced Monarch'.

'Old Velvet' and 'Laced Hero' displaying their exquisite almost black red.

Double hybrid dwarf pinks of Alpine origin. 'Pike's Pink', 'Chastity' and 'Hidcote'.

Old Pinks provide a steady supply of scented flowers for picking from May to August and combine well with old roses and violas.

Flowers which may all be found in tapestry embroidery and paintings from early Tudor times.

'Red Sim' spray carnation.

Sweet williams.

Perpetual-flowering carnation
'Queen's Reward' raised by Colin
Short, whose achievements in this
field are widely acknowledged.

Dianthus barbatus. *Grown since the sixteenth century, this well-loved member of the family has changed little.*

'Doris', most successful of Montagu Allwood's cultivars.

'Admiral Lord Anson', strongly
perfumed old carnation.

Old border carnation from a garden
in Usk.

forebears, though it seems more likely that recent work has simply started again from new vantage points and in any event the once despised 'pink ground laced' now seem widely accepted. Notable breeders of fine white ground laced pinks in recent years have been the late J. Douglas and Stanley Webb of Oxford. However, few if any of these mens' cultivars are available commercially and other interested prospective hybridizers would find this honourable and ancient field of activity wide open for a revival of interest.

8

MODERN BORDER PINKS

For many years I have realised that with the great development and competition of other flowers, the pink, in its old form, could never hold a prominent position as a garden plant, and so I set to work to create a plant which was perpetual flowering during the entire spring, summer, and autumn, which was exceedingly hardy, robust, and easy to cultivate, and yet, at the same time, had the perfect perfume and lovable flowers of the pink; in short, a plant that really was a Perpetual Pink in actual being, and not simply in name. I also strove to develop a plant which would find a place in every garden and required no skill in cultivation.

Montagu C Allwood in *Carnations for every Garden and Greenhouse*, (*Country Life* 1926)

History

By Allwood's own account he worked for nine years experimenting with various crosses between the Perpetual Flowering Carnation (*see* Chapter 10) and the 'old-fashioned, hardy, old fringed White Pinks'. To the immense frustration of subsequent hybridists he does not disclose exact details of his work, but writes of his dogged and finally triumphant battle to work away from the harsh magenta shades of the species forms and achieve new hybrids displaying the best qualities of their parents. He discarded many progeny before finally selecting a seedling, 'Mary', which though not in itself of lasting merit was to become a parent of many varieties and sports, several of which remain in cultivation today.

His best known creation remains the inimitable 'Doris', which nurserymen tell me still probably sells more than all other cultivars put together, some forty years after its original introduction. 'Doris' has sterling qualities of good temper and hardiness, and produces repeated flushes of long-stemmed, perfectly behaved flowers, which are lightly scented. Its outstanding ability to produce reliable and heavy crops of bloom has made it a prime subject for commercial growers as well as for enthusiasts of the show-bench and ordinary gardeners, and it is, of all pinks, the one cultivar most flower lovers can readily name. Its colour, of very fresh poached salmon with a darker eye the colour of its smoked counterpart, is unique and much in demand. Flower arrangers love

'Doris' for its long stems, and long-lasting flowers. Its subtle shade of pale pink, described as 'light neyron rose',[1] harmonizes softly with the ivory, cream, peach and apricot colours enduringly popular for summer weddings and festivities. In the garden I find the colour of 'Doris' presents a challenge to place successfully, for while the salmon tone can look well with several of its modern sisters it can jar crudely if grown near the softer pinks and purples of the older varieties. Allwood himself is said to have been unsure of Doris's worth in the early days, but encouraged by colleagues he took it to Chelsea for its début to observe the truest test for any realistic nurseryman – the reaction of the public. The response, registered in overwhelming orders for his new hybrid, was clear enough. Doris has been reselected over the years and collected its First Class Certificate, the ultimate accolade awarded by the Royal Horticultural Society, in 1956. It was to prove a masterpiece indeed, a fitting legacy and enduring memorial for this dedicated, meticulous and self-deprecating plantsman (in print at any rate, for I never had the good fortune to meet with him in person!) whose work as a hybridist spanned some 50 years. As he wrote in 1926 'The raising of new varieties is perhaps the most absorbing of any function connected with flowers . . . and if I have helped to develop pinks and carnations by raising new and improved varieties then in turn they have helped me to enjoy life with the peace and happiness that close contact with nature always brings'.

The epithet 'allwoodii', strictly speaking, applies only to pure clones of Montagu Allwood's original stock. However, many breeders continue to make use of his cultivars as parents for their own lines, and the phrases 'allwoodii-type' or 'allwoodii blood' are commonly encountered, being generically applied to various modern cultivars showing certain distinctive features and characteristics. Foremost among these is the valued capacity to produce successive flushes of flowers over some six months of the season. Maiden, or newly propagated and planted allwoodii will produce a strong 'crown' stem bearing a single, branched or clustered flower head in May followed by a heavy flowering in June and, if dead blooms are removed, there will be repeat flushes through the remaining months of summer, often into October, November and even December. This characteristic, as well as being an obvious bonus in the open garden, has meant that modern pinks are an immensely attractive subject for commercial production. A recent survey at Rosewarne Experimental Horticultural Station recently showed

---

[1] Neyron is a colour which appears on the RHS colour chart.

that 'Doris' could, with skilful management, be expected to produce some 440 stems per square metre per season under glass. Growers, large and small, in this country and abroad grow *allwoodii* and their descendants by the acre in conditions from the most sophisticated modern glasshouse to the open field, to be harvested for the insatiable demands of the wholesale and retail trades. While the vagaries of the British climate and depradations by pests can undermine the profitability of the best-laid plans in some seasons, this branch of horticulture is a significant one and the Ministry of Agriculture collects separate figures in its annual horticultural census showing substantial British acreage devoted to culture of this intensive and specialized crop. While contemporary florists' windows and bouquets now usually include carnations and other dianthus hybrids flown in from Columbia, Israel, Spain or Greece 'Doris' and her British-raised counterparts are invariably to be found as well, jostled but not eclipsed by these foreign-grown relations.

ROOTS, FOLIAGE AND BLOOMS

The genetic influence of the carnation on *allwoodii* pinks is evident from their overall habit and appearance. Compared with the older sorts these cultivars are relatively broader of leaf, thicker of stem and more regular of flower shape. In general the plants are faster and more vigorous in growth, making longer limbed, loosely branched plants which in my experience tend to earlier woodiness and hence a shorter lifespan than their older counterparts in the garden. Healthy young individuals will establish themselves quickly and firmly on a good fibrous root system. The fragile-looking young white rootlets like well-drained soil which is in good heart and though organic mulching is best avoided many expert growers make liberal use of proprietary granular or soluble feed in early spring in order to encourage heavy crops of flowers. Foliage is variable in colour according to variety, but is typically bushy, vigorous and firm, forming a substantial rather open plant, at its best in its first, second and third seasons. Commercial growers usually discard their plants after a year or eighteen months, but a three or four year lifespan is probably a reasonable expectation for the general gardener. Plants are easily renewed from midsummer cuttings and it is well worth this trouble in order to maintain the neat elegance of growth which these plants should contribute to the garden even when not in bloom. Foliage colour varies from greeny-blue through battleship grey to pale silver, having a waxy glaucous quality showing, at its healthy best, an iridescent grape-like bloom. This foliage can look superb in November frosts and the bluish tinge, accentuated in winter, is often outstanding for its fresh look in our dank winter spells. Growth often restarts in January and well-grown plants with their classic angular habit and silvery sheen can be highly complementary to the earliest flowering lime-green hellebores in February and March – *foetidissimus* with its bottle-green fan-shaped leaves, and *myrsinites* with its prostrate snaking stems clothed with waxed open scales of blue-grey.

Stems of *allwoodii*-type pinks are typically 12–18in (30–45cm) long, being firm, elastic, and able to support their own inflorescence without flagging except in severe rain which can coincide, in midsummer, with blooms standing open at their heavy best. Some gardeners insert a small stake at planting time but my own preference is to flank the plants well with close-growing complementary sub-shrubby neighbours such as lavender, decorative sage or penstemons, in order to provide a protective microclimate and an attractive, naturally supportive frame. Pleasing contrasts and similarities in colour, form and scent will rapidly suggest themselves as you plant and, as always, unintentional effects are often the most successful. I find the colour, habit and persistent good looks of the nepetas particularly good as immediate neighbours for the modern pinks, and also have been pleased with companion planting with several of the artemesias whose fine silver growth on elastic stems can insinuate itself into remarkably effective frames for these pinks. Their glowing, some would say strident colours, need to be boldly offset and deep-blue flowers of aconitum, delphinium or veronica are good strong foils.

The individual flowers of modern pinks are more regular in shape than the older forms, being mainly double or semi-double and more resembling the composed rosettes of camellias than the irregular, shaggy cabbages of the old doubles. On good, named modern forms the calyces are strong and should not split if well cultivated. Petals are held firmly and gently in an elastic tulip-shaped cup, whose five, gracefully pointed segments expand evenly holding the petals, some 20–30 in number, to present an even flower of circular outline. Petal edges are often almost smooth but can present an undulating or regularly notched margin. For show purposes the five petals of singles or the outer, guard petals of doubles should be held at right angles to the stems, and keen exhibitors sometimes encourage their flowers to this perfection by attaching a light, loose collar of card around the opening bud, which is removed before the show. Inner petals of doubles are laid in regularly diminishing size and proportion towards the centre of the flower, which should be pleasantly arranged to present a composed and uncluttered centre. The flower shape is generally of a flattish, upturned domed dish though fuller petalled doubles often present a somewhat raised centre and this is acceptable to the *cognoscenti* of the showbench as well as the less exacting eye of the general observer.

Scent

Scent in the modern pinks, though valued, has not proved a consistently strong characteristic of the race. While most breeders would wish to select for perfume as well as other qualities, the trait has proved elusive in otherwise fine show and commercial cultivars. While 'Doris', other *allwoodii* and several other easily accessible new forms do have a light, sweet scent, many other perfectly behaved hybrids which are widely sold have, alas, no scent at all. Scent, then, has proved a recessive element in many modern pinks, but growers, as always goaded by a challenge, are working to recapture it. Notable new lines of pinks are being raised by amateur as well as professional hybridists which again possess good clove scent as an added bonus to their clear colours, large blooms and good garden habits. Commercial growers and distributors are quick to realize the importance of fragrance in modern pinks for the almost universal response of anyone encountering a dianthus flower is to raise it to the nose in the hope of a pleasant feast of scent, so often these days to be disappointed. Interestingly, many amateur and professional hybridists have lost their own sense of smell as a result, perhaps, of working closely with the plants. The condition is thought to be similar to the 'violet sickness' said to have similarly afflicted those working with strongly scented violets when these, too, in their day were a heavily produced market crop.

In the face of these odds, however, several recently launched named forms do present perfume among their other recommendations. H R Whetman and Son, the largest growers of wholesale dianthus stock in the U.K., send out cuttings and young plants of well-scented varieties to commercial growers all over the country. Plants grown on from this stock, which is regularly kept cleaned of virus through the technique of meristem culture, find their way into retail and commercial outlets, and account for the bulk of the dianthus plants and flowers encountered today. In the hands of the commercial growers blooms are produced through seven months of the year, and their availability and consistent quality has ensured them a permanent place as a staple ingredient of the present-day florists' working material.

Colour

Visitors to Chelsea or any of the larger shows will no doubt have vivid impressions of the professional nurserymens' stands, bearing spectacular exhibits of these modern pinks, their perfect blooms held on long stems in fanned and tiered display. The reds extend from deep velvet to scarlet and flame, the pinks and violets from the pale fondant shades of soft-centred chocolates to the bold paintbox colours of boiled sweets. There are soft salmons, pale ivories, pristine creams and whites. There are striped 'fancies' like shot silk, laced beauties, plum on pink and purple on white. There are dark-eyed bicolours and perfect, pure 'selfs' or plain colours. However, there are, so far, no satisfactory clear yellows! Observers at the shows commonly assume these modern pinks are carnations, and some nurserymen display a notice pre-empting this mistaken assumption.

CULTIVATION

Cultivation of the modern hybrid pinks indeed requires 'little skill' as Allwood hoped, but as in all gardening enterprise a little forethought and an idea of the effects one wishes to achieve will reap its own reward.

A free-draining, loamy soil with a pH of at least 6.5 is the perfect base material, and suggestions on how best to coax less-than-ideal ground into this condition are offered in the previous chapter. Having achieved this basic prerequisite, decisions must then be made about planting times and positioning for the purpose or displays you wish to achieve.

PURCHASE AND PLANTING

Received wisdom has traditionally recommended two main planting periods for modern pinks: the first from September to the end of October and the second from March to May. The main suppliers still adhere more or less to these schedules, and send out orders of young plants accordingly. However, enthusiastic gardeners are liable to acquire plants at many other times of the year and modern pinks, being generally good-tempered subjects, will adapt well enough to unorthodox planting times as long as basic safeguards are observed.

Where to Buy

Garden centres, often unfairly derided, now offer a year-round service for all types of plants, and usually carry good stocks of containerized hybrid pinks. Offering cheerful pictorial labels and well-tended plants they are a good and easily accessible source of supply. More unusual and interesting plants often may be obtained from small nurseries or gardens open under the National Gardens Scheme, and treasures unobtainable elsewhere may be acquired in this way at odd times of the year. Potted plants of cultivars on display at the shows are often obtainable from the nurserymen exhibitors, and opportunities to purchase on these occasions should not be missed. Small supplies of newly raised or scarce forms often find their way to the fortnightly shows at the Royal Horticultural Society in Vincent Square, London, or to the various tented halls or open stalls which spring to life at the hands of growers, large and small, as they make their seasonal pilgrimage around the country. All such treasures may tempt the keen-eyed gardener to buy at the 'wrong' time of the year, when the ground is baked hard by drought or the gardener is about to leave for a summer holiday. These trophies usually arrive home somewhat the worse for their journey, having been squashed on public transport, and bumped around the knees in a hot polythene bag for longer than is reasonable. They may need a period of recuperation in a calm and undemanding spot but can be usually planted in the normal way fairly soon as long as the ground can be made moist enough to receive them and kept reasonably damp until they are obviously established.

More traditionally acquired plants sent from nurseries should be unpacked at once and afforded whatever sensitive reception appears due. For my own part I like to pot up any newly arrived individual and leave it to settle for a week or two, under observation in a corner of an unheated greenhouse. Traumas of transit include light starvation, sweated slow roasting in hot weather and sweated slow fungal attack in cold. There are also the various assaults of shaking, breaking and bursting of packages with which any receiver or sender of plants through the post is familiar. Plants snapped or damaged beyond redemption should be kept while the supplier is informed of the accident, for the firm will wish to make an insurance claim and the carrier may wish to conduct its own post-mortem. Total losses are comparatively few, but if your own package of looked-for treasures happens to be one of them this is scant consolation. Over some ten years of sending out orders, boxed in polystyrene, cardboard and other containers we have found an average failure rate of some 2½–3 per cent per year need replacement owing to damage or simple disappearance. It is a disappointing and irritating process, and sadly many nurseries in these days of expensive labour are unable to maintain the mail order service that has been a staple source of good plants for enthusiastic gardeners for generations.

After-Care

A close watch should be kept on newly acquired plants of whatever provenance. A suspicious lookout needs to be maintained for the very fine webs and strands signalling infestation by red spider mite – a frequent pest in commercial nurseries – as well as the more familiar greenfly. Plants showing any signs of either should be quarantined until disinfected. Fungal complaints, if obviously debilitating, should be treated with a suitable proprietary drench. Distorted leaf or stem growth may indicate early attack by thrips. Specific treatments for all such complaints are suggested in Chapter 10, such problems being easily overcome once recognized.

I like to nurture newly bought plants under cold greenhouse or frame cover until their roots comfortably fill a 2½in (6cm) pot. If held until growing well in this way they should grow on smoothly once set out in the open ground where less-than-ideal conditions may have to be overcome. The plants should be set out when conditions are congenial, to the same soil depth as established in the pot. Any plant showing premature desire to flower at the expense of good leaf growth should be pinched back in order to divert resources into bushy, low sprouting foliage or breaks, most of which will elongate to provide their own flower stems in due course. Many experienced growers recommend routine thinning of the developing flower stems even of well-established plants, for the tendency of some of these modern cultivars is to attempt a heavier crop of bloom than the individual can healthily withstand. In order to encourage a more prudent channelling of the plants' prodigious cropping energy Mrs Desmond Underwood, renowned personality and late proprietor of Ramparts Nursery, would urge her customers to follow her example and carry out drastic pruning of the lengthening bud stems in April and May. She pointed out that plants allowed to carry a bloom on each shoot will rapidly become overstretched, and by midsummer will show sparse foliage and disinclination to bush up again attractively by the following autumn. Individuals allowed to exhaust themselves in this way quickly become gawky and messy looking in the garden, and are not a credit to the race. While the first flowers carried on such a plant may be fine enough subsequent stems produce blooms of progressively poorer colour, scent and form since the roots and basal shoots are simply unable to maintain a supply of adequate nourishment. Plants behaving in this reckless manner will continue to pour energy into producing yet more flowers which are, after all, a bid for insect pollination and continuation of the line by seed at the expense, in the extreme, of the parent. Sometimes what looks like a glorious explosion of bloom is simply a brave and terminally exhausting swan song. To avoid such melodramatics Mrs Underwood recommended removing up to two-thirds of developing stems on modern pinks. Growers will wish to establish their own methods by experience, and may find themselves unable to execute this sacrifice which should, if it is to be effective, consist of removal of stems below the first shoot in order to prevent further attempts to flower from any weak side bud lower down. Stems will snap off in spring and early summer, and the process, though painful, is to be recommended.

Once planted and established, modern pinks need only regular removal of spent flower stems and the odd tidying of any senescent lower leaves to keep them healthy looking and in good form. Skilful cultivation and sympathetic soil may extend their acceptable lifespan, but few gardeners claim they can be maintained at their best for longer than five years.

Planting Ideas

Planting ideas for modern pinks may be stimulated by summer visits to the various parks and gardens open to the public, as well as more informal observation 'over the hedge' as one walks through any British town or village. Municipal gardens and show parks often use bold plantings of these dianthus as a staple ingredient of their permanent display. Their long flowering season makes them a good subject for such gardens with an extended open season and their drought resistance and salt tolerance mean they are a popular choice for seaside public gardens, perhaps the most exacting of all habitats. City parks often use them as an edging for beds of hybrid tea roses, where their foliage will make a complementary skirt to such formal planting, and their flowers will appear in roughly synchronized flushes with the roses through the summer. The tonal range of modern hybrid teas and modern pinks are complementary, and can be effectively matched in beds of bold or soft colour. Those gardeners of traditional taste will find such plant associations offer a reliable and pleasing return in their own gardens, though a watch should be kept to ensure that heavy organic manure traditionally spread among the feet of the roses is kept away from the pinks.

Owners of country houses or small private gardens open to the public through the summer are also great growers of modern pinks. These gardens display the more individual hand of their present owner or original guiding spirit, and the success or otherwise of different planting styles may be judged in the raw. I have seen inspired combinations of plants in such settings, as well as lamentable failures, and would recommend any mobile gardener to purchase the 'Yellow Book' published by the National Gardens' Scheme and take every opportunity to visit the gardens listed yearly therein. Some are open almost throughout the year, others for only a few Sunday or holiday days in their best season. Most will offer personal welcome, several a cup of tea, and a few sumptuous home-made cakes, all in congenial surroundings.

Notably successful uses of modern as well as older pinks may be found at Hatfield House and at Hidcote, where they are planted lavishly to flank and tumble over paths and walls. At Sissinghurst they are a significant ingredient of the much photographed White Garden with its subtly textured and restful planting of grey, silver and white. At the other end of the scale, the gardens of friends, neighbours and those of unknown ownership glimpsed from car windows or on walks will often contain good ideas which may more easily translate to our own settings. Among those I have encountered in this way are particularly successful massed associations of modern pinks with nigella, or 'Love-in-a-Mist', with its ornate white and blue flowers and complementary feathered foliage. Often such combinations are half accidental, and all the more successful for that. Almost every British garden, provided its owner is not very tidy minded, will establish its own particular mix of self-sowing annuals such as these, which will become naturalized over the years. Left, within reason, to their own devices they can become a unifying thread in your garden, framing and softening more angular subjects such as the modern pinks and helping them to blend into the lush growth of the summer border. Old gardens will often carry a flavour of previous owners' predilections and, like the eryngium 'Miss Wilmott's Ghost' continue to haunt subsequent owners. In my own garden plants of double opium poppy, antirrhinum and forget-me-not which have not been introduced in our time continue to assert their place and were perhaps sown by some Victorian or even earlier gardener here. Of more permanent plantings I have seen campanulas, in their varied forms and shades of blue providing good complementary partnership to the pinks, for their colours are clear and strong and their foliage, habit of growth and flower shapes make satisfying contrasts to the lighter outlines of the dianthus.

PROPAGATION

Cuttings

Modern pinks are readily renewed by cuttings which are easily managed with a little instruction and experience. Most amateurs will find it convenient and easy to carry out the process from early to late summer when natural warmth and light mean a cold frame, cool windowsill or even a sheltered spare patch of open ground will provide a good enough environment to promote adequate rooting. Cuttings may also be struck well enough at other times of the year providing a bottom heat of 65–70°F (17–21°C) can be maintained, and a small heating unit can be bought or devised easily enough to provide this. While summer cuttings have nature, as it were, on their side professional as well as amateur growers can produce high-quality plants from cuttings taken in the winter months excepting perhaps December and January, though extra care will be needed to avoid fungal attacks which thrive in conditions of cold and damp unless skilfully watched and checked.

Cuttings of *allwoodii*-type hybrid pinks should be taken from strong non-flowering shoots of well-established, healthy plants which show no sign of lengthening and running to flower. We remove them with a small sharp-bladed knife or fine, sharp scissors and cut them just below the fourth or fifth node. Experience will soon teach you the sort of shoots to look for and a few early successes will build your confidence. The bottom leaves of the cuttings are gently pulled off, the cut edge dipped into rooting powder or gel and they are quickly set, a finger's breadth apart, in pots or trays to a depth of about ½in (1cm), each being firmed as necessary to stand upright. They should be watered in to the rooting medium, which can be any combination of grit, perlite, proprietary peat-based compost or sterilized loam, and left in a humid, shaded place. A prudent watch should be maintained to ensure that the cuttings remain turgid and show no signs of flagging through undue exposure to heat, drought or draught, and if conditions are arid they should be syringed regularly. While we find cold frames perfectly adequate for rooting hundreds of thousands of these cuttings per year, mist units are the choice of larger growers and many keen amateurs. Those using such equipment find that while the cuttings root more quickly the young plants need sensitive care once removed from the mist, and must be weaned and re-acclimatized in gradual stages. When robust enough the newly rooted cuttings should be potted up and left to grow on. Elongating central stems should be 'stopped' or snapped out in order to encourage bushy 'breaks' further down the stem. It is possible to omit this stage when dealing with the older types of pinks with their naturally bushy, tufted habit of growth. However, the task is essential with modern pinks which will otherwise tend to produce a single long-stemmed, bud-bearing shoot which, once delivered of its flower, will leave foliage that is sparse, exhausted and unattractive on a root system which will never produce a sound garden plant.

Assuming the success of the above processes healthy young plants will be ready for planting out within three to six months of the initial cuttings stage. They should be planted out in an open position as outlined above, and kept watered until growth is established. Gardeners who like to use the hoe should make every effort to desist from this practice around the pinks, for their topmost roots extend horizontally only some ¾in (2cm) from the surface and will be certainly disturbed or damaged by such activity. Hand weeding with the aid, if necessary, of a small table fork, is a requirement here and will remain a pleasure if the surrounding soil is moist or can be moistened as you work.

Seed

Modern pinks may also be grown from seed, available from the specialist dianthus nurserymen as well as larger seed companies. You may also, of course, collect your own from bee-pollinated plants in your garden, or your own expert activities in the greenhouse. Seed should be sown in boxes or pans in late summer or spring and will germinate easily, the young plants being ready for pricking out at the four leaf stage and for potting up when their growth appears strong enough and you have opportunity and bench space to cater for their needs. Soft, central leaf growth should be kept pinched back in order to promote nicely bushed growth and the plants should as in the case of cuttings be grown on under cold cover or in the open air until large enough to withstand the rigours of the open ground. Plants grown from seed cannot, of course, be named forms as seeds from hybrid pinks do not come true to type and each will have a unique genetic mix. Such home-raised occupants of your garden will thus be of particular interest and, as their flowers open for the first time, you may cherish fantasies that one could emerge a real winner. True gardeners, like the many-times married, are exemplary believers in the triumph of hope over experience.

HYBRIDIZING

High-quality new seedlings and colour sports from established cultivars can indeed emerge from experienced amateur hands and may be taken up by the trade to become a commercially viable proposition. Of more interest to many keen growers is recognition by their peer group of fellow showmen, for any success here is hard won and therefore much cherished. Several new named forms of modern pink are introduced annually by the major firms. While most are the fruit of many years development by hybridists such as Donald Thomas or the late Cecil Wyatt the field is open and keen amateurs may also make a bid for a place in this company. Off-the-cuff reactions to promising looking seedlings may be solicited from the professional nurserymen, who may be relied upon to give you an immediate and straight reaction as to the commercial viability of your treasures. As their opinion will be unvarnished a stiff upper lip should be prepared.

Establishing a Hybrid

Alternatively you may submit stems for competition in a seedling class at one of the British National Carnation Society's shows, or proffer your flowers for the expert opinion of their Pinks and Carnations Committee which includes representatives from the Royal Horticultural Society and sits twice each year at the time of the Vincent Square shows. For this purpose at least three stems of a new pink, sweet william or carnation are presented with appropriate paperwork recording the pedigree, type, date of raising, grower and exhibitor. There are also separate categories indicating whether the cultivar is intended for exhibition or open border use. Plants of those flowers receiving the Committee's admiration may subsequently be requested for trials at the RHS Garden, Wisley, where they will be planted out and judged in the raw as growing specimens alongside other established cultivars which act as a control. Good reports from this quarter may result in a 'Commended', 'Highly Commended' or, exceptionally, an 'Award of Merit' certificate and further selection for the following season. Continuing strong performance at Wisley, where the soil and conditions are exacting for these plants could eventually result in further accolades on an ascending scale with the finest earning First Class Certificates, sometimes after a meteoric rise to early stardom, though many achieve recognition only in their mature years. The 1990 season at Wisley saw 28 cultivars of garden pinks on trial in the open beds, which may be visited by interested members of the public. Many received preliminary certificates and the commendations thus bestowed have been honourably won for the judgements of the Joint Committee members are made with seasoned eyes and meticulous care. Interest from a professional grower may be attracted by an amateur-raised cultivar performing well in this setting, and an offer could be made to take up, propagate and distribute such a plant. In recent years a royalty scheme has been set up aiming to pass on (to the original raiser) a percentage of any proceeds raised for an initial period. This attempt to protect plant breeders' rights to their progeny has similarities to the rules of copyright for authors and publishers though there are obvious weaknesses and the system is far from foolproof. While some breeders have been pleased to receive some small financial return on their named cultivars which have been distributed by the trade, the system is hard to administer tightly owing to the ease with which new plants can be propagated once parent stock is acquired.

Comments and suggestions made in previous chapters on hybridizing other forms of dianthus apply without major change to this branch of the family. The hopeful amateur hybridist will discover however that many apparently ideal candidates for parenting new lines such as 'Doris' are effectively sterile and cannot be used in the work. While 'Doris' presents sports from time to time many of which are hailed and marketed as equal or superior to the mother stock, she has been found to produce little viable pollen and no viable seed and therefore can not be expected to be a parent to new cultivars by conventional means.

The melting pot of dominant and recessive genes from which

modern pinks have been drawn contains, as we have seen, components from very old, scented fringed pinks as well as perpetual flowering and border carnations. Seedlings then, from highly developed and correctly behaved 'modern' parents can present surprising throwback qualities typical of earlier forms for each new individual, like a child, is a unique remix from a wide genetic palette. Those seriously interested in the fascinating study of plant genetics will be absorbed by the specialist textbooks available on the subject, and will find perusal of the charts and highly complex mathematics a delight. Such works are expensive and prior loan from a library is to be recommended before investment in what could become a 'bible' for a consuming interest.

Individual hybridists will build expertise over years working with their own personal favourite parents and may, in due course, develop lines which are recognizably their own. Conversations with such men (they are all men as far as I am aware) reveal a rich seam of knowledge and creative expertise and their tenacity and enthusiasm for the work joins them over two centuries to Florist predecessors who were, like them, dedicated, practical and patient innovators in the plant world. Several such amateur hybridists produce exquisite cultivars of laced pinks which find their way no further than their own gardens, for not every personality is interested in the public razzmatazz of the showbench or disposed to send his progeny for a brief and testing time 'on trial' at the hands of others at Wisley.

Other hybridists, however, are revealed to be firm *habitués* of the scene, and a perusal of the Royal Horticultural Society's annual lists of raisers and senders of plants for trial shows a familiar and select company of names, some of whom have been involved in this way for a generation and more. They have made their mark indeed, and future researchers will no doubt wonder at the industry of Messrs Galbally, Robinson and Varlow as we do at their Victorian predecessors Hogg, Davey and Maclean.

What to Do

Jim Gould of Aldridge, who has offered me the benefit of his expertise as a hybridist, tells me that he has found several modern cultivars particularly suitable as fertile parents, and a beginning enthusiast might care to start with some of his recommended subjects. He finds the white 'Iceberg', the red 'Crimson Ace', the fancy (or striped, to the uninitiated) 'May Jones' and the white bicolour Alice excellent and fertile male and female parents. Having chosen his intended brides and their suitors he pots the plants into 6in (15cm) pots and brings them under cover in order to avoid the opening flowers being drenched or otherwise assaulted by the weather, which as all British gardeners know, can ruin the best laid of plans, particularly summer weddings such as this. A few days after the flowers open two long slender pistils, first curving then curling gracefully at the ends, reach out visibly from within the centre of the flower, extending to stand proud of the surrounding petals in many cases. When they glisten they are ripe for pollen. Alas many desirable modern double pinks have sacrificed stamens for petals and there is often a frustrating search for anthers showing ripe pollen from a suitable parent. The pollen, yellow or greenish and light as the finest dust, will remain viable on the plant for only twenty-four hours and will be spoiled by rain, overhead watering, condensation or heavy dew. Fortunately the pistils will remain receptive for several days, though they must, of course, be isolated when in this fertile state (*see* Chapter 2). Likely male parents showing ripening anthers should be carefully watched around midday; in warm weather the anthers will gently swell and burst, releasing the fine dry pollen. While some breeders use thin individual strips of blotting paper as a transferring medium others simply pick the male parent flower, strip it of its petals, and wipe the recipient pistils directly with the pollen. Plants in pots may, of course, be picked up bodily and held under the arm for this process without such need for removal of a stem. The practice of removing petals may seem brutal and may not be deemed necessary by all, but does serve the purpose of clearing the field of operation so you can see clearly what is going on. The process of transferring pollen to stigma should be carried out in a calm and careful manner. There is no need for undue finesse of technique and the flowers will forgive a fair amount of less-than-perfect handling. Observation of the somewhat cavalier and determined attentions of bees – who could be said to have been the first hybridists, scrabbling in and out of the flowers and unwittingly doing the same job – should reassure a beginner who may be daunted by textbook descriptions which can give the impression that perfectly steady hands and laboratory conditions are essential.

If fertilization of your pistil-bearing mother flower has occurred the petals will close up within a few hours. If not, try again another day. A plastic label should be written and attached to each fertilized flower, giving the date of the operation and identity of the successful male parent. After fertilization it is as well to pull down the petals and segments of the calyx to avoid undue moisture

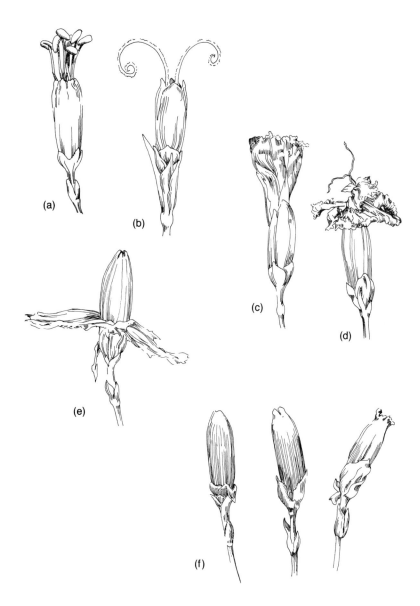

Hybridizing pinks: (a) Petals removed to show ripe anthers
protruding from calyx. (b) Ripe stamens curling over with glistening
stigmas. (c) Successful fertilization indicated by collapse of healthy
petals within 24 hours. (d) Unfertilized flower with petals withered
through ageing. (e) Calyx torn down from enlarging seed pod.
(f) Ripening seed pods.

resting here, though the pistils and seed pod should be left carefully undamaged and the flower stem allowed to remain in position on the plant. When withered, the petals and calyx claws can be gently removed. The mother plant needs continuing ordinary nurture in its pot while the centrally placed ovule changes from a green juicy blob, shaped like a fat lemon, into an elongating buff then brownish seed pod. Eventually seeds rattle within, turn black, and are revealed as the crackly pod tips curl and arch backwards. The stem can now be snipped off and the seeds carefully shaken out into a labelled bag. They may be sown at once for plants to flower the following summer or stored carefully until the following spring though there may be an eighteen-month wait for blooms from these plants and your impatience to see the fruit of your joint labours may dictate immediate recourse to the seed tray. Such seed, freshly gathered, should germinate within two weeks in the warm late-summer and autumn season, and plants may even be sturdy enough to set out by October. In my own view, however, it is more prudent to overwinter such individuals under cold cover for planting early the following spring, as they are irresistibly delicious to the slugs who may feast away in the fogs of November and the muds of December knowing that my back, at any rate, is likely to be turned. Flowers should be borne on these plants by midsummer and promising seedlings can be picked out at once. Sowing in spring means that plants will not bear flowers until the second summer and thus occupy space for two years, reducing turnover.

Assessing the Results

Breeders differ in the proportion of new seedlings they expect to find worth keeping. Many have no expectations of breakthrough from the first generation, or F1 products, and look to them only as possible parents for future crosses when desired qualities recessive at the first hurdle may re-emerge in the second, third or subsequent years' work. Breeding programmes of dazzling complexity and daunting time span may lie behind the eventual achievement of a single promising new cultivar.

Hybridists' judgement of the merit or otherwise of their own progeny is notoriously fallible. Mr Rickaby, present proprietor of Allwoods, has recently confirmed the apocryphal tale of Montagu Allwood's own reaction to his masterpiece 'Doris' which he originally considered a seedling of no merit at all, casting it aside as of no interest. Employees however covertly nurtured the rejected child in a part of the nursery seldom visited by the boss. Plants were grown on and Allwood, eventually permitted to have a look, acknowledged the sincerity of their efforts and let himself be persuaded to take it to a show. The rest is history.

Any seedling that you and an objective friend believe to look promising should be given your own reference number and cuttings taken for growing on the following year when a better idea can be formed of the individual's general character as an all-round plant. If it is decided to persevere with a seedling it should be named in not more than two words which do not already appear in the list of dianthus published by the registrar at the RHS. While many of the old cultivars bear wonderfully evocative names – 'Caesar's Mantle', 'Fair Folly', or 'Damask Superb' – the art of enhancing and describing new cultivars at their christening eludes many present-day raisers I feel, though often a touching sense of paternalistic pride is evident from the wives, children, nieces, nephews and favoured godchildren thus honoured into immortality.

Registering

While the process of registration is a paper exercise and involves no arbitration on the merits or otherwise of the living plant or its flowers, it is an important step designed to safeguard the interests of the raiser and every effort should be made to comply with its administration. The joint efforts of the RHS and BNCS have succeeded in the herculean task of recording all known cultivar names including those of flowers long lost, and since the first edition of the *International Dianthus Register* in 1974 order has prevailed in a previously chaotic field where synonyms abounded and the same cultivars were marketed with wrong or newly coined names. The *Register* is now updated with an annual supplement and felt to be working well enough though inclusion of foreign-raised new cultivars cannot always be guaranteed. The effectiveness of such a project depends on the maintenance of goodwill on all sides, for registration of names is a voluntary affair and no teeth can be bared at persistent defaulters. As the current supplement states: 'Raisers and introducers of all classes of dianthus are urged to ensure that all their plants have been registered and are reminded that registration should take place *before* a plant is released or the name is mentioned in print'. We have only ourselves to blame really if we disregard the cautionary tone of this advice and find that cuttings of a favourite plant turn up, as does happen, named, propagated and marketed by a nurseryman with no reference to the original finder or raiser.

Registration, then, does make sense and a form for this purpose may be requested from The Secretary, Royal Horticultural Society, Vincent Square, London SW1P 2PE. The form requests details of pollen and seed parent if known though if the cultivar is 'old' or of unknown provenance clearly such information cannot be supplied. A description of the plant type, its colour (according to the RHS colour chart if one can be obtained) and a photograph of the bloom should be supplied if possible. Information is also requested as appropriate on dates and details of the raiser, hybridizer, grower, selector, introducer and the person registering the cultivar in question. There is no charge for this service or the processing of the information which will be published in catalogue form in due course and the system works efficiently and effectively. It would appear that a fine job has been made of the considerable challenge issued to the RHS at its appointment as 'International Registration Authority for Dianthus' at the International Horticultural Congress in 1966. Having said this, the system, like any other, is open to abuse, its weak point being that there is no inbuilt critical faculty to monitor the quality of cultivars put up for registration. Undoubtedly now, as in the past, many seedlings of little lasting merit are dignified with a name and find a fleeting place in print only to be discarded within a short while. To save the *Register* being cluttered with too much material of questionable value it is as well to join the British National Carnation Society and enter your finds or seedling blooms in the relevant show classes. You will receive an immediate reaction from fellow competitors and judges. Peer group opinion is always telling, if painful, and you will return home with a clear enough indication of the true value of your blooms.

Accidentals

Several of the most commercially successful new cultivars introduced in recent years have arisen not from seedlings but from sports or mutations, which are sudden breaks showing entirely different flowers from their parent plant. Cuttings taken from such stems will hold the altered form, which may be a significant improvement on the original or indeed quite the reverse. Sports from 'Doris' and 'Joy' have been selected, named and widely sold in their own right. A large, West Country firm is always interested to hear of such sports which can appear at any time on any plant and whose cause is not perfectly understood. Plants under some form of stress seem most liable to produce such behaviour and extremes of weather or an imbalance in nutrition seem likely to produce these mutational changes though the conditions cannot yet be reliably replicated. 'Claret Joy', an excellent bright-coloured, crimson double appeared spontaneously as a sport of the carmine rose 'Joy' on a plant grown in open ground in 1985 at the nursery of Donald Thomas in Herefordshire. Recognizing its potential he lost no time in propagating from cuttings on this stem and the form is now separately registered and credited with his name. Such sports when registered with the RHS must contain the name of the parent plant, as this correctly does. In such a way 'Ruby Doris', a ruby red, bright rose flower with a dark centre was noticed and registered by Whetmans in 1978 and 'Doris Supreme', with stripes and ticks of magenta on salmon was fittingly selected and distributed from the home of its parent, Allwoods Nurseries, also in 1978. This same year saw several such sports and it may be conjectured that the after-effects of the 1976 British drought had triggered these mutational changes in the plants.

Such sports are submitted for trials at Wisley in the manner already outlined for seedlings where they await comment and possible acclaim alongside their fellows for a brief season in the public eye. What conversations they could hold! These trial beds are well worth seeing at a summer visit to Wisley, being at their best in June and July but often offering a truer test of the plants' garden viability at other seasons.

PESTS, DISEASES AND DISORDERS

Comments on the various troubles to which the race is prey have already been made above and suggested techniques for their avoidance and treatment differ little for these modern pinks.

Red Spider Mite

Commercial or amateur growers cultivating extensively under glass or polythene may be troubled by red spider mite. This pest thrives in arid, hot conditions and can become a real problem as no chemical control is totally effective. Its limitation is best effected by maintaining an inhospitable habitat through thorough regular drenching of paths as well as thorough spraying of the plants and soil in hot dry spells. Many amateur growers assert that a brisk blasting from the hose will see off this and other insect pests, and others have their own pet proprietary remedies to keep it at bay. However, the more adventurous growers who find their plants victim of this pest may be interested to try control by a natural predator, *Phytoseiulus persimilis*, a fellow insect which preys upon the offending mites. The creature is available to amateur growers and advertisements may be found in the gardening press. Instructions on the care and distribution of the imported insects should be studied carefully and carried out to the letter, for their successful establishment will depend on your own care that their needs are met. Most importantly, your own customary brand of insect control spray will need changing to a Pirimicarb based product, otherwise you will murder the invited as well as the uninvited guests.

Leaf Rot
Diagnosis of the various Fusarium rots and wilts specific to *dianthus* can only be offered by expert personal appraisal of any malingering plants. For the purpose of the amateur grower a general recommendation would be that any obviously sickly plant failing to respond to the usual fungicidal treatments such as a Benlate drench should be destroyed and replaced with healthy stock. Leaf rot, *Heteropetella valtellinensis*, appears occasionally and seems particularly prevalent on 'Doris' and its sports. Recognizable as apparently water-soaked areas on the green parts of the plant, it is favoured by wet conditions and causes most damage when growth is slow.

Rusts and Other Leaf Diseases
These can look unsightly but rarely have significant effects on the performance of the plants or appearance of the flowers. 'Haytor', the popularly grown white 'self' seems particularly susceptible to these disorders.

As always, plants which are growing well and have not been subjected to checks during the early stages of establishment will be troubled only slightly, if at all, by such conditions. Plants showing signs of distress should be pulled up and burnt without ceremony and the site rested a while or given a thorough cleaning by good cultivation. Maintenance of a buoyant atmosphere under glass or polythene, careful control of watering and general good husbandry should prevent build up of any serious trouble.

Soil Exhaustion
Some growers of pinks in the open garden tell me that they have encountered eventual crop failure due to apparent exhaustion or 'sickness' of the soil when the plants have been grown intensively for many seasons. Should your plants exhibit any sudden failure to thrive without other obvious explanation such a condition should be suspected and the site rested from dianthus for a while. Mineral

deficiency may be the simple cause, and you may be able to obtain a soil analysis which can suggest the trace elements which could do with replacement.

EXHIBITING

The tradition of growing and exhibiting flowers for competition reaches back for over three hundred years and continues to thrive today. While all gardeners value the private pleasures of tending plants many also welcome the opportunity to broaden their horizons and share the fruit of their work with others. The British National Carnation Society, whose own history is an absorbing study in itself, will supply details of shows all over the country where members meet to compete or simply enjoy their flowers, and classes for modern pinks are invariably part of the scene. Entries of pinks at some shows outnumber both border and perpetual-flowering carnations and it is a good idea to meet the flowers and their growers personally before deciding which you are likely to wish to cultivate yourself. The BNCS produces newsletters and a stylish yearbook giving lists of the winning cultivars in each class in the fifteen main shows which are held annually over the country. Interestingly, as ever, there are remarkable differences in those cultivars popular in the north and south of the country. New named forms come and go quickly in these lists for, as ever with dianthus, the pace at which new cultivars are produced encourages the rapid demise of earlier forms. A recent article by Audrey Robinson, historian to the Society, notes that of the many favourites grown some thirty years ago only three remain as regular prize winners today.

The Society's rules determine division of the pinks into six main classes for show purposes though there are local variations and a specific show schedule will help you better to understand the way things are organized. On a first, spectator visit to such a show it is worth while to acquire a schedule without which you are unlikely to appreciate what you are looking at as an unpractised eye will not immediately observe the nuances in the various classes. The flowers are grouped in five main categories which are the same for singles (those with five petals) as doubles.

Selfs
Selfs are generally listed and placed first, being flowers with plain-coloured petals bearing little or no trace of the 'eye' common to all

species forms. They are generally divided into separate classes for 'whites' and 'other than whites'. Several names crop up frequently at the shows, and an outstanding winner on the showbench is 'Haytor', with 'Allen's Ballerina', the lovely 'Swanlake', and the clove scented new form 'St Cuthbert', following on.

Of pink selfs, the new 'Oakwood Dorothy' has been well in the lead in recent years, followed by 'Diane'. The scarlets show 'Becka Falls' and 'Allen's Huntsman' as winners, and the crimson 'Houndspool Cheryl' and 'Crimson Ace' appear regularly. Self types falling outside these major colour bands are the pretty, cream-coloured 'Oakwood Sue' and the red-purple 'Bovey Belle'.

Bicolours

Bicolour pinks have a dark, circular central zone showing at its best a clear contrast to the outer or ground colour. The old Florists had a separate class for whites showing a clearly marked crimson or deep purple centre with the darkest, largest and most clearly delineated centres being most highly esteemed. The group, then known as 'black and whites' is lost today though the old 'Argus' remains an honourable exception and the red-centred 'Alice' is perhaps best known of this type today. A new white bicolour, 'St Oswald', is winning well on the showbench but grows rather tall for the garden and may have an uncertain future. Bicolours with an 'outer colour other than white' include 'Doris' which sometimes has a class all to itself, and 'Monica Wyatt', a personal favourite of mine. Its soft pink double flowers have a blackberry-coloured centre framed by perfectly formed flowers looking as if made from soft crinkled tissue paper. 'Valda Wyatt', also a winner from the late Cecil Wyatt's work as a hybridist, is a deep lavender-mauve with a darker centre, sometimes showing so faintly that it qualifies as a self for exhibition. Both these last have scented, fine-looking flowers.

Fancies

Pinks with spotted, flecked, striped or otherwise oddly disposed colour patterns are classified as fancies. Many are fascinating in their similarity to the old and extinct carnations with their elaborate markings. Of these 'Oakwood Bill Ballinger' is currently winning all the prizes, with 'Old Mother Hubbard', another sport from 'Doris', and 'Strawberries and Cream' also doing well.

Laced

Laced flowers, or those with a clear band of colour around the edge of the petal, are now accepted with pink as well as white backgrounds, with the former predominating in availability and current culture. The finest of the white ground laced pinks probably remains the old 'Dad's Favourite', though Allwoods's 'Laced Hero' can show well and newly cleaned stock of the red laced 'Gran's Favourite' bears excellent show blooms.

Pink ground laced pinks dominate the laced classes these days, though in the past would have been disregarded as merely 'run' colours. 'Prudence', 'Laced Monarch', 'Laced Joy' and my own favourite 'London Brocade' all show successfully and there is no runaway winner in this class.

General comments on the process of showing dianthus flowers have already been made above but there are extra points to bear in mind when showing modern pinks because a higher level of good looks and symmetry of bloom are expected in this class. Broken calyces, while expected and permissible in the Victorian and Edwardian 'bursters' are unacceptable in modern pinks and a split calyx even if on one of a number of otherwise perfect blooms will automatically disqualify an entry. Disbudding, or removal of secondary buds either beside the crown flower or further down the stem is frowned upon, and stems should be presented as they have grown naturally on the plant excepting the removal of any flowers which have gone over on a bunched or branched stalk. As in all other show flowers, obvious infestation by insects of any kind will result in the immediate disqualification of your entry.

Blooms of hybrid pinks should be picked twenty-four hours before your journey and stood in deep water out of bright light. Flower arrangers will tell you that a drink of fizzy lemonade (for the flowers!) will extend the vase life of pinks and carnations and this, or a proprietary mix available from your local hardware or garden goods supplier is worth experiment. If you are unable to travel in person to a show officials may, with prior arrangement, agree to collect your boxed blooms which can be reliably transported by the Red Star train service. While this may sound a hazardous method of transport I have seen prize-winning exhibitors bring their own blooms to shows in various kinds of cardboard box, the flowers sometimes having been out of water for some twelve hours before emerging from darkness to take the most sought-after trophies. One may also see spray and perpetual carnations arriving at airports and florists' shops in long boxes after several days' transport by aeroplane from Israel, Columbia or the various European sources. They survive, looking good, for we have a tough subject here. Those driving to the shows will devise their own methods of transporting the flowers, and various home-made strokes of genius may be glimpsed in backs of cars designed to prevent overturning buckets and jostled flower heads.

The process of judging, while bound to have a subjective element, is a fascinating and meticulous business. I am told that a chance to act as steward is most instructive and should not be missed. Many judges are approachable for comments on their methods and criteria and while it is now considered unacceptable to query their judgement, unlike the old Florists who often fell into hot dispute when disappointed, it can be worth while to seek out an informal chat, generally freely given to an interested newcomer to the scene.

The BNCS is aware of its need to continue attracting new members and is currently on the lookout for younger recruits. The entrants in the 'Novice' classes today could be winners one day of the silver cups and bowls now carried off by the experienced hands of the senior growers with well-known names in this small but intense world of the show pink.

PLANT LIST

Cultivars listed below may be bought from major suppliers or obtained through other nurseries listed in the invaluable *Plant Finder* compiled by Chris Philip and published by Headmain Ltd for the Hardy Plant Society. Those joining the BNCS and partici-pating in its activities may soon find themselves part of a network of fellow enthusiasts where exchanges, always the most satisfying of plant acquisitions, are a regular feature. In this way cuttings of an interesting seedling or cultivar no longer maintained by the trade may be accessible.

'Allen's Ballerina'
Double pure-white of excellent form and symmetry raised in 1984 by Donald Thomas of Herefordshire. The smooth fullness of the flower reminded him of a dancer's skirt, hence its name.

'Allen's Huntsman'
Large glowing blooms descibed as signal red, by the same raiser in 1985.

'Allen's Maria'
Gently suffused bicolour blooms of deep rose and pink, 1985.

'Becka Falls'
Double scarlet raised by the late Cecil Wyatt. A good garden and exhibition plant, 1980.

'Bovey Belle'
Another of Wyatt's raising, dark magenta with a clove scent, 1979.

'Cranmere Pool'
Striking creamy white with a dark-magenta centre. Wyatt 1984.

'Doris'
Widely available.

'Doris Elite'
Larger flower than its parent with a more pronounced red eye.

'Doris Majestic'
Brilliant salmon-pink sport of 'Doris'.

'Doris Supreme'
A 'fancy' sport from 'Doris' with carmine flakes and stripes on the original shade of salmon-pink.

'Frances Isabel'
Dark crimson, pink ground laced, introduced by Allwoods in the mid-1970s. Raised by H. V. Calvert.

'Gran's Favourite'
Said to have been raised as a chance seedling by the young grandson of Mrs Desmond Underwood and introduced by her in 1966. This is my own favourite of the hybrid pinks, being a good garden plant with well-scented often beautifully laced flowers, raspberry on white.

'Haytor'
Pure white double widely grown by large-scale as well as amateur growers. Wyatt 1971.

'Haytor Rock'
Scarlet and pale pink double fancy, very striking flower. Wyatt 1979.

'Houndspool Ruby'
Dark-pink sport of Doris with redcurrant-coloured centre, selected by Whetmans in 1977.

'Joy'
Carmine rose double self *allwoodii*, much grown for trade sales and has given rise to several good sports, all characterized by Joy's distinctive brownish eye. Allwoods, 1935.

'Laced Joy'
Crimson lacing on rose-pink ground. Prolific flowers popular for the showbench on a large, rather straggling plant. Allwoods, 1947.

'Laced Monarch'
Handsome laced flowers, deep magenta on glowing dark pink. Strong blue-grey foliage and a dramatic plant in the garden where it can behave impeccably for several years. Allwoods, 1972.

'Monica Wyatt'
Soft pink double of pleasing shape and petal texture with blackcurrant-coloured centre and light scent. Wyatt 1981.

'Rose Joy'
Heavy cropping brilliant rose sport from Joy, selected by T. A. Percival in 1973.

'Strawberries and Cream'
Subtle pink streaks and ticks of deep purple on pale pink. A fancy of intriguing character, raised by Wyatt in 1984.

'Valda Wyatt'
Warm lavender-pink with dark centre, Wyatt, 1977.

COMMERCIAL CULTIVATION

Census figures published by the Government Statistical Service show a steady rise in commercial production of hybrid pinks for the cut-flower trade over the past three years. A total area of 47 acres (19.5 hectares) of glasshousing or plastic-covered structure sheltered land registered for growth of this crop in 1989. There are further, less extensive plantings in the open ground though no separate figures are available. Significantly, in the same period the area devoted to British culture of greenhouse carnations has taken an inverse curve, more or less mirroring the rise of the pinks, and the tender carnation now occupies only 24 acres (9.43 hectares) of land. These carnations, more tender relations of our bone-hardy pinks, are now produced in quantity elsewhere in the world and are no longer as economically viable an investment as they were for British growers. The winds of change would seem to be blowing chill for carnation growers in this country at present despite the buoyant look of the pinks figures, and the total acreage devoted to the culture of dianthus for the wholesale flower trade has declined substantially in the last three years.

While commercial cultivation of hybrid pinks is by no means an easy source of profit, small-scale market production may have appeal for some keen amateurs. A venture of this kind may be appealing and realistic to proprietors of large under-used vegetable plots or vacant smallholdings, though as with any business enterprise due research should be thoroughly undertaken into local demand and marketing practicalities before any investment is made. Availability of local labour at harvesting time is an important consideration as intensive and efficient work is required, often at short notice, when the blooms are ready to pick and the British climate, predictable only in its unpredictability, can precipitate or delay flowering times and surprise the most experienced of growers.

PLANTING

Unrooted cuttings or small 'plug' grown plants may be obtained in minimum multiples of 100 from major growers and suppliers to the trade. Stock from a reliable source will be true to type and obtained from disease-free parent plants which are regularly tested and treated to ensure they keep free from virus-related ills. The small plants are generally grown on into robust individuals occupying 3in (8cm) or 4in (10cm) pots before being set out in late July–September, or March–April. Assuming good cultivation three flushes of bloom may be expected from each batch of plants and after 12 or 18 months the stock is discarded, either propagated anew on site from healthy plants or, more usually, destroyed and bought in afresh.

From a summer planting a first flush of flowers may be expected in late April or mid-June, a second from September to October, and a third in May or June the following year. A spring planting will yield a first flush in July, a second in April–June the following spring and a last in September and October. In both cases the crop is semi-dormant during the four winter months. When finally lifted the soil is thoroughly sterilized and cultivated ready for replanting in due course. Some variations to the timing and quantities of the flowers may be promoted by stopping, or pinching out the lengthening bud stems at different stages of growth, for blooms will fetch varying prices at different points of the season and the crop may be managed to take advantage of the market. Small numbers of maiden or 'crown' stems on newly planted stock which would normally be pruned away may, for instance, be allowed to develop early in the season. These will fetch a good price but there will be some expense to the number of breaks, or new bushy stems, the mother plant will subsequently produce and therefore a somewhat lighter crop will be born later in the season. The appearance of these crown stems may be further influenced by careful but time-consuming removal of the fat, topmost bud as the stems develop, for early in the season cultivars such as 'Doris', the deeper salmon 'Diane' or the pure white 'Haytor' produce a branched stem carrying up to eight nascent buds. Removal of the first of these at the correct moment will result in several of the others developing and opening simultaneously in due course and resulting in a multi-headed stem presenting a fan or spray of flowers. However, as any amateur or professional grower knows, the elements are well able to wreck the best-laid plans and the efforts of the most skilled cultivators may be overtaken by a sudden heatwave which can send the nation's plants into simultaneous flower, swamp the market place and send demand and prices tumbling.

Husbandry and harvesting of hybrid pinks is a labour intensive and skilled job. The flowers are normally gathered in early morning at the point of bud opening. Stems of 12–18in (30–45cm) will snap off safely without harm to themselves or the plants. They are usually presented in bunches of ten, the blooms being 'faced' or laid together in order to present an attractive appearance to the customer, with their heads placed to 'look' in the same direction. Two rubber bands secure the stems which, once prepared in this way are plunged into deep water under cool dark cover. Earliest blooms may sometimes be marketed in groups of five and placed in cellophane wraps, helping to attract the good price they deserve. Their life may be prolonged by chemical treatment at this stage and proprietary solutions containing silver nitrate and sodium theosulphate may be made up and added to the water, the plants being left therein for a minimum of four hours. As these elements are corrosive plastic tanks, buckets and due caution for oneself should be used.

Glasshouses and Polythene Covers

Plants of hybrid pinks can be grown successfully in the open in the east and south-east of England, though those with pale-coloured flowers are a better subject than dark cultivars, being less susceptible to spoiling from weather or insects. However, glass or polythene-clad structures obviously offer a more controllable environment where control of weeds, pest, irrigation and nutrition can be more accurately supervised. The plants are frost hardy and may be grown perfectly successfully in an unheated setting, though lifting glasshouse winter temperatures above 40°F (5°C) and providing artificial lighting by tungsten filament bulbs can advance flowering some three to four weeks. Flower quality or quantity is not, however, improved by such measures and detailed guidance should be obtained from the Agricultural Development and Advice Service (listed under ADAS in your local telephone directory) before considering any outlay here.

Single-span polythene-covered tunnels 20 or 40 yards (18 or 36 metres) long are the least expensive form of cover to erect and maintain though common sense should dictate caution if your site is particularly exposed or slopes awkwardly. Such tunnels are prone to condensation and should have wide openings left or made at each end in order to promote free air-circulation. Multi-span structures will need extra fan assistance for this purpose or use should be made of netted or webbed materials available to the trade for partial or complete covering of the structure. The relatively sudden atmospheric changes experienced under polythene-covered structures will obviously have a bearing on the performance of the crop and though temperature and atmosphere under polythene in spring can be excellent, promoting better quality blooms than under glass, sudden soaring summer temperature and stubborn humidity in autumn and winter can adversely affect second and third flushes by, respectively, heat stress and frost damage. No irrigation at all is advisable for pinks under polythene from November to February, when the crop should be allowed to dry out, thus avoiding the unhealthy combination of cold damp soil and stagnant moisture-laden air which can encourage rapid infection by fungal diseases.

Glasshouses should have glass to the ground with plentiful ventilation. Plants grown with some heat can be brought into production some two weeks earlier than cold-greenhouse plants, which in turn should flower some two weeks earlier than those grown under polythene. Careful consideration needs to be made before embarking on any investment in heating systems for which British growers, unlike their European counterparts, receive no subsidy.

Preparing the Ground

Cultivation of soil in preparation for the crop is generally undertaken mechanically and a thorough process of weed and pest control should be carried out while the site is entirely empty of plant growth. An annual subscription to ADAS will enable you to contact and obtain expert advice from one of their horticultural experts whose profession it is to keep abreast of current research. They are thus ideally placed to advise on techniques of soil sterilization and the selection and use of appropriate chemicals for weed, disease and insect control. For a fee ADAS will provide an analysis of your soil, will arrange for a personal visit to your holding, and an offer suggestions on a programme of soil fertilization and subsequent feeding of the crop. Any irregularities or problems with production may also be referred for their consultant opinion.

Before planting, a ground plan should be devised taking into account the need of the workers to reach plants without undue difficulty. Planting distances will depend on season, the individuals being set some 8in (20cm) apart in autumn and 12in (30cm) apart in spring and summer. Some sort of supporting skirt at path edges is often used and can be helpful in saving damage to the plants and flowers from passing feet and clothing. Watering should be tailored to the season, the weather, but above all an understanding of the plants' character and developmental stage. In winter it should be all but discontinued and in summer carried out soon after dawn in order for the leaves and buds to dry before the heat of the sun builds up. Afternoon irrigation should be early enough for the crop to dry off thoroughly by nightfall. Liquid feed may be incorporated at each watering and will obviously be easier to administer if an automated system is installed. Precise details of appropriate chemicals and their ratio per gallon may be learnt from ADAS literature or gleaned from trade suppliers or other growers, if they will tell you. Top dressing of granular feed which can be watered in and release its nutrients slowly will serve well enough for smaller producers without sophisticated equipment.

Blooms, once harvested, prepared and bunched, are packed into glazed or wax-paper lined cardboard boxes, in multiples of 10, 15 or 20.

9
CARNATIONS

Now, as ever, the word 'carnation' means different things to different people. To many flower lovers of mature years 'carnation' may evoke memories of the 'Malmaison' forms, those exquisitely scented huge flowers which were fashionable and widely grown in large establishments in Edwardian times. To Americans and most non-gardeners however the word would probably suggest the thick-stemmed, heavy-flowered, scentless carnations which were developed in the United States by William Sim, a Scots emigré who ran a hugely successful nursery in the early years of this century. These 'Sim' forms, together with their 'spray' mutants are the staples of the international cut-flower trade. They are grown in this country but are also raised and harvested in vast quantities in Israel, the Mediterranean and Jersey from whence they are air-freighted around the world. We meet them in bouquets, buttonholes and wreaths sent from florists' shops, as cut flowers in supermarkets and village shops, and in plastic buckets outside petrol stations. The 'Sims' and their hybrids are 'perpetual-flowering', in other words capable of blooming throughout the year, and are an important commercial crop. The flowers and stems are stiff-looking things, lasting long in and out of water and forgiving extremes of harsh treatment. They perform their duties in stoic fashion but, to my eye, have lost something in grace and charm along the way.

Other flowers encountered today under the general name 'carnation' are the huge blooms grown on standard perpetual-flowering plants, many of which are raised as in Parkinson's day and before, in Holland. Flowers borne on carnations of this type are often ornately patterned and exquisite to look at but often have little or no perfume and for some people, though by no means all, they are somehow without soul. They and the Sims are the result of intense hybridizing work from a strain of 'remontant' or repeat flowering carnation originally selected by Dalmais in France in the mid-nineteenth century. The plants are tender, requiring a minimum heat of 40°–45°F (5–7°C) in winter to flower successfully. Some British growers produce these blooms commercially but the vast bulk arrive in our markets from Bogota in Columbia, where a regular day-length of twelve hours and a constant temperature of around 65°F (17°C) ensure they perform at their optimum capacity. These are the type grown by enthusiastic amateurs for the show bench in this country, and in the hands of these expert growers the individual blooms can reach extraordinary size and perfection of form. While many of these cultivars are relatively short-lived and new forms are frequently introduced from abroad, several of our own showmen hybridize and perfect their own cultivars.

Yet more hybrid 'carnations' are raised and named yearly, arriving from various parts of the world and reaching our garden centres and chain stores described as 'miniatures', 'dwarfs', 'pot sprays' and so on. I have recently seen new Dutch hybrids in commercial glasshouse production which are results of crosses between perpetual-flowering carnations and *Dianthus barbatus* or sweet william types. These tall growing plants bear several stems of laxly bunched semi-double flowers in brilliant colours. Blooming within fourteen weeks of planting this new hybrid, named 'Queen Diana' would seem likely to become a sound commercial proposition. A further attractive and imaginative new cross has recently been launched, being a hybrid of a *barbatus* type with gypsophila, a related cousin within the genus. The result, a pretty, multi-headed spray of single five-petalled flowers of brilliant pink on a tall, dark-leaved stem would, I imagine, have immediate appeal to the flower arranger. It is to be named 'Gypsy', yet is a new form of 'carnation' to the layman.

There are also the annually raised carnations of 'Chabaud' strain, a popular and easy type for the amateur grower. While they are often a little irregular of flower and ungainly of habit, they have scent, strong colours, and undoubted personality. They are the favoured 'carnations' of many gardeners. A striking deep-maroon double, edged and backed with silvery white has recently been launched by the seedsmen Thompson and Morgan, named 'Black and White Minstrel'. It is elegant indeed, and resembles in looks the old 'painted ladies' of several hundred years ago.

One can only focus on selected spots over this very wide spectrum and it would seem convenient for the present purpose to subdivide the carnation into the two main types likely to be considered by the average gardener with an interest in the subject: the hardy, or 'border' carnation, and the tender or 'perpetual flowering' type. Both of these are widely grown by many skilled enthusiasts in Britain and as there are substantial publications already devoted to details of their care and culture the following section will attempt no more than a brief introduction to the plants.

Hardy carnations fit for outdoor culture in the British Isles have, as we have seen, been grown at least since the end of the sixteenth century. Their clove scent meant that they had a real part to play in English life for at this time it was the practice to mask rather than attempt to remove musty odours and sweet-smelling flowers were at a premium. The plants were regarded as having intrinsic value and from the late Middle Ages there are records of their having been handed over in part payment for goods or rent. The clove scent of both simple and sophisticated 'border'-type carnations remains their great source of attraction for many. In Elizabethan times the flowers were used in cooking as an ingredient of conserves, syrups, vinegars and cordials. Their essence was believed to 'cheer the heart' and recipes adapted to our present-day kitchens, with suggestions on their use in pot-pourri, are in the final section (see pp 202–10).

While, as we have seen, carnations have never lent themselves easily to classification, our present categories of 'border' and 'perpetual-flowering' carnation can be traced back to distinctions noted very early on in respect of the plants' general temperament and hardiness. From earliest times they have tended to fall into rough categories: the clove 'gillofloures' which tended to be tough and easy to grow, and the more odd and interesting novelties, mainly imported from the Low Countries perhaps via the East, none of which seems to have proved hardy in Britain for very long. While the 'perpetual flowering' habit of the tender carnation only appeared during the nineteenth century, its behaviour and patterning would suggest its genetic roots belong in this latter category.

First, then, a brief outline of the earliest traces of the plants we now grow as 'border carnations', for while many of our present-day cultivars in this category are of comparatively recent provenance several forms still grown look very like those known to our forebears in the late Middle Ages and perhaps even before.

HARDY CARNATIONS

Early History
Of Clove Gillofloures – The Kindes

There are at this day under the name of Cariophyllus comprehended divers and sundry sorts of plants, of such various colours, and also several shapes, that a great and large volume would not suffice to write of every one at large in particular; considering how infinite they are, and how every yeare every clymate and country bringeth forth new sorts such as have not heretofore been written of.

John Gerard in 'Gerard's Herball – The History of Plants' 1597

While we may draw on a wealth of botanical material from the time of Gerard a coherent account of the earlier cultivation and development of the carnation remains elusive at this point. I feel sure, however, that further material is available and that there is opportunity for much pleasant study for any who may care to take up this inviting task. Since the earliest records of its culture are scant, fragmented and often hard to interpret correctly, we must look elsewhere for traces of the flowers. Anyone who has an interest in classical, ancient Eastern and oriental works of art, and the inclination and freedom to look again at medieval European paintings and artefacts will discover appearances by the carnation as yet unknown to those interested in its botanical history. Scraps of information from such sources could well, if pieced together with our present knowledge, add to our understanding of the early culture and shed light on symbolic meanings as yet only half understood.

Like all compelling mysteries, the gaps in the story become more intriguing than the facts. There is no known incidence of the dianthus appearance in Greek art, or conclusive record of its use in contemporary medicine. We have the legend, from a French source, that the wild flowers sprang from the pierced eyes of the lovers of the Greek goddess Artemis, but this classical 'myth' appears to be a fake, albeit of some 400 years' standing. Yet only two centuries later, around the time of the birth of Christ, large pale flesh-coloured flowers growing, unless I am much mistaken, on tall highly cultivated carnation plants, appear on the wall frescoes of Empress Livia's Roman villa.[1] The Romans were not renowned for their skill in cultivating or developing plants. Where had they come from, who had nurtured them to this point, and what became of them afterwards?

The clues in contemporary writing confuse rather than clarify, for the supposed evidence for the Romans' cultivation of the carnation has been re-examined of late by Dr John Harvey and found to be of doubtful validity. On looking again at the received belief that carnations were twice mentioned by Pliny, Dr Harvey finds himself unconvinced and concludes that William Turner, the mid-sixteenth-century translator of the original Latin, indulged in 'a deliberate piece of Renaissance neo-classicism' to draw a false link across the Dark Ages between the flowers he knew and a plant mentioned by Pliny which is more likely, he feels, to have been a convolvulus. Turner faces the charge, in other words, of deliberately

---

1 Anthony Huxley considers these flowers to be roses. See *The Painted Garden* 1988, London (Collins).

cooking the books in order to add a dash of spurious classical resonance to the plants so widely grown in his own day. If this is true perhaps we too are guilty of a similar tendency to fudge facts for the sake of romantic whimsy, for the Pliny connection continues to be repeated by present-day writers despite the publication of Dr Harvey's research some fifteen years ago.

There remains, however, the tantalizing matter of Empress Livia's large pink carnations, if such they are. Could there be other such representations? If Turner was right and they were indeed grown by the Greeks why do they not, like the lily and the rose, appear on the decorative vessels and other artefacts of the day?

From Turner also emanates the assertion, similarly reviewed in a critical light, that the flowers were used in the crowning or 'coronation' of athletes and nobles in classical times. This association is offered as one derivation of our own word, carnation, and indeed I have heard present-day gardeners refer to the flowers as 'coronations'. Whether Turner was correct in his assumption or not, the notion had clearly been taken up with a will by the time he wrote in 1538, for in the lovely series of tapestries *Lady with a Unicorn* woven in the Loire in about 1500, the panel depicting scent shows carnation flowers, apparently red doubles, woven into a circlet for the head. In several of these tapestries the 'lady' is shown passing on skills which would have cost some pains to acquire. Her work in this panel has been executed with some skill and one wonders if the tradition was indeed already established. Such clues and historical threads often seem to be untangled at one point only to mix again at another. In this instance we may query the validity of Turner's deductions from the original sources but must consider the possibility that he was writing from a knowledge of established custom of which no written trace remains. If so, are there further examples of carnations being used similarly from this or earlier times?

In search of the true roots of the cultivated carnation Dr Harvey has also turned his scholarship to the comparatively full accounts of plants grown in Moorish Spain in the Middle Ages. He finds the carnation conspicuous by its absence, in marked contrast to other genera, cheiranthus for instance, which is already celebrated for its display of striped and multi-coloured flowers. Did the cultivated carnation exist then, and if so where and who cared for it?

The received theory has been that it was being quietly cultivated by the Persians and Turks, for it springs apparently fully formed from the pages of a treatise written at Herat, now in Afghanistan, in 1515. Now called the 'clove rose' or 'clove flower' it is described in both single and double forms with '100 leaves' or petals, in white, liver-coloured and ruby. The gardens of the Ottoman Sultans were first revealed to Europe through the embassy of Ogier de Busbecq, ambassador of the Holy Roman Emperor to the court of Suleiman the Magnificent. As well as the graceful tulips, hyacinths and narcissi he admired and obtained, contemporary records show he also acquired carnations cultivated by the skilled hands of the Ottoman Turks. From the elegant, stylized outlines on contemporary Izhnik tiles and textiles we may imagine that slender, single flowers were as much admired as these full doubles. This is not, however, the whole story. The Ottoman-raised plants did not leave Constantinople until 1554 at the earliest. Yet red, pink and white carnations, apparently with developed double flowers on very tall plants, appear in Northern European tapestries and paintings some seventy-five years earlier. Where had they come from? The King of Naples, René d'Anjou, is credited by a French source with introducing carnations to Europe from Provence in 1460; but who had developed these, and how can we account for their extraordinarily rapid spread throughout Western Europe? Suddenly they were fashionable, in the way of any modern cultivar. They appear, in this first flush of popularity, in countless paintings. Planted in decorated pots, set in the ground within pretty ironwork frames, supported by canes or lolling elegantly against trellis or rails, they were clearly treated as pampered treasures throughout France and the Low Countries. Intriguingly a wide trellis depicted in a Netherlands painting of 1490 laid horizontally over the plants some distance from the ground performs the same function of supporting foliage and stems as the wide mesh of strings seen in modern greenhouse culture of the plants today.

Such ingenious custom-designed habitats suggest that the culture of the flowers merited some degree of thoughtful planning. Their careful placing, in an eye-level pot to be seen and smelt, or in splendid isolation in a specially designed bed, indicates they were afforded special treatment. Yet we know of no written record passing on suggestions about their culture.

The plants clearly captured the taste of the day in a remarkable fashion, and changed hands with alacrity. A closely observed portrait appears as part of a *millefleurs* tapestry delivered to Philip the Good of Burgundy in 1466, only six years after René d'Anjou's reported introduction of the first forms. The Arms of Philip, emblematic of the expansion of Burgundian power, are set in a densely woven verdure worked in gold, silver and silk. Crowded together like jewels on black velvet among irises, acanthus, pinks and violets are the tall outlines of double carnations, red and white.

Flemish and French painters of the Books of Hours obtained the flowers and used them. The Margaret de Foix book, dated 1470, shows tall, branched scarlet carnations among the periwinkles, violas, violets, birds and strange beasts. An illuminated prayer book made for Henry VIII shows a carnation in pale pink, in a blue-patterned pot. A snail climbs the stem. There are many more examples.

Interesting colours and patterns began to appear on the continent and Thomas Hyll, writing in 1568, wrote tall tales of how they might be acquired.

These gilliflowers you may make of any colours you please . . . and if you please to have them of mixt colours you may also by Grafting of contrary colours one with another, and you may with a great ease graft the gilliflowers as any fruit whatsoever by the joynings of the knots one unto another and then wrapping them about with a little soft silke and covering the place close with soft, red waxe, well tempered. And you shall understand that the grafting of gilliflowers maketh them exceeding great double and most orient of colour.

He also spins a fine yarn about improving the flowers' scent.

Now if you will have your gilliflowers of divers smels or odours, you may also with great ease, as thus for example: if you will take two or three great Cloves, steepe them for four and twenty hours in Damaske Rose-water. Then take them out and bruise them and put them into a fine Cambrick ragge and so binde them about the heart roote of the gilliflower near to the setting on of the Stalk, and so plant it in a fine, soft and fertile mould, and the flower which springeth from the same will have so delicate a mixt smell of the clove and the Rose-Water that it will breed both delight and wonder. If in the same manner you take a stocke of cinnamon and steepe it in Rose-water and then bruise it and bind it, as aforesaid, all the flowers will smell strongly of cinnamon.'
The Proffitable Arte of Gardeninge

A yellow form 'procured from Poland' and given to Gerard by his friend Nicholas Lete appeared on the scene by the end of the century, and by the time John Parkinson wrote in 1629 Hyll's fanciful techniques presumably had been superceded by more practical methods, for the range was indeed wide. Writing of the 'Yellow or Orange tawny Gilloflower' Parkinson states:

This Gilloflower . . . like unto the Clove Gilloflowers, and about the same bignesse and doublenesse most usually, yet in some much greater than in others; but of a pale yellowish Carnation colour, tending to an Orenge, with two small white threds, crooked at the ends in the middle, yet some have none, of a weaker sent then the Clou Giloflower: this kinde is more apt to beare seede then any other, which is small, black, flat, and long, and being sowen, yeelde wonderfull varieties both of single and double flowers; some being of a lighter or deeper colour then the mother plants; some with stripes in most the leaves: Others are striped or spotted, like a speckled Carnation or Gilloflower, in divers sorts, both single and double; Some againe are wholly of the same colour, like the mother plant, and are eyther more or lesse double then it, or else are single with one row of leaves, like unto a Pinck; and some of these likewise either wholly of a crimson red, deeper or lighter, or variably spotted, double or single as a Pinck, or blush eyther single or double, and but very seldome white; yet all of them in their greene leaves little or nothing varying or differing.

Parkinson is describing a range of highly developed cultivars here and enormous progress had clearly been made. He includes numerous illustrations in his great book, which he subtitled *A Garden of all Sorts of Pleasant Flowers Which Our English Ayre will Permit to be noursed up*. Many have enchanting names: 'Master Tuggie's Princesse', 'Lustie Gallant', 'Fair Maid of Kent', 'Master Bradshawe his daintie Ladie' and, most notable of all, the smooth-petalled 'Master Tuggie his Rose gillowflower'. (*see* illustration on page 25)

    This item, the last of fifty-two he describes, is picked out for the significant advance it was:

Mr Tuggie his Rose Gilloflower is of the kindred of these Tawnies (or those described above) being raised from seed of some of them, and only possessed by him that is the most industrious preserver of all nature's beauties, being of a different sort from all other, in that it hath round leaves (petals) without any jag at all on the edges, of a fine stamell (red) colour, without any spot or streak therein, very like unto a smal Rose, or rather much like the Red Rose Campion both in form and colour.

Parkinson also picks out a type of flower with stippled or otherwise coloured petal faces, with a pure white reverse. We may have a survivor, or at least a similar replica, in our old carnation 'Painted Lady'.

Mr Bradshaw his dainty Lady may well be reckoned among these sorts of Gilliflowers, and compare for neatness with most of them; the flower is very neat, though small, with a fine small jagge, and of a pure white colour on the underside of all the leaves (petals), as also the whole jagge for a pretty compass, and the bottom or middle part of the flower on the upper side also; but each leaf if of a fine bright pale red colour on the upper side, from the edge to the middle, which mixture is of wonderful delight.

Such carnations were a delight for painters and are rarely absent from the great Dutch flower pieces of the early seventeenth century. They are painted in plain colours of white, crimson, scarlet, pink, maroon and yellow but the red and white striped or flaked flowers were clearly at a premium. These blooms, though often small, show clear, regular radial markings extending from the petals' edge to the centre of the flower. A carnation I grow, sent by an anonymous donor from an old garden in Usk, looks exactly like one of these and could have been the model for a bloom painted by Ambrosius Bosschaert, the Flemish master whose best work appeared around the turn of the century. His flower is picked and placed with its face towards us, at the foot of a *bloempot* containing a contrived and wonderful display of striped tulips, elaborately patterned irises, fritillaries, cyclamen, anemones and columbines. Holes chewed in the dark rose petals are carefully silhouetted against a bright background; a bluebottle, dragonfly and caterpillar sit among the flowers and water droplets are held in creases of the leaves. Bosschaert seems to have painted the same or similar flowers in many of his pieces, probably copying from his own work for the lie of the bloom and its patterning are often scarcely altered and the combinations of flowers obviously cross many seasons. His displays sit, typically, in an arched window before a landscaped view leading the eye to infinity, with far hills, rivers, villages and churches; art and nature in studied repose. Such pieces abound and reproductions of the originals are widely available and easily collected as prints and postcards. They are clearly once again in keeping with our contemporary taste for they now appear on wrapping paper, shopping bags and the bindings of notebooks!

A favourite of mine, recently encountered on a postcard from a High Street shop, is a flower piece by Jan Baptist van Fornenburg. A fine blue-patterned jug with a twirling, snake-shaped handle and spout is gilded with grotesque metalwork faces, half animal, half human. Its slender neck holds an extravagant bouquet of lilies, violas, roses and streaked tulips. The bizarre container and its contents are set on a heavy, rough-hewn table top. Gazing up at the flowers is an oddly speckled green lizard with a brown stripe down its scaly back. A simple *Viola tricolor* like those we grow today sits on its own, and to the left is one perfect double scarlet carnation, its face turned sideways to display the smooth greeny grey calyx, shedding drops of water as if fresh-picked from the garden. The work is dated 1623.

More original works, outstanding for their disregard of contemporary convention, were produced later in the century by

Flaked carnations from an engraving dated 1850. 'Jolly Dragon'
(left) and 'Justice Swallow'.

Rachel Ruysch, also of the Flemish school. This lady, mother of ten children and mistress of a busy household produced few but extraordinary flower pictures, immediately recognizable by her individual, naturalistic style. She paints a withering leaf as it is, yellow and crisp at the edges; a bent grass stalk keels over and remains so, a double poppy turns away at a rakish angle and we see only the back of its neck. As ever, caterpillars crawl, bugs and slugs sit, and insects hover though for her they gleam in a shaft of sunlight as if from a high window. Carnations, now 'bizarres' with more than two colours in the streaked patterns are set centre stage, though in her hands the curving stems and oddly coloured blooms have a lightness and grace often absent from the more formal portraits of her day as well as our own. Her work, executed some three hundred years ago, is full of freshness.

Development of the carnation continued apace over the next century. Then as now its excesses were an easy target for ridicule. In a remarkable book from the early nineteenth century, *Les Fleurs Animées* flowers are personified and satirized. Illustrated by Albert Grandville with sharp-eyed humour the carnation makes an appearance as an overdecorated young lady, the epitome of artifice. She poses against a backdrop of classic Dutch seventeenth-century formality: a clipped yew hedge sports serried stemmed pyramids of green, held aloft on bare trunks looking somehow absurd and artificial, though indeed they were real enough and some just like them may now be seen, restored to this perfect formality, at the Westbury Court Gardens in Gloucestershire now owned by the National Trust. Within the contrived and enclosed space of Grandville's caricature fountains spurt, carnations behave as required within their framework of canes but, in gentle mockery of the Flemish works of art, gaudy butterflies stare boldly into the lady's face and a large hairy caterpillar is making a meal of her trailing silken sash.

If your appetite for glimpses of the carnation in art is now whetted there are many examples to be discovered, often in the most surprising places. I find myself shamelessly scrutinizing peoples' wallpaper, curtain and dress fabrics where they are often to be found; a recent bath hat produced by Laura Ashley is decorated quite beautifully with small scarlet five-petalled carnations which look as if they would be quite at home on an Izhnic Persian tile of 500 years ago.

Appearances in various tales, perhaps apocryphal, are also frequent. Many involve drama and passion. Marie Antoinette, for instance, when imprisoned in Paris during the French Revolution, is said to have been sent an escape plan written on a slip of paper concealed beneath the calyx of a carnation. The plot was discovered, on 18 August 1793. She was, however, allowed to make a vain response, agreeing to the proposed escape, though as she had no pen she pricked out her message on a scrap of paper with a needle. This poignant relic is preserved at the National Archives in Paris. Marie Antoinette went to the guillotine for execution only two months later.

Associations with shed blood recur in many tales involving the dianthus, and specifically the red and white carnation. Princess Grace of Monaco in her book on the meaning of flowers recounted the story of the tragic love of Margherita Ronsecco for her lover Orlando whose death by the sword became symbolized by a crimson-centred white carnation embodied on the Ronsecco family crest.

To this day every florist knows that red carnations should never be mixed with white flowers of any kind in an arrangement, and any nurse will confirm that such a combination is taboo in a hospital setting for its blunt message is 'blood and bandages' to the sick and any who care for them.

BORDER CARNATIONS

The great Carnation Gillo-floure hath a thick round wooddy root, from which riseth up many strong joynted stalks set with long green leaves by couples: on the top of the stalks do grow very fair floures of an excellent sweet smell, and pleasant Carnation colour, whereof it tooke his name.

John Gerard in *Gerard's Herbal – The History of Plants* 1597

Gerard's description, some 400 years old, serves well enough today. We have widened the colour palette and range of flower types since his time but not all would herald every modern cultivar as an improvement on the old forms. While none of the Florists' carnations survives today and only a handful of genuinely hardy 'old' garden types linger on there are still many cultivars of 'border carnations' available which bear resemblance to the forms grown in times past.

Growers of border carnations are divided in a rather partisan fashion into those who prepare blooms exclusively for show, disbudding the stems and protecting the blooms from the weather, and those who prefer to grow their plants without interference in the garden. Cultivars will obviously display features with particular points of appeal to these differing groups, for where the former will value a plant which can be encouraged to produce one or a few tall stems perhaps bearing single magnificent flowers, the latter will clearly choose a stockier-growing individual bearing several free-flowering stems though the blooms will be smaller and less fine.

Roots

Roots of hardy or border carnations are perhaps more biddable than those of other dianthus, for while they resent disturbance like all others of the species they will grow happily in an open border yet will also support quite large and healthy top growth without resentment when potted in a 'final' pot of 6, 9, or even 12 inch diameter (15, 22 or 30cm). Roots of open-grown border carnations establish themselves with vigour, making a fibrous mesh with a tendency to spread laterally rather than very deeply into the soil. Care thus needs to be observed when hoeing or weeding near the plants and it is a wise precautionary measure to make regular checks through the winter that frost has not lifted young plants, whose heavy brittle foliage is easy prey for buffeting winds. Border carnations are traditionally planted rather firmly, and most experienced growers recommend compression of the soil bed by trampling before planting time, assuming, of course, that the conditions are dry and the composition and character of the soil are in line with those already outlined for other forms of dianthus.

Foliage

There is always a tendency to exploit the plant for show purposes, developing it for perfection of form and colour, which are most attractive; but the plant may become a pampered pet, whereas its real value lies in the garden. Therefore the habit of the plant should be reasonably short and bushy, never more than 30 inches high, but, what is still more important, the constitution of the plant must be really hardy, and the flowers should have sufficient substance to withstand the elements unprotected.

Carnations and all Dianthus Montagu Allwood in *Country Life*

Foliage of hardy border carnations is greeny-grey with the tufted habit of all dianthus though on a larger scale befitting this largest member of the genus. While Montagu Allwood's comments on the ideal habit and behaviour of the border carnation are wise and prompted him to raise a new strain named 'cottage carnations' which though now extinct, were easy and happy in the open border it will soon be realized by any interested grower of borders that there is a wide variation in the hardiness and growth pattern of the different named forms. The individual gardener will soon decide which characteristics he can and cannot tolerate and will settle in his own manner on the type best suited to his taste and purpose.

The foliage of the border carnation differs from that of most of its relations in that it does not normally need to be 'stopped' or pinched out to the same extent as other forms, and indeed some growers recommend never doing so at all. Unlike the modern pink or perpetual-flowering carnation the border type needs little or no encouragement to produce bushy side growths, and as each of these bears only one flower stem every twelve months you will simply limit the number of flowers the plant will bear if you clip back their elongating limbs in the manner instinctive to any grower of pinks. Show growers, however, whose design it is to encourage all the plant's resources into a very few or even a single stem bearing a wonderful bloom will choose to do this very thing. The foliage and habit of their plants will, as a consequence, often look neater and more compact than plants left to behave as they will, though obviously the latter will produce more flowers.

Typically, first-year plants produce only one flower stem but this will become surrounded during the season with up to a dozen bushy side shoots, each of which, if allowed to remain on the plant, will produce a blooming stem the following summer. Foliage should be stiff, vigorous and resilient, its personality being best stimulated by hard rather than soft living. I have ten-year-old plants in my garden of hardy 'Clove Red' or 'Painted Lady' types which are the size and girth of small shrubs though their appearance cannot be said to be beautiful for much of the year, for these old plants will develop woody lower stalks which need a flattering disguise of summer annuals if they are to deserve a place in a good-looking border. Their extraordinary perfume, however, encourages a forgiving attitude. The more delicate or fine-flowered cultivars are not temperamentally inclined to such longevity, and most growers will aim to keep such plants in the open border for only three or four years at the most before layering the side shoots and starting again with fresh plants.

Most growers offer their first-year plants a single stick support early in the year, avoiding the use of a hollow cane which can harbour insects. The emerging maiden stem or stems should be gently tied to its support with raffia or other soft material, or encircled with a wire or plastic plant support. Such devices can be purchased in various designs from nursery suppliers or made at home. Their worth will be amply demonstrated when summer winds and thunderstorms threaten to capsize your plants, and you will be glad of the few moments spent in early spring devoted to prevention rather than cure. In subsequent years supports such as those described in the following section (*see* pp 187–201) on perpetual-flowering carnations may be found ideal.

Blooms

The old Florists were very clear on the properties expected of their carnation flowers. James Douglas's standards for exhibition, published in *Hardy Florists' Flowers* in 1880 are often quoted, but were preceded by George Glenny's *The Properties of Flowers and Plants* in 1836.

1. The flower should be not less than 2½ inches across.
2. The guard or lower petals not less than six in number. They must be broad, thick and smooth on the outside, free from notch or serration and should lap over each other sufficiently to form a circular rosette flower, the more round the outline the better.
3. Each row of petals should be smaller than the row immediately under it, with not less than five or six rows of petals laid regularly. The flower should rise and form a good bold centre or crown and in quantity should form half a ball.
4. The petals should be stiff and slightly cupped.
5. The ground should be pure snow-white without specks of colour.
6. The stripes of colour should be clear and distinct, not running into one another, not confused, speckled or broken, but dense, smooth at the edges of the stripes and well defined.
7. The colours must be bright and clear. If there be two colours the darker one cannot be too dark or form too strong a contrast with the light. With scarlet the perfection would be black; with pink there cannot be too deep a crimson; with lilac or bright purple the second colour cannot be too dark a purple.
8. Faults. If the colours run into white and tinge it, or the white is not pure, the fault is very great, and pouncy spots or specks are highly objectionable.
9. The pod of the blooms should be long and large, to enable the flowers to bloom without bursting it; but this is rare; they generally require to be about half way, and the upper part of the calyx opened down to the tie of each division; yet there are some which scarcely require any assistance, and this is a very estimable quality.

Performance to such draconian specifications was a compelling lure for many growers and modern-border-carnation enthusiasts who enjoy showbench competition will recognize the spirit if not the detail of the old Florists' serious quest for perfection in their flowers. At the other end of the spectrum there have always been carnation lovers for whom competition holds no interest. The flowers they grew and still grow to this day may be smaller and less magnificent than these show beauties, but have equal claim to serious mention here. While exhibition border carnation blooms today can reach three or four inches across, the flowers of garden forms like the ones that I grow are quite different in character; they would win no prizes, being often irregular in shape and shaggy of petal, but they have a perfume and personality of their own. While they lack symmetry of form and have the dishevelled, loose look of Parkinson's day they also possess that extraordinary scent which means many country people still refer to them simply as 'cloves' to this day. While many exhibition cultivars are designated to a 'clove scented' class of their own there are many who feel that this attribute, once acknowledged as the most remarkable feature of the carnation, has been one of the casualties of the flowers' development in our hands.

SHOW BLOOMS TODAY

Modern border carnations are divided; like the pinks, into groups according to the colour and pattern of their flowers. While many growers may have no interest in showing the blooms, nurserymen classify their cultivars according to the categories devised by the showmen. These include 'selfs' or plains of different colours; 'fancies', those of striped, ticked or otherwise patterned form (known to the old Florists as 'flakes' or 'bizarres'); 'cloves', for their scent; and 'picotees', survivors from a very old type of flower, patterned with a narrow edge to their petals and renowned for their outstanding delicate beauty.

Selfs

These are separated into white, yellow, apricot, pink, scarlet, crimson, grey (often looking more like iridescent purple) and 'any other colour' groupings. They are judged, like the show forms of perpetual-flowering carnation, for various distinct attributes.

First of these is form and condition of flower and calyx: the flower shape should be as near circular as possible, with smooth-edged petals and an uncrowded, elegantly disposed centre. The calyx should be unbroken and although various devices are acceptable and normal to keep it that way during preparation for the show, such aids must be removed before judging.

The colour of the flower and its trueness to class come next, followed by condition of stem, which should be healthy, vigorous, and capable of supporting the flower's head without aid and in a seemly manner.

If a group of blooms is being entered for judging the last criterion is that of uniformity, or the pleasing matching of the presented flowers, which should look well as a group.

Fancies

These are divided into those with a 'ground' or base colour of apricot, yellow, white, or 'any other' type. The Florists of the nineteenth century admitted only white ground blooms as fit for show and would have found many of the colours and marking admired today unacceptable.

For them 'flakes' were flowers displaying clearly contrasting radial streaks in unbroken lines from petal edge to centre.

'Bizarres' showed two or more such colours which were sometimes allowed to suffuse together. However, for all the Florists' discernment and finesse of display not one of their hundreds of cultivars remains, for in their search for perfect faces the health and vigour or the parent stock was neglected with inevitable consequences. Their achievements are commemorated only on paper, in numerous exquisite surviving plates from contemporary journals, a few original drawings by Redoute and other unknown artists, but mainly and most frustratingly by extensive lists of names – 'Admiral Curzon', 'Dolly Varden', 'Master Fred' of whom only mouth-watering descriptions remain.

All such flakes and bizarres, as far as we know, are extinct, though one form (passed on through several hands but said to have come originally from the garden of Oscar Moreton) named 'Admiral Lord Anson' first recorded in 1750 gives some idea of their form and character. The flower of this plant has a pure white ground, marked with magenta streaks, ticks and spots. With such mongrel markings it would not have been acceptable as a show flake, but it has charm. It flowers in August with a three-foot stem on a perfectly hardy, rather massive plant. The blooms are more than 2in (5cm) across and many, but not all, split their calyces. The perfume of this apparently old cultivar is quite astonishing and perhaps in the hands of a dedicated showman it could bring back scent – that most lamented and nearly lost quality – with a vengeance.

Cloves

Cloves are judged in a class of their own and are often beautiful to look at in the various ways outlined above and are supposed to retain the perfume for which the flowers have been valued so long. Many in this class were raised by the late James Douglas of Bookham, a renowned breeder and exhibitor of border carnations. Unaccountably, to me, excellence of scent is not among the qualities marked in the judging of this class and many winning blooms have only the lightest perfume compared to other members of the genus.

Picotees

Picotees are those flowers of a plain white or yellow ground or main colour whose petal edges are marked with a contrasting rim at its lightest, like the tinted edges of a finely produced book, and at its heaviest like the dipped rim of a delicate bone china plate. Markings on present-day cultivars are said to be 'wire', 'medium' or 'heavy' edged and their beauty invariably draws real admiration even from those, and there many, who care little for the vast and highly coloured 'PF's' and other rather blowsy-looking modern border carnations. 'Eva Humphries' is believed by many to be the finest picotee, being pure white with a delicate edging of purple. Santa Claus, oddly named for he is yellow with pin-sharp purple edging, is also renowned and may often be seen exhibited to breath-taking effect.

These modern border picotees are direct descendants from a type of edged flower developed in France in the early eighteenth century, though the earliest mention of an edged flower appears un 1683 when Samuel Gilbert in his *Florists' Vade Mecum* described a form named 'Fair Helena', a plain white 'only edged with purple'. Once developed as a type, these flowers were separated from other forms and have long been shown in a class of their own. Their culture reached its zenith in the mid-nineteenth century, at the time of Thomas Hogg of Paddington Green, whose writing is so rich a source of material on the cultivars and gardening practices of the time.

Many beautiful and accessible coloured prints of these old flakes and picotees survive, and may be discovered and collected at little expense. Of the hundreds of vanished named forms many commemorate otherwise unknown nurserymen, though some flatter patrons or royalty or celebrate contemporary events or figures of notoriety. Some in my own possession show pure white, unblemished circular blooms traced with the finest scarlet or more boldly edged with plum or almost black-maroon. Some have regular small ticks extending from the petals' edge as if stitched with the finest embroidery silk. They bear the names of their raisers, 'Youell's Zenobie', 'Youell's Duke' and 'Crask's Queen Victoria'. How proud these now unknown men must have been of the results of their skill.

The old picotees and flakes were 'dressed' for show, their petals painstakingly rearranged or plucked out if poorly placed. The large heavy heads were supported on cardboard collars and presented in serried ranks on a board with only their faces showing, like pieces

'Youell's Duke'. Border carnation redrawn from original early Victorian engraving. Pure white with deepest red markings, typical of the genre.

of jewellery or pinned insects. The flowers themselves had weak stems and went out of favour when challenged around the turn of this century by the celebrated grower Martin Smith. Mr Smith introduced the showing of flowers on long stems in vases and soon flushed out the weakened beauties of the day. His exemplary culture of healthy border carnations braving the elements in open beds is recorded in early photographs and the performance of the robust flowers reaching the shows from him marked the demise of the old, lovely but fragile flakes and picotees.

CULTIVATION

Plants of all strong-growing cultivars will do well in the open ground and many strains have been developed with a particular eye for outdoor culture, requiring little in the way of staking, and performing well in a mixed border. All the older and taller forms may also be grown in pots, as they have been for centuries, and it is only in this way that fine blooms may be nurtured on the less robust and free-flowering cultivars. Some growers do produce excellent show flowers on open-border-grown plants, though a sheltered garden and some method of protecting opening blooms from rain and wind is needed. Most showmen, however, containerize their plants, leaving them outside for much of the year and bringing them under cover when the buds are forming and the flowers opening. There is no commercial cultivation of the border carnation for the cut-flower trade as far as I am aware, and the plants are therefore the exclusive province of the general gardener and specialist amateur.

Beds for open-grown carnations should be carefully prepared and need the same well-cultivated, well-drained, open kind of position as other border dianthus. Some extra nourishment in the form of well-rotted stable manure or compost may be incorporated before planting, and a top dressing of granular feed added in spring, for although these plants do not need rich living their appetite is greater than their smaller dianthus cousins. Established pot-grown young plants, with a rootball of at least 3in (8cm) should be planted firmly and not too deeply, some 12in (30cm) apart. Autumn is the preferred season but plants may be potted on and overwintered in a cold frame or cold greenhouse if a March planting better suits your circumstances. The open-grown plants should be staked in their first spring, and supported with more substantial encircling devices in second and subsequent years unless you can arrange, as I try to do, a suitably firm-limbed set of neighbouring plants to hold them up.

Plants intended for a life of containerized culture are potted up as growth dictates in spring and are traditionally set in pairs in loam- or peat-based compost according the pet methods of their grower. A brief glance through the various accounts of the various growers' composts will indicate that a vast range of materials is used for the pot culture of border carnations, and as always, the best are simply those with which the individual feels comfortable and at home. Good drainage is important, and the traditional terracotta-coloured earthenware pots look attractive, work well, but should be well cleaned and well 'crocked' with broken bits of rough china or whatever is to hand. Terracotta pots, alas, are prone to frost damage and the soft-coloured old ones are becoming scarce. They may still be picked up cheaply at country auctions or newly made ones may be acquired, though they have not the patina of the earlier types. Plastic, of course, has arrived in the garden as everywhere else, and many growers find the convenience, cleanliness and lightness of these pots, easily available and in plenty of sizes, quite adequate for all their border carnation needs.

Careful watering of pot-grown border carnations is obviously essential, and feeding with a proprietory fertilizer is suggested as the buds form. Staking, ready for the elongating flower stems, should be done before the pots fill with roots. The potted plants are best placed in an airy spot in the open or, if under glass, given plenty of ventilation. Those who wish to encourage fine large flowers may remove, by degrees, all but a few or even the single topmost bud though others will leave each to develop as it will, to give a succession of flowers on one stalk. Experienced growers advise that this disbudding is carried out in stages and not too early in the year. Mistakenly premature or sudden removal of young buds can cause a sudden diversion of sap and nutrient into the topmost bloom causing the calyx to split and the flower to be spoilt. Calyces have a tendency in some forms to split however careful one's culture, and this may be avoided by attachment of a rubber band or loose cardboard collar as the bud swells. Such devices are available commercially and cheaply but many growers make their own.

When about to flower, the plants are generally moved under cover if not already there, where the atmosphere should be kept cool and buoyant. The colour, form and longevity of the flowers will be much improved if this shelter can be devised. Growers without the facility of a greenhouse or the muscle power to shift their plants may chose instead to erect their own forms of shelter over the flowers, or simply trust to luck and congratulate themselves if successful on raising fine flowers in the open.

PROPAGATION

Border carnations are traditionally propagated by layering, which may be carried out either in the open border or in the greenhouse. As soon as flowering is over (around July in the south and August in the north) good strong side shoots are selected and a compost high in sharp sand or perlite is prepared near the parent plant to receive them. In the open border it may be necessary to tease away a little soil from around the topmost roots of the mother plant, in order to arrange a depth of about 2in (5cm) of the fresh rooting medium around its skirts, for it is here that the work of creating new plants will take place. In the case of outdoor or greenhouse standing pots, nearby containers will need to be filled with the

Border carnation showing layering process: (a) Mature plant with leaves removed from lower stems ready for layering. (b) Preparing stem for layering having made an upward cut. Remove tongue as shown. (c) Layers pinned down keeping cut surface open. (d) Rooted layer ready to be severed from parent plant.

rooting medium to present themselves at a judicious height for the operation. Lower leaves of the selected shoots are removed leaving about six healthy leaves at the end. Now comes the process, daunting to the beginner, of making an upward slanting cut into the plant tissue, using a sharp knife or blade to create a tongue in the stem, about two nodes down from its end. Any ragged end of loose tissue is carefully cut off, a device such as a small stone used to hold the tongue open, and the elbow-shaped plant tissue buried and firmly held down by a hairpin or curved peg into the rooting medium. It is as well to ask an experienced grower to show you the first time. In my own case I had the good fortune to be visited by Fred Smith of Birmingham, then President of the British National Carnation Society an expert and respected grower of these plants, who was kind enough to demonstrate a process I now find easy enough but had previously avoided.

The pegged 'layers' need to be watched carefully as they must not dry out. Their owner is thus unable to leave for a summer holiday or even a weekend unless a conscientious neighbour can be relied upon to keep them well- (but not too well) watered at this tricky time of year which can be boiling hot or muggy and chill. If all proceeds as it should vigorous cultivars will produce a healthy crop of roots in four weeks, though others may take up to two months. When the layers seem well enough established they should be severed from the parent plant and potted up separately into suitably sized pots. Such newly raised plants need consideration and care, and will appreciate nurture in a cold frame until obviously well established. Layers rooted in the garden will also appreciate an interim stage of containerized care, and it may be prudent to overwinter the less vigorous new plants in a cold greenhouse or frame.

Some growers believe that layering is unnecessary and find acceptable results from cuttings of border carnations, taken in July and August. Such material is handled and treated in exactly the same manner as hardy pinks, and the cuttings are kept in a frame or propagator with a bottom heat of 70°F (21°C). While I find this method successful for the tougher old cultivars and some more vigorous border carnations many tragic losses have been experienced by other growers entrusting valuable stock to such a technique which is not to be recommended for the beginner.

The skill required to propagate the border carnation (of all members of the family) is then, perhaps the greatest. Partly because of this, it is predicted by many that its future as a commercially available plant may be bleak. A leading BNCS member has recently said to me that growers these days are simply not prepared to wait a year for one brief flowering and are turning instead to the Perpetual-flowering or 'PF' and other mongrels of the race offering bright colours, a longer flowering period, and ever larger blooms. Many nurserymen agree, with regret, that the writing is on the wall for the border carnation. Though several still carry impressive lists of cultivars, the time involved in producing saleable plants, most of which are still propagated by the layering process, is simply not cost-effective nowadays. Other growers, however, are more hopeful, for there is still a brisk market for the plants, particularly in the north of England and several commercial nurserymen tell me that they can sell every plant they can produce.

Cultivation of the border carnation, then, requires some skill but those gardeners who cherish them are in line with an ancient tradition, and we may hope that these plants will continue to flourish under their care. For use in the general garden I find them a little challenging, for their tall habit means that they must be placed rather far back in the border, and in such a position their need for uncluttered, airy footspace can be at risk. Planted, however, in association with the larger artemisias and senecios, which also appreciate similar open, well-drained conditions, they can look pleasing enough in leaf and spectacular in flower. While my own tendency is always to consider plants first and foremost for their potential contribution to the wider garden setting, many dedicated growers of border carnations plant them boldly in blocks and rows, in the businesslike style probably adopted by previous generations. Photographs in Montagu Allwood's and R. P. Brotherston's books show forests of plants set into beds in this way, uncluttered by other neighbours. To walk around such gardens in the height of the season must have been an extraordinary experience.

HYBRIDIZATION

Despite the rather gloomy prognosis for the border carnation's long-term future new cultivars are still grown and introduced by amateur enthusiasts at a smart enough pace, and the trials ground at Wisley is showing almost twice as many border carnations as pinks this year. Hybridizing principles already outlined for other forms of dianthus apply well enough though this specialized art is one I have never attempted. The arena is very much open to any keen amateur who may care to try his hand among these kings of the race a programme of work here could put his name into the archives, where growers such as John Galbally and Peter Russel, to name only two, already have firmly staked their claim.

SHOWING

Principles for showing carnations differ little from those already outlined for pinks. My suggestion to any interested newcomer would be to attend a show, see the final results of the grower's skill, and, if you are infected with the desire to know more, join the BNCS whose published literature will contain all the details you can absorb. Best of all, establish friendships with experienced growers, most of whom will be glad to show you the ropes.

PESTS AND DISEASES

The pests and diseases to which border carnations are prey are little different from those already outlined for other members of the genus. An exception peculiar to the carnation is the carnation fly, whose fat white maggots can cause considerable damage to the leaves and roots. Their activities are obvious from silvery white tunnelled markings beneath the epidermis of the leaves, and they should be winkled out at once without regret. Thrips, the tiny black insects, as big as a comma, which sit on this page as I write in July and commonly infest us as 'thunder bugs' at this season can also do damage, and their covert activities within still-closed buds can cause bad scarring to petals, being particularly noticeable on dark, plain flowers. Their control is difficult but vigilance and a ready supply of insecticidal spray applied before the buds open should limit their assault.

Larger pests can come in the surprising form of birds, which sometimes can be attracted to and peck out the tips of carnation shoots in winter. Caterpillars can also be a menace but may be picked off by hand.

Circular grey spots may appear on the leaves of border carnations, erupting into pustules of black-brown spores. This is the fungal condition, carnation ring spot. Affected leaves should be disposed of by burning or by other total destruction and the condition may be kept at bay by treatment with a proprietary fungicide.

10

PERPETUAL-FLOWERING CARNATIONS

However beautiful the border carnation, the pink or any other member of the dianthus family may be, none holds that charm and exhilarating beauty which the perpetual-flowering carnation possesses. Certainly there is great beauty in the border carnation, the tiny dianthus alpine, or even the common sweet william. In their correct setting they enhance any garden or rockery. What cheer a perpetual-flowering carnation can bring, however, during the sombre and dreary winter days when one enters a greenhouse, however small, filled with these plants in full flower – especially when they are the newer cultivars with their splendid habit, long erect stems, and with such a wide range of colour in their so well-formed blooms.

Steven Bailey in *Carnations*

Originally grown in France but considerably developed in the United States and Britain during this century, the perpetual-flowering carnation (known familiarly and from now on as the 'PF') is now more widely grown and shown than any other form of dianthus. It represents a huge slice of the international flower market and, nearer to home, accounts for the highest number of exhibits at the BNCS shows. Its appeal lies in many attributes, first of which perhaps is its talent for producing high-quality flowers, often magnificently patterned though rarely scented, through twelve months of the year. The PF is exclusively glasshouse grown in this country, needing a winter temperature of at least 40°F (5°C) to survive, though higher temperatures will induce a more even succession of flowers. While commercial growers produce 'American spray' and Sim-type flowers as well as the large bloomed PFs our showmen here confine themselves almost exclusively to the latter type and have developed the flowers to great perfection.

The precise origins of the PF are obscure though it would seem that a series of fortunate natural crosses, probably between *Dianthus caryophyllus* and *Dianthus sinensis* resulted in a form displaying a habit of extended flowering. First recorded in Mayonnais, France, in 1750 and developed by 1830 as the 'Remontant Carnation' by Dalmais, it was sent to the United States in 1852. Here the type was further developed as a result of intensive work, catalogued in detail by the American Professor Holley in his study of the history and genetic background to the perpetual-flowering carnation which was published in Iowa in 1963. The most significant breeders in the States were perhaps Frederick Dorner, Peter Fisher, Alfred Smith and William Sim, who progressively developed a plant grown under glass on a vast scale for cut-flower production. Results of their work recrossed the Atlantic and were introduced to our British breeding programmes. Some, but by no means all, were warmly welcomed by our own renowned breeders of the time, Carl Engelmann, Montagu Allwood and Steven Bailey, to name only a few. The work of these men is continued in style in Britain as the market for PFs is very much alive and interest in new forms is intense. The work of the expert amateur hybridist is again at a premium and the work of several of our own growers has had significant impact on the international scene.

ROOTS, FOLIAGE AND BLOOMS

The root system of the PF is perhaps the fastest growing and therefore quickest to establish of the species and because the plants can be kept growing through the winter months it is possible to continue the propagation and potting up or out process at all times of the year. Growers may choose to cultivate their plants in pots or, if ambition and opportunities expand, may care to construct open beds for their culture within the greenhouse.

Plants may be grown in either a loam- or peat-based medium and particular care should be given to maintaining its good health since much is expected of these plants and they cannot perform at their best unless their nutritional and health needs are well met. American studies have demonstrated in detail that adequate levels of nitrogen, potassium, phosphorus, calcium, boron and a cluster of trace elements are essential to healthy root growth in plants of whom high commercial yield is expected. While the average amateur will have no need to grasp the complexities of plant nutrition it is clear that the growing medium for these plants should be kept fresh and in good health, fed appropriately and replaced when exhausted. Given an open growing medium, correctly balanced nutrition and sympathetic growing conditions, the fibrous roots of PFs will settle to strong growth quickly and without check. Establishment of a healthy root system is of primary importance because the leaf and foliage it is to support will be the most massive and floriferous of the species.

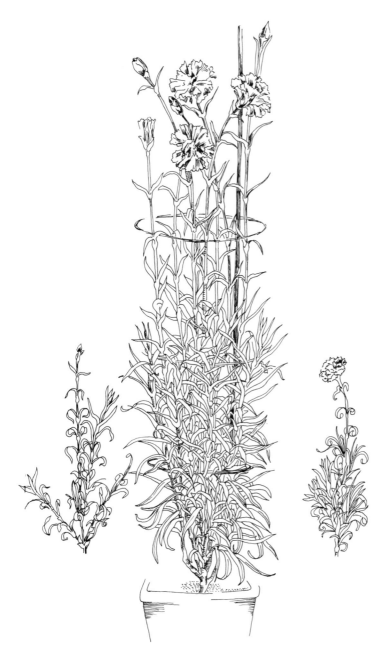

Perpetual-flowering carnations showing different habits of growth.

Foliage

Within the PF category there are, as always, considerable variations in height and habit of plants. While this type includes tall giants of the race – the 'American Tree' carnations can grow 8ft (2.5m) or more in height – many of the forms favoured by British amateurs are stockier by nature and typically reach only about 4–5ft (1.25–1.50m) in stature. In general, however, the PF is distinguished from its hardy cousins by having a faster-growing, comparatively tall and lean body outline, with wide internodal spaces and extended flower stems. The long, paired leaves of many PFs tend to curve away from the stem at the tip, and sometimes curl around in the shape of a twirling rams horn. Foliage colour is typically green-grey, but some cultivars have distinctly bluish foliage, while others tend towards greeny yellow. Texture of foliage is crisp and sappy on healthy plants, and cuttings or prunings are snapped off quite safely in the early morning when the plant is turgid.

Because of its height the leaf growth of the PF does need efficient support. Many amateur growers now use expressly designed metal stakes which are rot- and rust-proof. These can be carefully inserted into the growing medium in pot or beds, obviously taking care to avoid damage to the young root system. Lengths of wire can then be curved into a circle of appropriate size to embrace the foliage, and secured to a clip which can be slid and fixed at the appropriate height on the metal shaft. Other such rings can be added if necessary as the plant grows. Commercial growers, however, or those amateurs cultivating extensive plantings of PFs find such individual measures are not feasible, and use instead a system of horizontal strings and wires little changed in principle from the latticed supports visible in a Netherlands painting of 1490. Such a system is constructed on a framework of stout, vertical corner poles, at least as high as the plants will be, carrying a foundation frame of wires across which lighter strings are overlaid, one level on top of another, in order to create a series of horizontally stacked wide-spaced squares. The plants grow up and through these stringed supports, remaining accessible for husbandry and sufficiently supported to perform well.

Blooms

Blooms of PFs range from the small but numerous flowers held on cluster headed 'spray' forms to the astonishing huge beauties of the 'standard' PF which can be 4in (100mm) in diameter. Apart from appearances at the BNCS shows where these glamorous stars may be seen at their finest, both types are widely available to the high street shopper, and any florist's window will display these long-stemmed giants of the race. The individual flowers of spray carnations can be of many colours and are often heavily patterned. In shape and size they resemble well-formed, full-petalled pinks. They are rarely scented. The flowers of standards, however, are an entirely different matter. Their flowers are valued for size, shape and pattern as individual specimens and comments overheard at shows include comparisons, not always kindly meant, with peonies, begonias and bath hats. The flowers' patterns are often exquisite and their colours brilliant. In shape the blooms have, typically, a raised, crowded centre, a circular outline and a regular profile of well-disposed, often crinkled petals. Petal edges range from perfectly smooth to deeply serrated, though most are shallowly toothed or notched. Scent, alas, is often absent and while it is claimed as a feature in some cultivars it rarely approaches the penetrating sweetness of the old pinks or clove border carnations. Oddly, it is reported that cultivars can present and lose scent in successive years and that in some seasons southern- or northern-grown plants of the same variety can simultaneously lose or acquire perfume.

Flower colours and patterns in PFs are often astonishing. There are plain pure whites and creams, pinks, yellows, apricots, reds and purples. There are patterns of every kind already described in other members of the race, all in abundance. The variety of their forms and colours though remarkable can induce a sense of satiety in some observers, but we are dealing here with nature pushed to its limit by the hand of the hybridizer. These extraordinary flowers are the end-product of a developmental process which, as we have seen, has been afoot for hundreds of years. Since Shakespeare's day they have been seen as fair game for satire, but their lure remains strong and shows no signs of failing. The opening of these blooms, which I do not grow myself, is most exciting to watch and it is no wonder they inspire such dedication in their growers and such a spur to their hybridizers.

CULTURE

Although PFs may be grown outside in the open garden during the summer months in Britain they are not hardy in our winters and need glasshouse protection during this time. Detailed advice on the types of structure best suited to their needs is offered by many specialist books on the subject. Suffice it to say here that the plants need maximum light and a fresh, airy atmosphere, a minimum temperature of 40°F (5°C) in winter and the good care of the plantsman or woman whose love of the type will promote a rapid understanding of their needs. Culture of PFs can be of particular interest to the enthusiastic gardener who is happy within, or limited by, a smallish area for cultivation. A feast of blooms may be raised from a carefully maintained collection of plants in a compact greenhouse which, always comfortably warm in winter, can provide pleasant sanctuary for gardener as well as his or her charges. Most growers recommend setting aside a greenhouse for exclusive devotion to the culture of the PF. The height of mature plants dictates that eaves should be some 6ft (1.83m) high to allow easy access, and there should be ample ventilation and some screening from scorching summer sun. Every grower devises his or her own favoured method of arranging the internal space available. Plants may sometimes be set directly in beds which need a depth of at least 6in (15cm) and can therefore be raised if desired. Most amateur growers however start with setting their plants in pots at ground level, perhaps with their feet on gravel or a low bench. Mature three-year-olds will occupy a pot of up to 12in (30cm) diameter and plants of all sizes and ages can be a splendid sight, for in a well-maintained collection there are freshly opened flowers to enjoy every week of the year.

PROPAGATION

PFs are propagated from cuttings which root easily but need to be carefully selected from strong-growing mother plants. Commercial growers reserve stock plants exclusively for the production of cuttings and such plants are continually 'rogued' or scrutinized for performance, with any weak or otherwise undesirable stock immediately destroyed. It is generally advisable to buy in fresh stock regularly from professional growers since their standards of hygiene and quality are maintained at a higher level than the amateur can reliably ensure, and show-quality flowers can only be produced from the best available mother plants. Most suppliers in this country obtain their stock from Holland where, as in Parkinson's day, the best and highest-quality plants are raised and maintained.

Amateurs wishing to take their own cuttings in this country

generally do so in the winter months, between December and February, though they will root at any time of year and many keen gardeners are delighted to find they can propagate from quite small scraps of foliage taken from a bunch of florist's flowers. Though PFs are easy subjects considerable care should be taken in selecting cutting material, for the character and behaviour of plants of your own raising will be determined by the position and ripeness of their source and only poor results will be obtained from incorrectly chosen material.

Each stem of a well-grown PF carries approximately a dozen nodes or pairs of leaves, and each such node produces a side shoot. Near the top of the plant such shoots consist largely of buds, most of which the commercial producer as well as the showman will remove in order to encourage good form and size of the leading bud or buds. At the other end of the plant, the lowest nodes will produce thickset leaf growth. The central section of the stem, however, will produce material that is suitable, with short inter-nodes and semi-ripe appearance. In order to avoid spread of virus through infected blades it is the practice of most growers simply to snap cuttings off at a joint, for they will come away with a clean break. Tests have shown that there appears to be little difference in the rooting proclivities of differently trimmed cuttings, and most growers simply remove the lower leaves, dip the end of the severed growth in hormone rooting powder, and place the cutting as usual in the rooting medium. A bottom heat of 70°F (21°C) is ideal, but rooting will take place, though more slowly, at as little as 60°F (15°C). A mist unit is ideal, but hand spraying or an enclosed propagator will work well enough. Multipot modules are used by commercial growers and are available to the amateur if he feels confident of keeping them adequately watered. Such devices obviously avoid root disturbance as cuttings, once rooted, can be removed each on their own small rootball. Weaning should be carefully watched, with air and light admitted progressively as the young plants establish. Rooting of PFs should be adequately accomplished in three or four weeks, and the plants may be potted on as usual with the aim, as always, of producing strong sturdy young individuals whose character is best encouraged by keeping temperatures rather low and not overstimulating by premature feeding.

Plants should be kept growing without check, and only experi-ence teaches how to water and otherwise care for them. As a general guide, the foliage should always feel crisp and turgid, and while the soil should never be allowed to become dust dry the

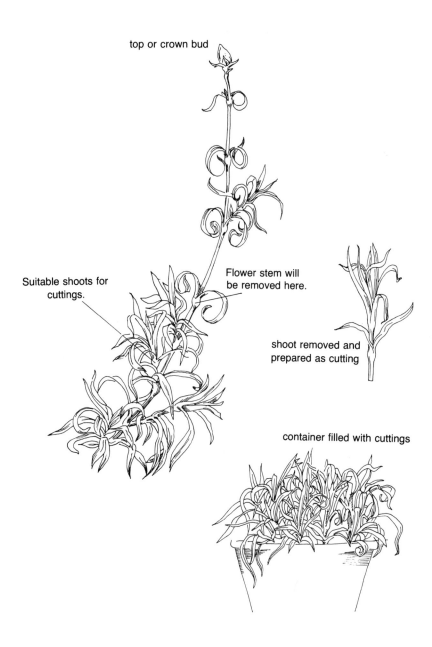

top or crown bud

Suitable shoots for cuttings.

Flower stem will be removed here.

shoot removed and prepared as cutting

container filled with cuttings

Growth habit of perpetual-flowering carnation showing disbudded stem bearing a crown bud.

plants must not be flooded and left in standing water which does not rapidly drain away. Watering in winter obviously calls for particular care and attention.

'Stopping' or removal of the growth point should be carried out when the plants are well established and occupying pots of some 5in (13cm) diameter. The purpose of stopping is to encourage side growths or 'breaks' and so to build up a bushy plant which will carry many flowering stems. Cultivars differ in their habit, but the average amateur may safely break out the lead growth when the plant is some eight to ten joints long, leaving some six joints on the stem, which will be left standing some 4in (10cm) high. Each node, or leaf joint, should now 'break' or sprout fresh growth naturally. If the stopping is done early in the morning when the plants are fresh and in good form the top-growth may be snapped out with a sideways movement. Each break or new shoot will produce flowers some six months from the stopping process, which is continued so as to encourage as bushy a plant as possible carrying as many flower stems as possible. 'Second stopping' is normally carried out (with the exception of spray forms for whom this is unnecessary) when the plants are well established, in 'final' pots or the greenhouse border. One or two leading shoots are broken out at a time, the aim being to induce a succession of bud forming top-growth. Experienced growers tend to work over their plants weekly when they are in good growth, stopping leading shoots as the plants' behaviour dictates, achieving a succession of buds and blooms at every stage of the season.

Plants thus nurtured should produce, from a spring planting, their first flowers during late summer and will continue through the winter months. They should remain in good health and vigour for two years, perhaps more, in the careful hands of the amateur though the commercial grower will tend to discard his stock plants annually and buy in afresh.

As well as 'stopping' the careful grower who wishes to produce show-class large blooms will need to master the process of disbudding, although this is again unnecessary for spray forms. Each week the buds large enough to handle should be removed, excepting the crown or topmost bud, by a firm pull sideways and downwards. The small buds nestling near the crown bud need particular care in their removal, for damage to the plant tissue here can affect the even development of the main flower and cause a lopsided or otherwise distorted appearance. It is recommended that buds should be neither too large nor too small at the time of removal, and the illustration will give some suggestion of the

(a)

(b)

(c)

Perpetual-flowering carnations. 'Stopping' of the lead growth should be carried out when the young plants are established and growing well in order to encourage 'breaks' of bushy growth at the base of the plant. Cultivars differ in their habit and some will 'break' naturally, but as a general guide the plants should not be allowed to grow unstopped past eight or ten joints (fig. a). The lead growth should be snapped out when the plant is turgid to leave four to six joints (fig. b). Each node will now sprout new leaf growth (fig. c) which can be left to elongate and carry its own flower stem.

appropriate moment in their growth. Experience will soon encourage the new grower to be confident when handling this process, which comes as second nature to any seasoned lover of the plants. Flowering stems of PFs are cut early in the morning when the blooms are almost open. Breaking rather than cutting is again the preferred method, and stems will snap readily at a node or just above. The node will now break to produce new growth which will, in turn, support a fresh flower stem.

Stems should be placed in deep water at once in a dark, cool place. A proprietary chemical mix may be added to the water or you could try a trick known to all flower arrangers who wish to prolong the life of the subjects: fizzy lemonade. If the plants have been growing well and conditions are favourable, a good stem of a perpetual-flowering carnation can remain looking in fine form for three weeks or even longer.

PESTS, DISEASES AND DISORDERS

Red Spider Mite

Of the pests which bother the PFs and their growers, red spider mite is undoubtedly the most trying. This tiny creature, hardly visible to the naked eye, loves the climate and contents of the carnation house and is a stubborn pest to eliminate effectively by chemical means. Losses of entire collections of plants are reported as a result of the piercing, sucking and web-weaving antics of this insidious pest and much has been written about the methods of various growers in combating its ravages. The best preventive measure is, of course, rigorous control of new plants coming into the greenhouse, and recently arrived stock should be closely scrutinized and quarantined for several days until you are sure it is clean. The small creatures are best searched out with the aid of a magnifying glass. The tiny mites are typically dark reddish brown, but can look yellow or greenish. They tend to congregate on the underside of leaves and first signs are mottling or slight distortion, followed later by a fine woven, random webbing which can, by the time it is noticed, signal that only destruction of the shoot or plant is now an option. Plants under attack should be removed from the greenhouse and treated elsewhere. Spider mites' resistance to standard chemical controls seems to build up in different seasons and different areas and a rotating programme of insecticidal preparations may need to be tried. Of the repertoire of available controls, Malathion seems most effective most often. Some growers, how-

(a)

(b)

(c)

(d)

Disbudding border and perpetual-flowering carnations.

ever, avoid all fuss and simply subject affected plants regularly to a sharp jet of water which, they maintain, drives off or drowns the creatures just as effectively. Others, including any large commercial growers, are introducing natural predators with a good measure of success, and comments on this process have already been made in the section on hybrid pinks (*see* p 151).

Red spider mite is said to have arrived originally in this country from South America and some experts have the chilling suspicion that its recent healthy and widespread appearances in Britain could be connected with the large-scale importation of PF flower stems from Columbia.

Carnation Tortrix Moth

The Carnation Tortrix moth is a second pest particularly familiar to carnation growers under glass, though consequences of infestation in this case are nothing like as dire. The moth's presence is not hard to diagnose. Leaf tips appear oddly rolled or glued together at their tips, and on investigation will reveal small greenish-yellow feeding caterpillars. These will grow to 1½in (4cm) long olive-green bodied, brown-headed fat larvae, which feed on buds and blooms and pupate in a dense web. Control is generally by time-honoured methods of sharp eyes and 'finger and thumb' though Derris is used. The adult moths are small creatures with lower wings of bright orange and uppers of brownish grey.

Thrips

Thrips, mentioned already, are generally controlled by dusting the lower leaves of the plants and surrounding areas with Gamma BHC dust. They are a particular problem in country areas and clouds of these tiny creatures invade houses as well as greenhouses, particularly at harvest time.

Rusts, Rots and Wilts

Rusts, rots, wilts and viruses of various kinds can affect PFs and are hard to diagnose with precision by any other than professional examiners. Such troubles and their symptoms have already been covered in the section on hybrid pinks. Maintenance of a healthy atmosphere and a healthy stock of growing plants is, as ever, the best form of treatment; PFs whose needs are well-catered for will generally throw off or 'grow through' minor ailments. Some of the wilt conditions can, however, prove fatal and plants showing sudden dieback and strawy looking leaves should be removed at once and destroyed, their sites being treated with a thorough drench of disinfecting mix of appropriate character.

Calyx Splitting

Of disorders, calyx splitting is perhaps the most troublesome to growers of PFs. Causes are various, but some varieties are more prone to weak calyces than others and advice should be sought from nurserymen by beginners on this point. Fluctuations in temperature, watering and nutrition have all been shown to contribute to the problem. Many who grow for shows will place an elastic or thin wire band around the calyx, as it begins to release its petals, to ensure a uniform appearance even if the calyx presents no obvious signs splitting. Such devices are quite acceptable though should, of course, be removed before the blooms are presented for show.

HYBRIDIZING

In the world of the perpetual-flowering carnation today, as for Gerard four hundred years ago 'every clymate and country bringeth forth new sorts, such as have not heretofore been written of'. Of all the branches of the family PFs probably receive more attention from the hybridizers than any at present. Large commercial firms in Holland sponsor their own breeding programmes, there are lines of work in many other European countries, and several British amateurs work on a large scale. Colin Short of Lancashire for one, flowers some five hundred cultivars annually of his own raising. Such work is made possible by the fruits of over one hundred and fifty years of post-Mendelian genetic research. Mr Short finds that, for him, chance is virtually eliminated and any desired combination of qualities can be produced in his subjects, almost at will. His achievements are widely acknowledged.

Physically, the PF flower is often the least accessible for the hybridist. Stamens are sometimes buried in a sea of petals and ripe pollen is hard to find. As a result many hybridizers use some border carnations as male parents for their breeding programmes, though this practice has some critics.

Many newly raised and named cultivars appearing in the *Register* in recent years are of Dutch, Israeli and Italian provenance. British-raised cultivars of the first rank may attract the interest of buyers from such large concerns, and their raisers may, exceptionally, be approached for the release of marketing rights. Advice should be sought from fellow growers if this should happen, for it may be advisable to apply for the cultivar's registration under International Plant Breeders' Rights, an expensive process but one designed to ensure a proper financial return to the breeder.

Outstanding new cultivars of PFs can receive an eager embrace from the market-place, both professional and amateur. Individual cultivars have a lifespan averaging only about twenty-five years because many have a tendency, not wholly understood, to weaken and become.progressively less worthy of culture after this time. Stocks of commercial cultivars are continually 'rogued' or scrutinized for poor-growing specimens which are ruthlessly destroyed; cuttings taken from mother plants of less than robust form can only hasten the process of a cultivar's untimely decline. The genetic ingredient determining longevity has clearly been pushed from centre stage in the breeding programmes of the modern PF, and some breeders are looking to the known older forms of border carnation to reintroduce a little more staying power.

11
PRACTICAL USES

Of Pinkes The Vertues

These are not used in Physicke, but esteemed for their use in Garlands and Nosegaies. They are good to be put into Vinegar, to giue it a pleasant taste and gallant colour, as Ruellius writeth; Fuchsius faith, that the roots are commended against the infection of the plague, and the iuice thereof is profitable to waste away the stone, and to driue it forth: and likewise to cure that have the falling sicknesse.

John Gerard *Of the History of Plants* 1597

July-flowers, commonly called Gilly-flowers, or Clove July-flowers, (I call them so, because they flower in July) they have the name of Cloves, of their sent. I may well call them the King of flowers except the Rose . . . of all flowers (save the Damask Rose) they are the most pleasant to sight and smell. . . . Their use is much in ornament, and comforting the spirits, by the sense of smelling. As they are in beauty and sweetness so are they in virtue and wholesomeness.

William Lawson *The Countrie Housewife's Garden* 1617

The conserve of the Carnation gillyflower is exceeding Cordiall eaten now and then.

Thomas Tryon *The Good Housewife* 1692

As we have seen, carnations and pinks have long been valued for their fragrance as living flowers, and have long challenged the skills of those who wish to preserve their qualities once the flowers have faded. Despite their strong fragrance when fresh they are not easy subjects, for whereas flowers such as roses and lavender are generous in yielding their essential oils, carnations and pinks are less obliging. Floris, the British perfumiers whose range of fine products remains based on flower fragrances, produce a range of bath essences, soaps, powders and so on with delicious 'Malmaison carnation' fragrance. The scent of these luxurious products is, however, based on a mix from sources other than the natural flowers, a fine example of the perfumier's artistry.

While John Gerard does mention an apothecary's specific use of the roots of pinks, his source here is the German Leonard Fuchs, a celebrated physician and botanist whose own *History of Plants* was published in 1542. I have found no detailed directions for medicinal use of the roots or flowers in the contemporary herbals, and emphasis seems more to have been on devising methods of preserving their fragrance and flavour for simple enjoyment. The phrase 'to cheere the hearte' often appears as a recommended use for the syrups, cordials and preserves based on the petals of scented carnations and pinks in the surviving Tudor and Stuart recipes.

Some three years before John Gerard's great work was published Sir Hugh Platt had written his *Delights for Ladies* containing many suggestions for drying, candying, and otherwise preserving various flowers. Among them is this one, which produces pretty sugared crisps, though the flavour of carnation (or rose, for the recipe covers both flowers) is actually fleeting.

Roses and Gillyflowers Kept Long

Cover a Rose that is fresh, and in the bud, and gathered in a faire day after the dew is ascended, with the whites of eggs well beaten, and presently strew thereon the fine powder of searced sugar, and put them up in luted pots, setting the pots in a coole place in sand or gravell: with a fillip at any time you may shake off this inclosure.

(Collect carnation buds or petals on a dry day after the dew has dried, dip them in beaten egg white and sprinkle with caster or icing sugar. Place them, layered with the sugar, in a closed pot in a cool place). These are attractive to strew over summer soufflés or iced cakes. The sugar assumes a delicate flavour of the carnations – choose the deepest red cloves and it will turn a pretty pink colour too – and can be used to make a special addition to sweets and puddings.

Sir Hugh Platt also suggests candying the flower thus:

How to Preserve Whole Roses, Gillyflowers, Marigolds Etc.

Dip a Rose that is neither in the bud now overblowne, in a sirup, consisting of sugar, double refined, and Rose-water boyled to his full height, than open the leaves one by one with a fine smooth bodkin either of bone or wood; and presently if it be a hot sunny day, and whilest the sunne is in some good height, lay them on papers in the sunne, or else dry them with some gentle heat in a close roome, heating the room before you set them in or in an oven upon papers, in pewter dishes, and then put them up in glasses; and keep them in dry cupboards neere the fire.

(Make a syrup of water (rose water if you can get it) boiled with sugar and dip a half-open carnation or pink for some ten seconds. Arrange the petals as best you can with a narrow metal knitting needle or similar and leave the flowers in the sun or a warm room until more or less dry. Then place them on a metal or pyrex dish in gentle warmth above an Aga or in an airing cupboard. After several days they should be thoroughly dried out. They can be used to adorn special puddings and are interesting in texture and flavour for those in the family who must eat them. They should be kept in an airtight tin or glass jar and regularly inspected for soundness.)

Many scented flowers were processed and preserved by the house-wife in Tudor and Stuart England. Several recipe books survive from the latter part of the sixteenth century, passed on through succeeding generations of women in families. Hilary Spurling, who has recently published such a book which had been in the possession of her own family since 1600, has pointed out that such documents are a rare, probably unique, instance of property being inherited and preserved exclusively at the hands of the female line.

Of garden flowers appearing in such books, the rose is perhaps most often mentioned. However 'gillofloures' also feature large. Lady Elinor Fettiplace's Receipt Book, dated 1604 but probably containing records of practices from much earlier times, makes several references to their use. She made a 'Conserve of red Jilloflowers' made with amergreece and musk which, washed doen with spiced claret wine, was a prescription 'For the Passion of The Harte'. She used the petals, perhaps dried as suggested by Sir Hugh, to decorate 'Claret Wine Water', a winter drink of spiced wine and spirits. While the true extent of the flowers' use in drinks has been questioned of late (unravelling another tangled etymological skein over the origin of 'sops in wine') they do make a pretty and lightly flavoured addition to summer drinks. There is no question that Friar Daniel in the late fourteenth century was delighted with his pink which 'spiceth every liquor that it be laid in' and while we do not find the fresh petals make any impact on the lightest of red wine, there is a discernible impact on white sparkling wine, home-made lemonade, elderflower champagne and, perhaps best of all, plain spring water. Such cool drinks sprinkled with the shot silk and deep red petals of the July clove-scented carnation are quintessential summer.

The scent of the dianthus is, however, best transmuted into flavour by various forms of pickling, and, as Gerard records, the flowers' 'pleasant taste and gallant colour' is admirably elicited by vinegar. The following recipe, reproduced from Hilary Spurling's edition of Lady Fettiplace's Book, is to be highly recommended.

To Make Sallads of Gilloflowers

Take Red gilloflowers and Cutt of all the whight from them soe lett them stand all night, then take strong wine vinegar and as much sugger as will make it sweete boyle it 2 or 3 walmes then take it from the fire and when it is through cowlde, put yor gilloflowers into it and soe keepe them for your use this way you may doe any other fflowers.

The white base of the petals should be nipped off because it is said to be bitter. Weight the petals, which must be perfectly dry, measure out an equal weight of sugar and dissolve it in white wine vinegar (which should do no more than barely boil or it will set solid). Allow one fluid ounce of vinegar to each ounce of sugar . . . the recipe is worth trying even with only one or two ounces of petals, packed well down in small stone or glass pots (the little, dark, screw-topped containers used for pills are ideal as they keep out the light). Pour the cold syrup over them and seal tightly. They will keep their bright colour so long as neither air nor light gets at them.

Hilary Spurling *Elinor Fettiplace's Receipt Book* 1986

Petals treated in this way become succulent, brilliant red, sweet and sour morsels with a faint though definite clove flavour. They are an odd and delightful decorative addition to green or rice salads and well worth making. The scarlet vinegar syrup, mixed with hot water, is a pleasant and comforting drink for chill weather or when a sore throat or cold needs nursing. Cordials of this type were also made with lemon juice and honey, and I have found that any combination of these ingredients with the petals is successful. Lavender flowers and herbs may be added as available and the resulting concoctions kept, bottled, in the fridge where they will last at least a year though if your children find them they will soon be gone. The syrups, with clear strong colours, unusual flavour and pleasant sweetness, make delectable topping for ice cream.

12
PRESERVING THE SCENT

If thou hast wisdom, hear me, Celia.
Thy baths shall be the juice of July flowers,
Spirit of Roses, and of Violets.
The milk of unicorns, and panther's breath
Gathered in bags and mixed with Cretan wines.

Ben Jonson 'To Celia'

If odours may worke satisfaction, they are so soveraigne in plants and so comfortable that no confection of the apothecaries can equall their excellent virtue.

John Gerard, 1597

As anyone picking up this book will already know, the sight and scent of flowers does us profound good, and our awareness of the fragility and transience of freshly picked flowers is perhaps part of the magic. The ancient Egyptians and Greeks buried crocks of rose petals with their dead, presumably wishing to include scent among the other earthly pleasures needed for the journey into the unknown. We still cover graves with flowers and at times of overwhelming community sorrow scarlet carnations are often strewn, a spontaneous gesture which we have seen in recent years in this country when, following the tragic death of many in a crowd of football supporters, the Hillsborough pitch was carpeted with the flowers. Such language is international; we have seen mourners of the victims of the recent Rumanian earthquake throwing red carnations into the graves of their loved ones, so thickly that the coffins were covered. Such gestures somehow combine defiance and acceptance. For many of us sending flowers at time of grief or joy seems always appropriate.

The desire to capture and preserve the scent of fresh flowers, a quintessentially fleeting thing, is perhaps motivated by deeper impulses than we recognize. In any event the process of picking, drying and processing fresh leaves and petals is a delightful one, and the creation of home-made pot-pourri has much to recommend it.

Roses yield their essential oils more readily than any other flower and remain the most successful subject. Although pinks and carnations retain little fragrance when dried they are an asset when mixed with other more pungent dried petals, herbs and spices, for the shape of the flowers when dried whole remains recognizable and the colours can remain bright and attractive if carefully treated. As already suggested in Chapter 11, the scarlet colour transfers well when pickled in vinegar or wine and, if you wish to feel like Jonson's Celia, you may add this elixir to your bath instead of drinking it, though its efficacy may be limited if you cannot obtain the unicorn milk or panther's breath.

The art of making pot-pourri (from the French, literally 'rotten pot') became popular in the sixteenth century, and recipes were recorded and passed on in most household books. Methods were basically the same as those we use today, petals and leaves being either dried simply and kept in an open bowl, or layered in a closed crock in order to ferment and hold a richer fragrance.

Flowers for a simple, dry pot-pourri should be gathered in early morning, after the dew has dried but before the sun has encouraged the release of too much of the volatile oil which we recognize as scent. Some whole blooms may be placed in containers of powdered borax or silica gel, which should be carefully trickled between the petals and into the centre of the flowers. The deep red and white striped carnations are most successful to use here. After three or four weeks the flowers will emerge as desiccated, pretty additions to an open bowl and will retain some scent. Other petals should be stripped from the flowers and set out in a thin layer to dry in any place, out of hot sun. I use large oval old china plates for small quantities, but those working on a more ambitious scale may wish to rig up tiered racks of cheesecloth to separate and aerate the petals which, after a week or so, should be dry and crisp. Herb leaves and other petals may be dried in a similar manner depending on their availability in your garden. After roses, lavender and dianthus, I find good subjects are bay leaves, 'Eau de Cologne' mint, thymes, lemon verbena and some of the scented pelargoniums, but the mix depends very much on your own taste. When all ingredients are ready they may be gently folded together with the hands, with a fixative of about 2 tablespoons per pound dried weight of powdered orris root, which may be acquired without trouble at any large chemist and some health food shops. You may add bought scented oils if you wish, and dried peelings of lemon or orange and whole cloves, cardamom pods or sticks of cinnamon are traditional additions. Dried petals of orange marigolds, blue florets of larkspur or delphinium or white gypsophila are attractive but inessential additions. The finished result makes an immediate and satisfying impact on any room, piled into china or glass bowls. If you have too much for your own use and are sure your mixture is perfectly dry you may pack it into cellophane bags which should be stored in a cool, dry, dark place. The pot-pourri will remain fresh and wholesome for several months, and is an excellent standby for presents at any time of the year, particularly if emptied into a small basket.

Refresher oils are now very widely available and may be sprinkled into the mix at intervals when you feel the fragrance needs a boost. Through the winter months I fill a fireproof bowl with this simple summer pot-pourri which, set near a wood-burning stove or other source of heat, becomes a constant source of fragrance. The volatile oils, activated by the warmth, demonstrate the original derivation of the word 'perfume' (from the Latin *per* meaning 'through' and *fumare* meaning 'smoke') and with an occasional fillip from scented oils of lavender, rose or violet your rooms will be laden with luxuriant warm scent through the cold months. The petals will remain crisp and looking good, too, as Sir Hugh Platt wrote in his *Delights for Ladies* in 1594: 'You should hang your pot in an open chimney or near a continual fire so that the petals will keep exceeding fair in colour and be most delicate in scent'.

A stronger smelling, longer lasting but less visually decorative pot-pourri can be made by layering half-dried petals with salt in a closed crock. The flowers should be picked and the petals set to dry as usual, but before they crisp up, (at about the 'chamois leather' stage) they should be closely packed into an opaque jar, petals first, interspersed in layers with roughly equal quantities of salt. The jar should be firmly corked when about three parts full. The mixture will take about a month to cure and will eventually form a dull-coloured, crumbly textured cake. Look at it from time to time and give it a stir to check progress. Sometimes the petals exhude juice which should be tipped away. Collect it in a pot and put it in your bath, or use as a final rinse for hair or special fine clothes. When more or less dried out the concoction should be emptied out, broken up gently with the fingers and mixed with powdered orris root at about a tablespoon per pound, and then folded together with your chosen blend of spices and other dried herb petals. This is the type of pot-pourri to store in round-bellied oriental ginger jars or any of the odd and interesting china or earthenware pots one may have about the house, so long as they have a lid, cork, or can be otherwise closed at the top. When you need to remind yourself of summer lift the lid, stir the contents, and the scent will be full-bodied and powerful.

Pot-pourri carefully made in this manner and kept enclosed is said to last in good heart for fifty years and more. Though its life expectancy will be reduced by exposure to the air I find it excellent to use in closed drawers or wardrobes and a seldom-used room can be quickly made to feel inviting by stirring the pot and leaving the lid off for a day or two. Good containers for such purposes abound in flea markets and the glass pots with perforated metal tops once used for face powder are inexpensive to buy, attractive and just right. The pot-pourri may also be displayed in a glass jar or open bowl though its life expectancy will obviously be reduced. Its appearance may be improved by addition of dried petals or flower heads which keep their colour though their scent value may be negligible. The pink or white dried daisy heads of *Acrolinium* can be used successfully to line a glass jar and fixed with beaten egg white or a dab of glue, their faces looking outwards, before the pot-pourri is carefully packed in behind them.

FLOWER ARRANGING

Carnations and pinks are widely used by professional florists and amateur flower arrangers. Carnations in the hands of the florist may find themselves the resplendent centrepiece of a buttonhole, their stems impaled upon wire. White flowers may be turned into curiosities their water being spiked with dye, turning them odd hues of green and blue. Petals may be stripped from one flower, gathered together and reformed into another. More usually, however, the flowers are used simply as they are, for their long-lasting brilliantly coloured heads are right for many settings. The huge standard Sim carnations are a staple ingredient for formal work in grand settings for their circular outlines provide satisfying focal points and their long buds can be used to lead the eye wherever the arranger chooses. Spray carnations are perhaps more adaptable and may be broken up for use in small-scale work or used as they are where their many heads on one long sturdy stem are a source of well-disposed immediate colour. Scarlet spray carnations are at a premium at Christmas, when their blood-red makes stunning impact against glossy dark-leaved holly and black-berried twirling ivy. White carnations can look equally dramatic with variegated holly in church at this season.

Flower arrangers use carnations and modern pinks extensively. Their work may be seen at almost every agricultural show through the summer and wherever trestle tables groan with sponge cakes, hand-knitted garments, enormous vegetables and miniature gardens ostensibly made by children, the flower arrangers' work will be at hand. Whether or not their interpretations on a theme or posies in a candlestick are to your taste, the dianthus family invariably features large. Brightly coloured carnations are set like firecracker sparks in ambitious formal displays, 'Doris' and her relations are surrounded by eucalyptus and gypsophila, tiny pinks from the garden are lovingly bunched and put into eggcups with rosebuds and the last of the forget-me-nots. There is a scent of trodden grass, apples and freshly pulled carrots but not, alas, of full-bodied clove pinks, unless you stoop to catch their fragrance in the eggcups.

APPENDICES

I SELECT BIBLIOGRAPHY

Allwood, Montagu C., *Carnations and all Dianthus* (Allwoods, 1935).

Bailey, Steven, *Carnations, Perpetual-Flowering Carnations, Border Pinks* (Blandford, 1982).

Coats, Peter, *Flowers in History*, (Weidenfeld & Nicolson, 1970).

Duff, Gail, *A Book of Pot-Pourri*, (Merehurst Press, 1985).

Duthie, Ruth, *Florists' Flowers and Societies*, (Shire Press, 1988).

Fish, Margery, *Cottage Garden Flowers*, (Faber, 1961).

Genders, Roy, *Collecting Antique Plants*, (Pelham Books, 1971).

Genders, Roy, *Garden Pinks*, (The Garden Book Club, 1962).

Gerard, John, *The Herball*, (1597).

Harvey, Dr John H., *Mediaeval Gardens*, (Batsford, 1981).

Hyll, Thomas, *The Proffitable Arte of Gardeninge*, (1568).

Ingwersen, Will E., *The Dianthus*, (Collins, 1949).

Lawson, William, *A New Orchard and Garden*, (1618).

Lyte, Henry, *A Newe Herball or Historie of Plantes*, (1578).

McQuown, F. R., *Carnations and Pinks*, (Garden Book Club, 1965).

Moreton, C. Oscar, *Old Carnations and Pinks* (Rainbird Press, 1955).

Parkinson, John, *Paradisi in Sole Paradisus Terrestris*, (1629).

Platt, Sir Hugh, *Delights for Ladies* (1554).

Ray, John, *Synopsis Methodica Stirpium Britannicarum*, (3rd edition, 1753).

Turner, William, *The names of herbes in Greek, Latin, Englishe, Duche and Frenche with the commune names that Herbaries and Apotecaries use*, (1548).

Tusser, Thomas, *Five Hundreth Points of Good Husbandry*, (1573).

Sinclair-Rohde, Eleanor, *The Scented Garden*, (Dover, 1920).

Sinclair-Rohde, Eleanor, *A Garden of Herbs*, (Dover, 1936).

Stuart, David and Sutherland, James, *Plants from the Past*, (Viking, 1987).

II GLOSSARY

Adventitious root   Root developing from part other than the basal root.

Annual   Plant which completes its life cycle within a year or growing season.

Anther   Head of stamen containing pollen or fertile male spores.

Axil   The angle between a leaf and a stem, often containing an axillary bud or flower.

Biennial   A plant that lives for two seasons, flowering and seeding in the second year.

Calyx   The outer covering of leaf-like envelope of a flower, its segments being called sepals.

Carpel   Reproductive unit of a flower consisting of an ovary, style and stigma.

Corolla   The part of the flower within the calyx consisting of petals.

Cotyledon   Primary leaf of the seed embryo, important in the early feeding of the plant.

Flower   A specialized reproductive shoot, usually consisting of sepals, petals, stamens, and ovary.

Gene   The hereditary factor which is transmitted by each parent to offspring and which determines hereditary characteristics.

Genus   A term of classification for a group of closely related species. It is the first of the two Latin names normally used to describe plants.

Hybrid   A plant produced from the cross-breeding of two different species and possessing characters from both parents.

Inflorescence   A general term for the flowering part of a plant, whether of one flower or many.

Node   The position on a stem where one or more leaves arise.

Ovary   The basal part of the carpel containing the ovules and later the seeds.

Ovule   The egg cell that once fertilized develops into a seed.

Perennial   A plant living for more than two years and usually flowering each year.

Petal   A segment of the corolla surrounding the sexual parts of the flower.

Pollen   The fertilizing dust of the flower.

Pollination   The process by which pollen is transferred from the anther to the stigma.

Seed   A structure within the ovary produced by fertilization of the ovule and consisting of a seed coat, food reserves and an embryo capable of germination.

Sepal One of the segments of the calyx, serving to protect the flower bud.

Species A group of individuals with similar characteristics, that can interbreed, but do not normally breed with individuals from another species. The specific name is the second of the two Latin names used to describe a plant.

Stamen One of the male sexual parts of the flower consisting of a filament and an anther containing pollen.

Style The middle, often elongated, part of a female sexual organ of the flower between the stigma and the ovary.

Turgid The swollen state of plant cells when they have taken up water to their fullest extent.

Vegetative propagation Asexual reproduction in which part of a plant becomes detached and subsequently develops into a new plant.

III USEFUL ADDRESSES

Alpine Garden Society   Hon. Secretary, Lye End Link, St John's, Woking, Surrey, GU21 1SW.

British National Carnation Society   Hon. Secretary, 3 Canberra Close, Hornchurch, Essex, RM12 5TR.

The National Gardens Scheme   Hon. Secretary, 57 Lower Belgrave Street, London, SW1W 0LR.

The National Council for the Conservation of Plants and Gardens Hon. Secretary, c/o Wisley Gardens, Woking, Surrey, GU23 6QB.

The Royal Horticultural Society   Hon. Secretary, Vincent Square, London, SW1P 2PE.

The South Island Carnation Society   The Secretary, Omawiti, R&I Lyttelton, New Zealand.

The North Island Carnation, Gerbera and Carnation Society   The Secretary, 73a Maioro Street, Avondale, Auckland, New Zealand.

IV LIST OF SUPPLIERS

Allwood Bros   Mill Nursery, Hassocks, West Sussex, BN6 9NB
Steven Bailey   Silver Street, Sway, Lymington, Hants SO41 6ZA
The Margery Fish Plant Nursery   East Lambrook Manor, East Lambrook, S. Petherton, Somerset, TA13 5HL
R. & T. Gillies   22 Chetwyn Avenue, Bromley Cross, Bolton, BL7 9BN
Mr and Mrs J. Galbally   11 Robin Close, Eastbourne, East Sussex, BN23 7RJ
Hayward's Carnations   The Chace Gardens, Stakes Road, Purbrook, Portsmouth, PO7 5PL
Hoo House Nursery   Hoo House, Gloucester Road, Tewkesbury, Gloucester, GL20 7DA
W. E. Th. Ingwersen Ltd   Birch Farm Nursery, Gravetye, East Grinstead, West Sussex, RH19 4LE
Reginald Kaye Ltd   Waithman Nurseries, Silverdale, Carnforth, Lancs, LA5 0TY
Kingstone Cottage Plants   Weston-under-Penyard, Ross-on-Wye, Hereford, HR9 7NX
E. Parker-Jervis   Marten's Hall Farm, Longworth, Abingdon, Oxon, OX13 5EP
Plants from the Past   The Old House, 1 North Street, Belhaven, Dunbar, EH42 1NU
Three Counties Nurseries   Marshwood, Bridport, Dorset, DT6 5QJ
Woodfield Bros   Wood End, Clifford Chambers, Stratford-upon-Avon, Warwicks., CV37 8HR

INDEXES

GENERAL·INDEX

INDEX OF DIANTHUS SPECIES FORMS

INDEX OF DIANTHUS NAMED FORMS

Other Gardening Titles published by The Crowood Press

Bonsai	Dave Pike
Cacti & Succulents	W. C. Keen
Camellias	Logan Edgar
Chrysanthemums	H. B. Locke
Clematis	Keith & Carol Fair
Climbing Plants & Wall Shrubs	Stephen Taffler
Conservatory Gardening	Yvonne Rees & David Palliser
Container Gardening	Yvonne Rees & David Palliser
Dahlias	Philip Damp
Delphiniums	Colin Edwards
Flowering Shrubs	David Carr
Fruit Growing	Peter Blackburne-Maze
Fuchsias	George Bartlett
Garden Design	Brian Leverett
Garden Trees Book	David Carr
Geraniums & Pelargoniums	Jan Taylor
Herb Gardening	Jessica Houdret
Indoor Bonsai	Dave Pike
Organic Gardening	Dave Pike
Pansies, Violas and Violettas	Rodney Fuller
Pelargoniums	Jan Taylor
Primulas	Mary Robinson
Soil Care for Gardeners	Jim Mather
Successful Greenhouse Gardening	Jonathan Edwards
Topiary & Plant Sculpture	David Carr
Vegetable Growing	Peter Blackburne-Maze
Wildflower Gardening	Yvonne Rees